T0317207

WHAT'S THE MATTER WITH DELAWARE?

What's the Matter with Delaware?

How the First
State Has
Favored the Rich,
Powerful, and
Criminal—and
How It Costs
Us All

Hal Weitzman

PRINCETON UNIVERSITY PRESS

PRINCETON AND OXFORD

Published by Princeton University Press
41 William Street, Princeton, New Jersey 08540
99 Banbury Road, Oxford OX2 6JX

press.princeton.edu

All Rights Reserved
ISBN 9780691180007
ISBN (e-book) 9780691185774

British Library Cataloging-in-Publication Data is available

Chapter 8 excerpt from SUMMERTIME BLUES/Words and Music by EDDIE COCHRAN and JERRY CAPEHART/© 1958 (Renewed) WARNER-TAMERLANE PUBLISHING CORP./All Rights Reserved./Used by Permission of ALFRED MUSIC.

Editorial: Joe Jackson, Josh Drake
Jacket Design: Jenny Volvovski
Production: Erin Suydam
Publicity: James Schneider, Kate Farquhar-Thomson

This book has been composed in Adobe Text Pro with Gotham

Printed on acid-free paper. ∞

Printed in the United States of America

10 9 8 7 6 5 4 3 2 1

For Lorna

CONTENTS

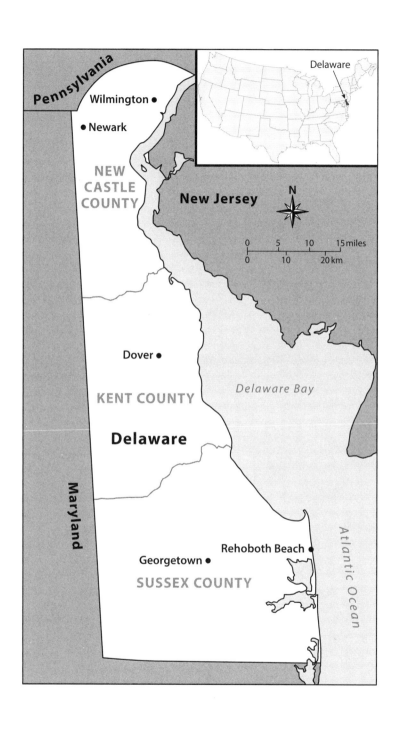

I grew up in Wales, and observed since childhood that size comparisons often seem to mention my country. We learned in our schoolbooks that the Holy Land was "about the size of Wales." Reporting from the Amazon rainforest, a BBC reporter noted in 2006 that "an area the size of Wales is chopped down every year."[1] A mangrove swamp in India is half the size of Wales, the *Economist* reported in 2010. The surface area of the moon with the capacity to trap water is "twice the size of Wales," *Scientific American* informed its readers in 2020.[2] The notion that this reference point would be meaningful to non-Welsh readers always struck me as fanciful.

When satellite images revealed in 2017 that one of the world's biggest icebergs had broken off from Antarctica, the British media, once again, described it as being "about a quarter of the size of Wales."[3] But the *New York Times* and *Washington Post* described the same chunk of ice as "nearly the size of Delaware."[4] (Which makes Wales four Delawares big, to use my own preferred mnemonic.)

So I discovered that, like my own small country, there is an even smaller US state that seemed to act as a convenient yardstick, usually to measure disasters. A swarm of locusts that hit Argentina in 2016 was "about the size of Delaware," according to the *New York Times*.[5] That same year, the Fort McMurray wildfire, one of the most damaging wildfires in the history of Canada, was "roughly the size of Delaware," *USA Today* told its readers.[6] The amount of land in Louisiana lost to erosion in the past century was "an area nearly the size of Delaware," the Associated Press reported in 2015.[7]

This discovery gave me a natural affinity for Delaware. Like Wales, Delaware is small: the second-smallest US state in terms of land mass, measuring just shy of two thousand square miles (about half as big as Connecticut, or twice the size of Rhode Island, if you prefer) and the sixth-smallest in terms of population, with some 974,000 residents in 2019, according to the US Census Bureau— about one-third of one percent of the overall US population.

But unlike Wales, the laws passed in tiny Delaware have global implications. Its part-time legislature approves the legal code that governs the behavior of corporate leaders, both in the United States and overseas. Wales exports celebrities such as Shirley Bassey, Anthony Hopkins, Tom Jones, and Catherine Zeta-Jones. (And, like many noncelebrities, I followed these stars in leaving Wales to live abroad.) Delaware exports corporate laws. Wales famously has more sheep than people.[8] Delaware has more registered companies than people.

During my twelve years as a *Financial Times* journalist, I often heard Delaware mentioned and never quite understood why. America's "First State" (a name it claimed after becoming the first state to ratify the US Constitution in 1787) always seemed to crop up as the location of great corporate legal battles—over mergers and acquisitions, shareholder lawsuits, or bankruptcies. I vaguely understood that Delaware was somehow critical to the infrastructure of global business. It was only when I stepped away from the day-to-day mire of being a news reporter that I found the time to look into why this state, just one-quarter the size of Wales, was of such international importance. And the more I learned, the more questions I had. There was a lot more to Delaware than met the eye.

WHAT'S THE MATTER WITH DELAWARE?

1

Introduction

WILSON'S GIFT

John Cassara first became aware that Delaware was a problem around the turn of the millennium.

Commanding, chiseled, and intense, with a thatch of graying hair, Cassara spent twenty-six years investigating international drug traffickers, arms dealers, and terrorist cells for the US government.

Cassara began his career as a CIA operative in the late 1970s, recruiting spies in Angola and writing reports that often found their way into President Ronald Reagan's daily CIA briefing. He went on to work for the Secret Service and then the US Customs Service. He went undercover to expose arms dealers trying to break the US trade embargo on apartheid South Africa. He worked with the Italian authorities to investigate money laundering by the Mafia. He worked in the Middle East, probing cases of fraud, intellectual property rights, smuggling, and high-tech crimes.

The United States at that time was a global leader in countering money laundering. In 1986, it became the first country in the world to make money laundering a crime, enacting a powerful law with tough penalties and extraterritorial reach and authorizing civil penalty lawsuits by the government.

These days, Cassara is widely recognized as an expert on the subject. He's one of very few people to have been both an intelligence agent for the Secret Service and a US Treasury special agent. He's testified to a string of congressional committees on complex issues such as alternative remittance systems and trade-based money laundering.

In the late 1990s, he was working back in Washington at the US Treasury, in the Financial Crimes Enforcement Network (FinCEN), a somewhat obscure department that had been established a decade earlier to help detect, investigate, and prosecute domestic and international money laundering and other financial crimes. Cassara toiled away in FinCEN's small international division, tasked with cooperating with similar agencies in other countries to investigate financial wrongdoing.

In 1995, the United States joined the Egmont Group, an alliance of these agencies from 152 countries that have pledged to share their expertise and financial intelligence to combat money laundering and terrorist financing. The group took its name from the location of its founding meeting: the Egmont Arenberg Palace, an elegant sixteenth-century mansion in Brussels that hosted the fencing events for the 1920 Summer Olympics. Today the palace houses Belgium's Ministry of Foreign Affairs.

FinCEN, which employs a few hundred people, takes in financial intelligence such as currency transaction reports, analyzes that information, and distributes it for law enforcement purposes. The agency shares the information with its colleagues in the Treasury, with other US government departments such as the FBI and the Drug Enforcement Agency, and with states and municipal authorities.

As part of its commitment as an Egmont Group member, FinCEN also shares information with foreign governments, if it's working on joint investigations with them. Cassara recalls fielding calls from his law enforcement counterparts in other countries who were on the trail of suspects in a terrorist investigation or a money-laundering probe. When the trail led to the United States, the foreign agency would ask Cassara if FinCEN could supply information to help their investigation. Cassara wanted to help, but often he couldn't. There was no information to be had.

Cassara knew there was no point in even asking. "Every time that happened, we would have to say, 'There is nothing we can do,'" he recalls. "These weren't isolated incidents. This happened repeatedly, on multiple cases. There were so many that I can't even remember which the first one was, the first time I ever heard about it."[1]

One dead end that Cassara and his colleagues frequently ran up against was the US state of Delaware. The process of creating a company in Delaware didn't require any information to be collected about the real, individual owners of companies—what lawyers call the "beneficial owners." Even if Cassara had secured permission from Delaware authorities to pursue the investigation, he would not have been able to find any useful information.

His department would go through the motions. They knew they couldn't get anything out of Delaware, but they would search their databases to see what they could find—information in the public domain or on commercial databases. It was rarely sufficient or particularly useful, and it made Cassara feel both irritated and embarrassed. "We'd write it up and send it back to them saying, 'We're sorry, we can't get anything out of Delaware. We can't answer your specific question, but we do have a little bit of additional information.' We would always try to give them something, but far too often, the answer was, 'There's nothing in the database. We can't assist.' They were frustrated and we were frustrated."

After Cassara left the federal government in 2005 he went around the world, training financial crime investigators in dozens of countries about money laundering and terrorist financing. During these presentations, Cassara would share his expertise and show the officials how to "follow the money." When there was a break, one of the local officials would invariably approach him, Cassara recalls. "They'd come up to me and say, 'Mr. John, we're working on a money-laundering case in my country, and the trail goes to this place in the United States called Delaware. Have you heard of it?' I'd nod, and they'd say, 'Can you help us follow the money?' It was extremely embarrassing. I was going out there telling them how to follow the money trail, kind of criticizing what they're not doing, and then they'd just throw it right back in my face, very politely of course. It underlined how hypocritical it was of the United States to preach to others when we didn't clean up our own mess."

Eventually, Cassara gave vent to his frustrations in a blistering op-ed in the *New York Times* in 2013. Delaware and a few other states allowed companies to wrap themselves in multiple cloaks of anonymity, Cassara argued, and had "become nearly synonymous with underground financing, tax evasion and other bad deeds facilitated by anonymous shell companies."[2]

That wasn't just speculation.

———

The first thing you notice is the lighthouses. You can't miss them on the way into Rehoboth Beach, a community on the Atlantic Coast in southern Delaware, about a 100-mile drive down the coast from Wilmington. The lighthouses are decorative rather than cautionary, adorning shopping malls and traffic signs. Rehoboth Beach is a typical seaside town—heaving in the summer, dead in the winter. It's about one square mile, with lots of trees almost all the way to the shore. Its main street is dotted with restaurants, bars, and curiosity shops selling shells and assorted maritime tchatchkes.[3]

The 1,400 or so permanent residents of Rehoboth Beach are a somewhat mixed bunch. Not racially—the town is overwhelmingly white—but they do include retired Midwesterners, assorted beach bums and hippies, middle-aged gay couples, and Tom Larson, imperial wizard of a Ku Klux Klan affiliate organization called the East Coast Knights of the True Invisible Empire.[4]

The town is particularly popular with the politicians, their staff, and lobbyists who work on Capitol Hill, roughly two hours away if you don't get stuck in a weekend traffic jam. In 2001, top Republican lobbyists Jack Abramoff and Michael Scanlon established what was billed to clients as a "premiere international think tank" with the generically pompous title the American International Center. Scanlon asked two of his childhood friends to run it: Brian Mann, a yoga instructor, and David Grosh, a lifeguard. They operated out of a small house at 53 Baltimore Avenue, across the street from the yoga studio where Mann worked and two blocks from the beach.

Neither Mann nor Grosh was qualified to run a think tank. In a 2005 Senate hearing, Grosh recalled his initial conversation with Scanlon, who he said had asked him, "Do you want to be head of an international corporation?" It was a proposal Grosh said was "a hard one to turn down," particularly after "I asked him what I had to do, and he said 'Nothing.' So that sounded pretty good to me."[5]

The think tank on the beach was part of Abramoff and Scanlon's scheme to steal millions from the Native American tribes who were their clients. This involved tribes paying money to the American International Center and other shell companies, which, in turn, paid money to Abramoff and Scanlon. The American International Center paid Abramoff about $1.7 million in lobbying fees from 2001 through 2003. Grosh got free accommodation in the beach house and $3,000 in cash. Mann did better, scoring four lavish trips to the Caribbean island of St. Barts, paid for by Scanlon. Meanwhile, Abramoff and Scanlon each bought luxury real estate in Rehoboth Beach.

In 2005, Scanlon agreed to testify against Abramoff, pleaded guilty, and was ordered to repay $20 million to his former clients. Abramoff was found guilty the following year and sentenced to six years in federal prison. In 2010, Abramoff's story was made into a feature film, *Casino Jack*. Barry Pepper played Scanlon. Kevin Spacey played Abramoff.

The scandal was merely one in a string of international criminal and otherwise dubious activities—some illegal, some strictly legal but less than ethical—linked to Delaware in the first two decades of the twenty-first century.

There were US political scandals. In 2018, Paul Manafort, the flamboyant and vain former campaign chairman for ex-president Donald Trump, was convicted on eight counts of hiding millions of dollars in foreign accounts to evade taxes and repeatedly lying to banks to obtain multimillion-dollar loans. Manafort's scheme was conducted using sixteen companies, nine of them registered in Delaware. The same year, Michael Cohen, Trump's bungling former lawyer and fixer, was convicted of campaign finance violations, tax fraud, and bank fraud. Cohen had become a household name when he was revealed to have tried to pay adult movie star Stormy

Daniels $130,000 to keep quiet about an alleged affair with Trump, via a limited liability company he formed in Delaware. Cohen used another Delaware LLC to pay $120,000 to former Playboy Playmate Karen McDougal to buy her silence.

There were domestic and international corporate scandals.[6] Jeffrey Skilling, Kenneth Lay, and Andrew Fastow, the most senior executives at Enron, perpetrated one of the biggest frauds in US corporate history using a sprawling, twenty-three-state network of two thousand corporate subsidiaries, 685 of which were registered in Delaware. In 2016, LAN, the Chilean airline, was found guilty of concealing bribes to Argentine labor union bosses by using a Delaware LLC.

There were cases of international kleptocracy and dirty-dealing. Malaysian officials used eight companies in Delaware to steal billions of dollars of public funds, some of which were used to produce the 2013 Hollywood movie *The Wolf of Wall Street*. Frederick Chiluba, Zambia's second president, siphoned at least $25 million from the impoverished African country, using a company registered in Delaware to help hide the money. In 2015, the government of the United Arab Emirates looked for hitmen to assassinate its political opponents in nearby Yemen. It hired Spear Operations Group, a company of mercenaries registered in Delaware.

There were cases involving the trafficking of arms, drugs, and people. In 2011, Viktor Bout, an international arms trafficker known as the "Merchant of Death," was convicted of conspiring to kill US citizens and officials, delivering anti-aircraft missiles, and aiding terrorists. He disguised the profits from his weapons sales in part with at least two businesses registered in Delaware. Meanwhile, Serbia's most feared crime bosses, Luka Bojović and Darko Šarić, laundered proceeds from their narcotrafficking empire through two companies registered in Delaware. In 2018, US federal agents raided the homes of the owners of Backpage, a Dutch classified ads website that served as a front for child sex trafficking. The company's US operations were registered in Delaware.

Delaware wasn't the exclusive US home of wrongdoing, domestic or international. Viktor Bout, for example, used ten companies registered in Texas and Florida. Paul Manafort set up companies in

Virginia, Florida, and New York. Frederick Chiluba had a company registered in Virginia.

But often when misconduct was exposed, there was a connection to a company registered in Delaware. What was it that attracted shadowy political operatives, sketchy lawyers, fraudulent lobbyists, hitmen for hire, thieving foreign officials and kleptocratic leaders, arms smugglers, international crime bosses, child sex traffickers, and manipulative corporate managers?

———

In his last days as New Jersey's governor in the first two months of 1913, president-elect Woodrow Wilson gave Delaware a lasting gift. The previous summer, Wilson had been selected as the Democratic nominee at a highly dramatic convention. The delegates took forty-six ballots to decide on their candidate, the most since the Civil War half a century earlier. The choice of Wilson, who was not at the convention itself but golfing at Seagirt, the governor's summer house on the Jersey shore, was something of a surprise. He had even been on the verge of releasing his supporters to other candidates. But Wilson had gone on to win the election handily that November against a split opposition: the sitting Republican president, William Howard Taft, and former president Theodore Roosevelt, who was running on a Progressive Party ticket.

A big issue in the campaign was how best to regulate America's fast-growing corporations. Candidate Wilson promised to introduce better regulation and inject more competition into American capitalism. Roosevelt taunted him, saying that as governor of New Jersey, he had done nothing to rein in the growing number of corporations there.

This insult stung. Back in 1888, New Jersey had become the first state to allow corporations to own the stock of other companies, a measure that gave birth to "holding" companies with operations in several states.

The US Constitution had left the power to charter corporations in the hands of state legislatures, although from the earliest days of the United States this was in dispute. Alexander Hamilton and Thomas

Jefferson, two prominent members of President George Washington's cabinet, had disagreed about whether the federal government should issue a federal charter to incorporate the Bank of the United States. Hamilton supported the idea and won the argument.

By the nineteenth century, the United States was gripped by fear of the growing power of corporations. Louis Brandeis, the Supreme Court justice, summed up the reasons behind this trepidation:

> There was a sense of some insidious menace inherent in large aggregations of capital, particularly when held by corporations. So at first the corporate privilege was granted sparingly; and only when the grant seemed necessary in order to procure for the community some specific benefit otherwise unobtainable. It was denied because of fear. Fear of encroachment upon the liberties and opportunities of the individual. Fear of the subjection of labor to capital. Fear of monopoly. Fear that the absorption of capital by corporations, and their perpetual life, might bring evils similar to those which attended mortmain [transfers of land to the church in perpetuity].[7]

But in the hunt for new sources of state government revenue, New Jersey had brushed aside these concerns and set out to make itself "the happy hunting ground of the large corporation."[8] In 1896 it loosened the law further, scrapping limits on the duration, purpose, and size of corporations, allowing them to carry on business anywhere, providing for mergers and acquisitions, and enabling them to change their charters more easily. All this happened without much corresponding increase in regulation.

If New Jersey was explicit in wooing corporations, corporations certainly reciprocated. By 1904, the Garden State was the registered home to the seven largest trusts in the United States, with a combined market capitalization of $2.5 billion—about $75 billion in 2021 dollars—as well as half of the United States' smaller trusts.[9] This process had a huge impact on New Jersey's finances. By 1911, a franchise tax amounted to nearly one-third of the state's revenues.

Delaware and other states watched jealously. "Little Delaware, gangrened with envy at the spectacle of the truck-patchers,

sand-duners, clam-diggers and mosquito wafters of New Jersey getting all the money in the country into her coffers, is determined to
get her little tiny, sweet, round, baby hand into the grab-bag of sweet
things before it is too late," observed an 1899 article in the *American Law Review*.[10] Along with a few other states, Delaware copied
New Jersey's legislative lead, winning some business by undercut-
ting New Jersey's fees, but it could not shake the Garden State's
first-mover advantage.

But the argument that had first flared up between Hamilton and
Jefferson resurfaced. In 1898, concerns about corporate power were
so pervasive that Congress created a commission to investigate the
issue. Four years later, the commission's final report fretted about
the competition for incorporations between the states: "Two or
three States have apparently, for the sake of securing a more certain
revenue easily collected, bid against each other by offering more
liberal inducements to corporations," the report noted.[11] The federal government, it recommended, should consider requiring all
corporations engaged in interstate commerce to be licensed and
registered with a federal bureau of corporations. At the time, some
of America's industrial titans welcomed the proposal. The leaders of
Standard Oil, Federal Steel, the United States Tobacco Company,
and American Steel and Wire all praised the idea of federal uniformity as superior to the fragmented patchwork of state variability.

On taking office in September 1901, President Theodore Roosevelt took up the charge. Within seventeen months, he had persuaded
Congress to establish the Bureau of Corporations as part of another
new federal government agency, the Department of Commerce and
Labor. Its first annual report to Congress in 1904 echoed some of the
earlier commission's concerns about the effects of interstate competition for business registrations:

> Each State naturally desires, chiefly for the purpose of revenue,
> to attract incorporation to itself by lax corporation laws. The
> ground has been cut from under the feet of objectors to such
> laws by the unanswerable proposition that if incorporators or
> organizers were not accommodated in the given State they could

incorporate in a more complacent State and easily come back
to the first State to do business. The logical result has been an
inevitable tendency of State legislation towards the lowest level
of lax regulation and of extreme favor toward this special class
of incorporators, regardless of the interests of the other classes
properly concerned.[12]

The bureau urged Congress to introduce federal licensing or
franchising for corporations involved in interstate commerce, but
to leave business formation in the hands of the states; it fell short
of proposing federal chartering of corporations themselves at the
moment of incorporation, which would have meant stripping the
states of their power to register businesses. This "modest proposal"
was met by industrial companies "with so much favor," the *Wall
Street Journal* noted, but the *New York Times* saw the idea as a Washington power grab, cautioning that "before resorting to the Federal
power, the resources of the State power should be more thoroughly
examined."[13] By 1908 a bill was introduced in Congress proposing a
system of voluntary registration for corporations with federal agencies, but with incentives for companies to comply. However, sentiment in the business community had turned against the idea, and the
bill was sent for a lingering death in the Senate Judiciary Committee.
The following year Roosevelt's protégé Taft became president and
once again took up the issue, proposing a national incorporation law.
But while there was still support for the idea in Congress, no specific
legislation emerged with any significant support. Taft became more
interested in pursuing his predecessor's antitrust legacy and lost his
focus on the incorporation issue.

Wilson's two principal opponents in the presidential election
of 1912, then—Roosevelt and Taft—both had records of trying to
assert federal power over the states' incorporation business. Wilson, a reformer by instinct, had promised to clamp down on New
Jersey's lax incorporation rules in his 1910 run for governor, but when
Roosevelt launched a fierce personal attack on him during the campaign for failing to follow through, Wilson had no ready defense. The
Democratic presidential contender had also been deeply affected by

meeting Louis Brandeis, an energetic campaigner against powerful corporations and monopolies, in August 1912. Wilson adopted the term "regulated competition" from Brandeis, whom Wilson would later nominate to the Supreme Court. Wilson was even under pressure from within his own state, where lawmakers and citizens were getting increasingly concerned about its reputation. A month before the election, both the Republican and Democratic state conventions included antitrust proposals in their platforms, with Wilson's own party pledging "an immediate investigation of the method of incorporation pursued in this State under our laws."[14]

In the wake of his November election victory, and with his inauguration scheduled for March, Wilson returned to New Jersey with a reforming zeal. He used his last annual governor's message of January 1913 to argue for improved regulation:

> It is our duty and our present opportunity to amend the statutes of the state . . . to provide some responsible official supervision of the whole process of incorporation and provide, in addition, salutary checks upon unwarranted and fictitious increases of capital and the issuance of securities not based upon actual bona fide valuation. The honesty and soundness of business alike depend upon such safeguards. No legitimate business will be injured or harmfully restricted by them. These are matters which affect the honor and good faith of the state. We should act upon them at once and with clear purpose.[15]

State legislators quickly introduced seven bills, dubbed the "Seven Sisters," to ban holding companies and anticompetitive practices, require official permission for all mergers, restrict the issuing of stock, and combat price-fixing and price discrimination. A howl went up. Richard Lindabury, a lawyer whose clients included John D. Rockefeller, the founder of Standard Oil (and of the University of Chicago, my employer), told the *Newark Evening News* that a strict interpretation of the legislation "would halt all business in New Jersey."[16] Others fretted about the effects on the state's finances. "Don't Kill the Goose," screamed the headline on an editorial in the *Daily State Gazette*. "Proper regulation of corporations cannot be reasonably objected to by anybody," the newspaper noted, "but there seems to be no demand from the people for corporation laws that will drive a great source of revenue from this to some other state."[17] But Wilson and his supporters were unmoved. The bills were quickly passed, and one of Wilson's final acts as governor was to sign them into law. Once in Washington, he took up his predecessors' attempts to extend the federal government's oversight of corporations, proposing a federal licensing law in 1919 and 1920. Congress demurred. (The echoes of Hamilton and Jefferson's original disagreement continued to simmer over the coming decades, bubbling up again in the early 1940s in an effort for a federal incorporation law. Calls for increased federal regulation returned in the 1970s but went nowhere.)

Wilson had moved on to a bigger stage, but the *Daily State Gazette*'s warning proved prescient. The number of corporations chartered in New Jersey declined rapidly and state revenues from franchise taxes plummeted, falling by more than $600,000 between 1913 and 1919.

Thus was Delaware, which had long coveted its neighbor's position as "the mother of trusts," reborn as America's incorporation capital.[18] It had not been an innovator. It had copied New Jersey's statutes, and only cemented its leading position once New Jersey dropped out of the few-strings-attached incorporation business.

Wilson's legislation had not even hit its mark. Since they were not retrospective, the laws failed to rein in big trusts. Existing New Jersey–based holding companies, such as US Steel and Standard Oil, were left untouched.

For New Jersey, there was little upside and a great deal of downside. Because of Wilson's efforts, spurred by campaign-trail barbs from Teddy Roosevelt, the state had thrown away its business-friendly reputation. All the benefits accrued to Delaware, which rapidly took off as the new leading state for incorporation.

By 1919, New Jersey realized what it had done. Its legislature hurriedly repealed the Seven Sisters. But it was too late. New Jersey had actually been losing business since before the legislation was passed,[19] and the trend had exacerbated so quickly that the state could not win the business back.

Meanwhile, Delaware had learned two important lessons. First, never let internal political debate endanger the incorporation business. In spite of its small size, the state had always been riven by social and political tensions. To this day, its leaders are vigilant and anxious about anything or anyone who might upset its social order or economic position. Second, Delaware learned that its neighbors' loss could be its gain. As we'll see, the First State became a specialist in taking advantage of other states.

Wilson's gift set Delaware on the road to becoming a facilitator of corporate secrecy, a host to money laundering and ill-gotten gains, and a harbor for criminals and tax dodgers.

———

Most Americans know no more than two things about Delaware:

1. It's where President Joe Biden is from
2. There is a lot of business activity there—they've heard of "Delaware corporations" or companies going to bankruptcy court in Delaware

Actually, many Americans don't even associate Delaware with the second point—only the first. But the two are intimately connected. To get a complete picture of our forty-sixth president, you need to understand where he is from—and that means understanding the industry that has come to underpin the economy of Delaware.

Delaware isn't the sort of place that typically inspires dreams or makes its way onto tourist bucket lists, like San Francisco, New Orleans, or the Grand Canyon (as famously parodied in an iconic scene from the 1992 comedy movie *Wayne's World*).

But even if you've never been there, you probably have many connections to Delaware. Most of us do. Delaware is inescapable. Delaware is everywhere.

If you bought this book (or anything else) on Amazon, you're giving money to a corporation registered in Delaware. If you used Google to find out about the book, you used a service run by a company incorporated in Delaware (as is its parent company, Alphabet). Perhaps you prefer shopping in real stores, so you went to Walmart. That too is incorporated in Delaware. If you're more upscale and went to Whole Foods, it's owned by Amazon, so that takes you back to Delaware. If you used a credit card to make your purchase, your credit card issuer may very well be incorporated in Delaware. If you got there in an Uber, you were generating revenue for a Delaware company. You may well be on Facebook or Twitter, which are also Delaware corporations. If you've saved money in a retirement account, like half of all working Americans, your funds are very likely invested in a range of companies incorporated in Delaware. If you have a student loan, your lender may well be a Delaware corporation. If you have a brokerage account to buy stocks, both your broker and most of the companies whose stock you're buying are likely incorporated in Delaware. Even if you just have a bank account, there's a good chance your bank is incorporated in Delaware. If you've ever given money to a US presidential campaign or a political action committee, it might well have been registered in Delaware. If you've ever bought anyone a gift card and they failed to spend all of it, you may have inadvertently paid into Delaware's public coffers.

To see how connected you are to Delaware, just think of the name of a company you do business with—a company whose stock you own, or the bank where your salary gets paid, or where you regularly shop. Type that name into a search engine (registered in Delaware or otherwise) and add "Edgar" and "10K." If it's a public company, you should easily find a document that the corporation is required to file annually with the Securities and Exchange Commission, the federal agency that regulates financial markets. At the top the document states where the company is incorporated. Once you start looking, you'll likely see the extent of your connections to Delaware. (You can also check out companies at opencorporates.com, a free database of company registrations.)

In fact, two-thirds of the companies included in the Fortune 500—the biggest companies listed on America's stock market—are registered in Delaware, accounting for about 45 percent of the United States' gross domestic product. They are global corporations that sell American products and services all around the world, employ tens of millions of people, and coordinate vast and complex international supply chains. They make money in a wide variety of ways, but one thing most of them have in common is their connection to Delaware.

For a sense of Delaware's relative importance, let's imagine what the Fortune 500 would look like without corporations registered in Delaware. Here are the other states where America's biggest companies choose to incorporate:

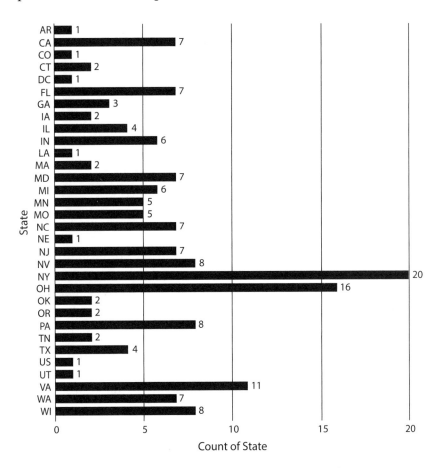

FIGURE 1. Number of Fortune 500 Companies by State (excluding Delaware) 2018.

But Delaware overshadows all of these states:

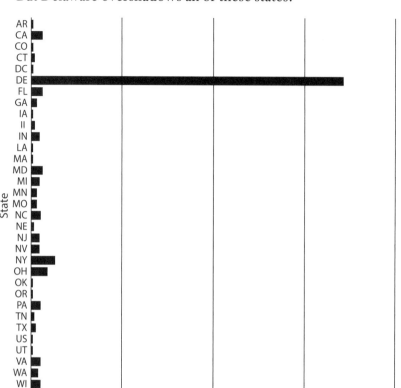

FIGURE 2. Number of Fortune 500 Companies by State Incorporation 2018.

The proportion of stock exchange–listed companies registered in Delaware has been growing over time. In the 1960s, 30 percent of companies listing for the first time on the New York Stock Exchange incorporated in Delaware. By the late 1990s, 77 percent of such companies chose the state as their corporate home.[20] By 2018, the figure was 82 percent.[21] By 2020, it was 93 percent.[22]

Publicly listed companies are just the beginning. The state has more registered businesses than residents—about 1.6 million companies in a state with a population of less than a million. Some 250,000 businesses register for the first time in Delaware each year—an average of 683 a day. Most of these are not large corporations that trade on the stock market, but instead are formed as structures such as limited liability companies. LLCs began spreading in the late 1980s and are now one of the leading legal structures of US businesses. And they make up more than 70 percent of Delaware's new business registrations. In 2020, there were 180,376 new LLCs registered in the state, compared to 51,747 corporations.[23]

LLCs have a number of advantages over traditional corporations. They can be used to pay less tax. They're more lightly regulated, so there's less paperwork to fill out. They have a lot of freedom to decide how to structure their management: in Delaware, an LLC's operating agreement need not be written down. It can be verbal, or even just implied. And you don't need a group of people to start a company—even an individual can form an LLC.

So it's a combination of both LLCs and corporations that have chosen to register in Delaware more than any other location. This is why Delaware matters. It is a critical component of the capitalist system. Think of Delaware as the closest thing the United States has to a registrar of corporate births, marriages, and deaths. Companies go there to get registered when they are first created. They go there to seek legal approval for mergers. They go there when they have legal disputes with each other. They go there when they enter bankruptcy. Delaware is for corporate life events.

While Delaware is, hands down, the business-formation capital of the United States, it is not, as it is sometimes mistakenly called, America's corporate capital. That would imply that lots of corporations physically locate themselves in Delaware. They do not. The large number of incorporations doesn't mean that any of these companies is actually based in Delaware or that they have much of a presence there. In fact, you're very unlikely to have much of a connection with a company that has its headquarters in Delaware. There are exceptions. Perhaps you live in Delaware. And you may eat foods that contain ingredients made by DuPont, an industrial giant (albeit less gigantic since its parent company was broken into three in 2019) based on the Delaware River in Wilmington—ingredients such as guar gum, a thickening agent used in ice cream, packaged foods, lotions, and laxatives. But for the most part, companies that are registered in Delaware are based in other US states or other countries. They get all the benefits of being in Delaware without actually having to locate there. And for the most part, the residents of Delaware have no more connection to "Delaware corporations" than the rest of us, and play little role in the incorporation industry.

So what does it actually mean to be incorporated or registered in Delaware?

It's what is sometimes called a "legal fiction." In fact, any company is a legal fiction, but given that most companies registered in Delaware do little actual business there, they might be considered more fictional than the norm. A company that is registered in Delaware can do business anywhere and doesn't have any obligations to the state, other than to pay annual fees to the Delaware Department of Corporations. In some years that could be the only interaction a company has with Delaware. But in many cases, when it goes to court it will do so in Delaware and be subject to Delaware's corporate laws. These state laws govern the company's "internal affairs," spelling out the rights of its shareholders and the duties of its managers. They guide what happens if there is a dispute between the company and some of its shareholders, or if a legal issue arises when another company tries to take it over, or if the company goes bankrupt. As we'll see, there are reasons that companies like to go to court in Delaware, if they have to go to court at all.

One parallel for Delaware-style corporate legal fiction is in the maritime world, where jurisdictions such as Panama and Liberia offer to register ships and fly flags for countries looking to evade international sanctions.

As a tiny state, Delaware has thrived as an exporting economy. In the seventeenth century, one of the state's top exports was tobacco; in the eighteenth century, wheat and lumber; in the nineteenth century, peaches; in the twentieth century, chemicals. Nowadays, Delaware's main export is laws. The standards set in Delaware govern a great deal of life in the United States and across the world. "The main benefit of Delaware incorporation is freedom from restriction by the corporate laws of other states and countries," argues UCLA's Lynn LoPucki. "The 'internal affairs' of a corporation are governed by the law of the state or country of incorporation. For a Delaware corporation, that means Delaware law, regardless of where in the world the corporation actually does business."[24]

If Delaware is such an important part of America's (and, therefore, the world's) corporate landscape, why is it so rarely discussed, outside of legal conferences, executive boardrooms, and analyst meetings? It may be because what goes on there seems obscure, complex, and arcane. It may also be because Delaware likes it that way. It wants to fly under the radar, largely unnoticed and taken for granted. It wants to be like background noise or telephone hold music, something that we tune out and live with, something whose ubiquity we don't even notice.

But Delaware's influence on US corporate life is immense. Its corporate code is the United States' corporate code. It has effectively set the rules on how much interest credit card companies can charge their customers. It has helped companies and wealthy individuals avoid paying taxes, harming the public finances of other US states. It has shielded the illicit and unethical use of corporate entities.

If you care about tax dodging, if you care about how corporations behave and how to hold them accountable, if you care about regulating the financial sector, if you care about the secret funding that flows into US political campaigns, if you are even just curious about what happens to the money on gift cards when the cards themselves get lost down the back of the sofa and the money is never spent, you should care about Delaware.

John Cassara describes the weary resignation with which he and his colleagues responded to their failure to secure financial information from one of the smallest states in their country. "The culture was: there's nothing weird about this," he says. "I'm not going to go to my superiors to question it. The general reaction at FinCEN was just to shrug our shoulders and say, 'This is just embarrassing.' We were all aware that Delaware was Delaware and there's not much anybody can do about it. Nobody can crack that nut."[25]

PART I

The Franchise

2

Enjoy Delaware®

Jeff Bullock likes to compare Delaware to Coca-Cola.

Bullock has been Delaware's secretary of state since 2009. Unlike most of his peers in other states, he was not elected, but appointed by the governor.[1] Tall, lean, and jovial, Bullock is an imposing figure with a bald, shaved head. Physically, he reminded me of Gareth Thomas, the former Welsh international rugby player. I met Bullock in his office in May 2018, and we went to a conference room next door to talk. One of the first things he wanted to talk to me about was Coca-Cola. "When you want to go and buy soda, there's this whole aisle of soda that you could pick from," Bullock said. He continued,

> There's all different brands—the name brands, the store brand, and the one-off brands that you never heard of. And a bunch of them are a lot cheaper than Coca-Cola, but you end up buying Coca-Cola. And you buy it because you know what you're buying. You know exactly what you're getting. You know how it's going to taste, you know how the bubbles are going to feel in your mouth. You don't have any questions about that brand. Certainty and reliability, that's what we sell.

It's an instructive analogy. For one thing, Coca-Cola does not take its market-leading position for granted, but advertises mercilessly.

Soda drinkers actually know how lots of different sodas are going to taste, but Coca-Cola's relentless promotion of itself as the "real thing" has created a sense that there is something authentic about the drink. What's more, Coca-Cola has learned that changing its taste will lose it customers. In 1985, the company suddenly replaced its many-decades-old beverage with New Coke, a drink with a different flavor, sparking a huge customer backlash as the more beloved original version disappeared from grocery shelves. Even Fidel Castro, the Cuban communist dictator, spoke out against it. The company was forced to change course after just seventy-eight days. It has learned to be careful when tinkering with the taste of Coke.

Similarly, Delaware is diligent about maintaining its position as America's incorporation capital and is reluctant to make substantial changes to its winning recipe. Ask a Delaware official why the state remains such a popular destination for business registrations, and the phrase you'll hear most is "business friendly." The state's official pitch for business uses a different analogy from Bullock's, one that hews closely to the "race to the top" position. "We are far more like Bergdorf Goodman or Tiffany than we are like the Dollar Store," it states in its marketing material. "You pay for quality and service."[2]

Whether you think there's a race to the top or to the bottom, or to stay one step ahead of the federal government, there's no doubt that Delaware wants to keep itself as attractive as possible for companies. Delaware may be the incumbent leader, but it cannot afford to rest and relax. Over the years, the state has introduced numerous tweaks to its corporate code, aimed both at being as business friendly as possible and at preventing the federal government from intervening. These tweaks, though, don't change the fundamental business-friendly aspects of Delaware law. The aim is to marry stability with flexibility.

Delaware's General Corporation Law, which governs the internal affairs of corporations registered in the state (and parallel laws for noncorporations such as LLCs and partnerships), is designed to be enabling, meaning that it generally allows corporations to develop their own specific ways of operating. There's a handful of more prescriptive elements. Investors have to be able to elect members of the board of directors and to vote on big deals. But even these provisions can be avoided, if both managers and stockholders agree.

As well as the law itself, one of Delaware's central attractions is the court system. Delaware has a separate legal track for corporate cases that is fast, efficient, and predictable. They go through the Chancery Court, where rulings are made by one of seven expert judges, without a jury to interfere. This unique system has given Delaware a rich body of case law. Judges write statements to justify their decisions, meaning that the outcomes of cases should not come as a complete surprise.

One key aspect of business-friendliness is that although Delaware expects managers to make decisions in the best interests of the corporation, in general, the state's law is guided by a "business judgment rule." Under that norm, if executives act in good faith, the courts will not subsequently second-guess their decisions—even if those decisions have disastrous results.

Another is that the owners of Delaware companies are protected from personal liability for business debts and judgments by a "corporate veil." This has traditionally been a key selling point. "A Delaware business owner is more likely to be struck by lightning than have this corporate veil pierced," boasted John Williams, who runs IncNow, a registering agent in Wilmington.[3]

Delaware law can also help businesses avoid taxes. The state does not levy corporate income taxes on earnings from intangible assets like trademarks. Corporations can transfer their trademarks to Delaware holding companies and then pay those Delaware subsidiaries to use the trademarks, avoiding tax in the states where they earned the money. It's called the "Delaware Loophole."

The process of setting up a company in Delaware is fast and efficient. The state has invested serious money in making sure that its bureaucracy is as customer friendly as possible.

There's also location. Perhaps in the age of the internet, physical location will become less and less important, but historically, Delaware has been lucky to be close to much of the United States' Northeast business world, the places where many corporations registered in the state are actually headquartered: New York, Pennsylvania,

Connecticut, the area around Washington, D.C., and, of course, Delaware's former rival for incorporations, New Jersey. Wilmington, Delaware's business hub and biggest city (population: seventy thousand), is roughly two hours by car or train from both New York and Washington. As a US senator, President Joe Biden famously boarded an Amtrak train in Wilmington every morning for more than three decades, preferring a lengthy round-trip commute to establishing a residence in Washington, as most out-of-town members of Congress do.

And, like Coca-Cola, Delaware is highly attentive to its branding. Officials from the state have an aggressive marketing campaign touting its benefits as a home for business formation, which they take on roadshows around the world in an attempt to attract non-US companies to register their American affiliates or subsidiaries in Delaware. The state's website details the benefits of incorporating in Delaware in nine languages other than English.

Often, Bullock says, the companies they pitch to have little sense of Delaware other than its role in incorporations. "I travel all over the world and they won't know where it is," he told me. "They won't necessarily even know *what* it is, but they'll have heard of Delaware and they will associate it with business and the corporate world in a positive way."

Delaware's size matters when it comes to the issue of business registrations. For one thing, it helps explain why it doesn't face much serious competition for incorporation fees. For most other states, with bigger budgets, the revenue from business fees is much less meaningful than it is to tiny Delaware. It does not make sense for them to even try to compete. This again punctures the idea of a genuine "race" for business registrations among all US states. Except for those with the smallest populations—such as Wyoming and South Dakota—most states have very little incentive to participate in such a race.

It's no coincidence that small states, like small countries, more often seem to convert themselves into service centers for corporations. Locations such as Luxembourg, the Cayman Islands, Bermuda, Hong Kong, Jersey, Singapore, and the Bahamas have traditionally attracted an outsized amount of corporate activity. "Havens are generally small states or countries that provide their services to the residents of large ones," observes UCLA's LoPucki. "Delaware is naturally suited to being a haven."

What makes Delaware different from any of these other jurisdictions is that it enjoys all the benefits of being part of the United States, such as the protection of federal law, the use of the US dollar, and unfettered access to other US states. "Delaware has a great, iron-clad contract—the U.S. Constitution—that grants Delaware the right to exploit the other 49 states," writes LoPucki. "The Constitution requires other states to give 'full faith and credit' to the 'public acts, records, and judicial proceedings' of Delaware. What Delaware does or decides, the other states are constitutionally obliged to honor."[4]

In Delaware they call the business-formation industry "the Franchise." If it did not have the Franchise, Delaware would almost certainly be in financial straits. In 2020, income from business registrations was the state's biggest source of revenue after personal income taxes. Together with the money from unclaimed property—a lucrative by-product of registrations, as we'll see—the Franchise accounted for more than 38 percent of the revenue flowing into the state's General Fund.[5] This makes Delaware far and away the US state most dependent on business-formation fees and related revenue. In fact, Delaware alone, with just 0.3 percent of the US population, collects more than one-quarter of the total fees paid in all of the United States for registering companies.[6]

This is not necessarily to say that Delaware fee-gouges (at least, not for incorporation fees). The state faces a delicate balancing act: the fees have to be set low enough so as not to turn off any company, but high enough to bring in a significant amount of revenue. It costs $89 to register a corporation or LLC, plus $50 for a certificate of incorporation. It takes a few weeks to get the paperwork back, but for an additional $50 you can get it the following day, or $100 to get it back the same day you file—or $500 to get it back within two hours, $1,000 if you can only wait an hour, or $1,500 if you need to get it registered in thirty minutes.[7]

Then every year, you'll have to pay a franchise tax, based on either the number of authorized shares the company has or on the overall value of the corporation. Because companies of all different sizes incorporate in Delaware, there's a lot of variation. The minimum franchise tax payment is $175, and the maximum is capped at $250,000. Until 2017, the top figure was $180,000, but Delaware determined that it could increase that figure for the biggest companies by 40 percent without losing any of them.

"There appears to be a fair amount of elasticity in what we can charge," says Bullock, "which doesn't mean you get sloppy or stupid." The calculation is that $250,000 is still peanuts to a Fortune 500 company, but in the aggregate, it brings in tens of millions of dollars in revenues for Delaware. LLCs and other "alternative entities" pay a flat franchise tax of $300. Companies that pay these fees in any year are considered to be "in good standing."

If, like the vast majority of businesses registered in Delaware, you are not actually doing any real business in the state, you do not have to pay corporate taxes there. So what makes the Franchise such a critical revenue generator is the fees: in 2020, for example, the state collected more than ten times as much revenue from fees than it did from corporate income taxes.[8]

But business-registration fees, franchise taxes, and unclaimed property revenues don't capture the full extent of the impact of the Franchise on Delaware's economy. Every company has to have a registered agent and there are hundreds of agents in the state, from mom-and-pop operations to vast companies with hundreds of employees. Then there are the lawyers that corporations hire to represent them in court (companies must have at least one Delaware lawyer in their teams) and their support teams. Then there are the ancillary services employees who work in the restaurants, bars, and hotels, the Uber drivers, office cleaners, and IT service technicians. "From couriers to caterers, all have thrived in the legal business ecosystem," notes Bill Freeborn, Delaware's former assistant secretary of state, who once ran the Division of Corporations.[9] All these people have the Franchise to thank for their jobs and all of them pay taxes to the state of Delaware. And personal income taxes are the state's biggest single source of revenue.[10] A good proportion of that comes from folks whose livelihoods depend on the Franchise.

Delaware's economy needs all the revenue from the Franchise because the state has struggled to diversify in the postindustrial era. In the 1950s and 1960s, more than 40 percent of the working population was employed in manufacturing.[11] But, over a three-decade period, Delaware went from the US state with the biggest manufacturing sector relative to its population to the state most dependent on services, many of them associated with the Franchise. In 1980, manufacturing accounted for 34 percent of Delaware's economic output, more than any other state in the union, and well above the US average of 21 percent. By 2010, the share of output attributable to manufacturing had fallen to 7.5 percent, smaller than thirty-eight other states, and well below the US average of 12 percent. Meanwhile, the services sector grew from nearly 20 percent of Delaware's economic output in 1980, roughly the US average, to 56 percent in 2010, the highest proportion in the United States, far above the US average of 36 percent.[12]

Since the Great Recession of 2007 to 2009, Delaware has become even less diversified and even more dependent on the Franchise. The number of workers in the state employed in manufacturing dropped by 22 percent between 2008 and 2021, while the number employed in leisure and hospitality increased by about 9 percent. (The increase from 2008 to 2019, before COVID-19 hit leisure and hospitality, was 18 percent.) The number of construction workers fell by 4 percent while the number of government employees grew by 4 percent.[13]

Delaware's industrial past is visible all around the state. The Chrysler plant in Newark, which made vehicles such as the Dodge Durango, closed in 2008. The GM factory in Wilmington that used to produce Pontiac Solstice convertibles closed in 2009, marking the end of large-scale automotive production in the northeastern United States. Between them, the two car plants had once employed 10,000 workers. Hercules, a chemicals company spun off from DuPont in 1912, employed 1,800 people at its Wilmington headquarters in the 1980s, but it was subsequently sold in 2008 and broken up. Its successor companies now only employ a few hundred people in Delaware.[14] National Vulcanized Fibre closed its Yorklyn factory in 2006, after 100 years at the site. Evraz Claymont Steel, a steel mill in Claymont that employed 500 workers, closed in December 2013. AstraZeneca laid off 550 of the 5,000 staff at its Fairfax office in 2011 and shed another 1,200 jobs in Delaware between 2013 and 2016. DuPont laid off 1,700 of its Delaware-based employees in 2016, nearly one-third of its workforce in the state. There has been some new manufacturing investment, but not nearly enough to employ the same sorts of numbers of people who used to work at the old facilities. The COVID-19 pandemic hit Delaware particularly hard. Hotels and restaurants, which depend on the tourism the Franchise brought in pre-pandemic times, were devastated.[15] By October 2020, the state had the second-worst economic recovery among US states, according to one measure.[16]

Over time, as Delaware's economy has become less and less diversified, it has become more and more addicted to the Franchise. In 2016 the state overhauled its corporate tax structure to try to attract more real investment, not just incorporations. It has not yet succeeded in diversifying the state's economic base. "Are we too dependent? Probably," Bullock says. Jack Markell, the state's former governor (and Biden administration nominee to be US ambassador to the Organisation for Economic Co-operation and Development), echoed that view when I spoke with him in 2019. But neither seemed too worried about it, so long as the money from the Franchise continues to flow in.

And as long as it does, all Delawareans will continue to benefit enormously from the Franchise. Delaware has the second-highest level of per capita spending among the fifty US states.[17] The only state that spends more government money per capita is oil-rich Alaska, which pays an annual dividend from its Permanent Fund to every man, woman, and child in the state. Delaware effectively pays its own dividend: the proceeds from the Franchise. Its residents may not receive a check every year, but they do enjoy several other benefits, thanks to the income from registration fees. Delawareans have the fourth-lowest tax burden among all states in the union,[18] and Delaware is one of only five states without a sales tax.[19] It has the United States' fourth-lowest property tax rate. If you include all the money that companies located outside the state contribute directly to its state revenues, Delaware residents end up paying just fifty cents for each dollar of service they receive.[20]

Joe Biden is perhaps the most high-profile beneficiary of the Franchise. In his 2020 presidential campaign, Biden received big donations from a wide range of business leaders. The Hollywood producer Jeffrey Katzenberg, Netflix CEO Reed Hastings, and Sean Parker, who cofounded Napster and was Facebook's first president, all gave more than $1 million each. But as a senator for thirty-six years, Biden's political campaigns had always been powered by money from Delaware—money that had been earned thanks to the Franchise. Among Biden's biggest and most consistent donors were Delaware corporate law firms that owed their success to the state's role as America's home for business registrations.

The leaders, the state, and the residents of Delaware have clearly benefited from the state's role as the incorporation capital of America.

But have the rest of us?

———

In 1974, William Cary published an explosive article in the *Yale Law Journal*. Almost fifty years later, Cary's opening lines still crackle with electricity:

> Delaware is both the sponsor and the victim of a system contributing to the deterioration of corporation standards. This unhappy state of affairs, stemming in great part from the movement toward the least common denominator, Delaware, seems to be developing on both the legislative and judicial fronts. In the management of corporate affairs, state statutory and case law has always been supreme, with federal intrusion limited to the field of securities regulation. Perhaps now is the time to reconsider the federal role.[21]

Cary was no radical. The son of a utilities lawyer from Columbus, Ohio, he had joined the SEC in 1938 after graduating from Harvard Business School. When the United States entered the Second World War, Cary rose through the Marine Corps before becoming a spy, serving in Romania and Yugoslavia in the final years of the war as an officer with the Office of Strategic Services, the predecessor agency of the CIA. After the war he went into academia, lecturing at Harvard, Northwestern, and Columbia, and became an expert on the law of corporations. In 1961, President John F. Kennedy appointed him chairman of the Securities and Exchange Commission.

But Cary was not afraid to upset entrenched corporate interests. He was an effective campaigner for more effective regulation of the financial sector. He increased the SEC's enforcement powers, tightened prohibitions on insider trading, ran a study that helped end fixed securities brokerage commissions, and oversaw the reorganization of the American Stock Exchange, one of the United States' most venerated trading venues. Cary was not combative, but he called it like he saw it. In a speech to the Investment Bankers Association in 1962, he said that the New York Stock Exchange, "though a public institution, still seems to have certain characteristics of a private club."[22] His observation outraged many on Wall Street at the time. Today many in the financial community would agree that it was an accurate and fair description of the situation at the time and perhaps still now.

It was after Cary returned to academia, as a professor at Columbia Law School, that he wrote his famous article on Delaware and the "race to the bottom" in corporate standards. The general idea of a race to the bottom among US states is now fairly mainstream. It takes a dim view of interstate competition, viewing it as an inexorable move toward the interests of corporations. It portrays the US economy as a series of match-ups in which states try to underbid each other, attracting investment by weakening environmental rules and lowering employment standards. They compete to lower taxes and business fees.

As New Jersey's rise and self-induced fall in the 1910s battle for business registrations illustrates, there have long been concerns in the United States about the wisdom of such a competition. Louis Brandeis was among the first to call the search for increasingly less stringent standards and weaker regulation a "race to the bottom." The race for charters, Brandeis said in 1933, "was not one of diligence but of laxity."[23]

Cary's 1974 article picked up on this idea. New Jersey had lost its leading position in company formations because it had tightened up its laws. Delaware had taken over because its laws remained relatively lenient. Other states had gradually been forced to loosen their corporate laws to match Delaware's, for fear of losing their business registrations to the state. Cary argued that the tendency had even infected the US Model Business Corporation Act (MBCA)—a legal template first drafted by the American Bar Association in 1950 for states to adopt in the absence of a federal incorporation law. The MBCA, Cary noted, had "been watered down to compete with the Delaware statute on its own terms rather than offering alternative approaches," thus helping accelerate and institutionalize the race to the bottom. In a way, the easing standards for corporate protections achieved the vision of Rockefeller and other corporate titans back in 1902, who welcomed federal incorporations as a way to bring uniformity to what was a fragmented system of different standards between states. The difference was that, in Cary's view, the standards were being set not in Washington but in Delaware. And changes to the law were mostly in one direction: "They have watered the rights of shareholders vis-à-vis management down to a thin gruel," Cary noted. It was up to the federal government to protect shareholders' interests, and it largely did so by policing how securities were offered and sold, setting up a distinction between securities law (a federal responsibility) and corporate law (made by the states). Cary argued that this distinction made little sense in practice:

> There is no justification for a federal law disciplining or holding a tippee liable for misusing inside information concerning management decisions but not monitoring the misconduct of management itself. Even if it is said that the securities laws focus exclusively upon protection of the securities market, confidence in the market generally and in any particular stock may depend as much upon the probity of management as upon the mechanism of the market. If we accept the soundness of the securities laws, then there should be a federal interest in providing a standard of conduct for management and the corporations on which much of the economy depends.[24]

Cary fell short of advocating federal incorporation, as Roosevelt, Taft, and Wilson had urged early in the twentieth century, but instead proposed federal standards of corporate responsibility on such issues as shareholder approval of deals, the provisions included in certificates of incorporation, and the duties of company directors, officers, and controlling shareholders.

Cary's paper was hugely influential and, for a while, even took hold at that bastion of free-market thinking, the University of Chicago, where the law professor Stanley Kaplan shared Cary's view. "When the faculty of the University of Chicago teaches that markets are bad, as Kaplan did, and that only federal regulation can save the day, you can be confident that there was an academic consensus," notes Frank Easterbrook, a US Court of Appeals judge for the Seventh Circuit who is himself a senior lecturer at the University of Chicago Law School.[25]

But, as with many an academic consensus, it was soon broken. In the late 1970s and the 1980s, legal scholars picked apart Cary's argument. Cary had barely accounted for investors, assuming they were widely dispersed, largely uninformed, and therefore largely unable to hold managers to account. But some shareholders are savvy—at least the big ones such as pension funds or money-management firms. If Delaware had lax rules that helped managers benefit at the expense of their investors, the counterargument ran, over time investors would put their money into companies registered in states with higher standards, or where the managers don't fleece the investors. Investors would then follow the money, going to companies that gave them the best returns and avoiding greedy managers. A series of studies appeared to confirm that idea, suggesting, for example, that when companies reincorporate in Delaware their stock prices rise (although subsequent research cast doubt on the durability of this "Delaware effect").[26] Instead of a "race to the bottom," in fact, there was a race to the top, the argument went, with states competing to establish the best possible environment for managers to create value for shareholders.[27]

This debate continues, having spawned a vast academic literature on whether Delaware leads in a race that is heading up or down. Although interesting, it's also something of an intellectual rabbit hole. It's hard to find data that comprehensively demonstrate the validity of either argument. Perhaps the competition for company registrations doesn't have a clear effect on corporate governance standards one way or the other.

And perhaps the metaphor of a race for incorporations between all the states may be somewhat misleading. It seems unlikely that before a company chooses a place to incorporate, it carefully considers the corporate code of every one of the fifty US states. Instead, what typically happens is that the company's lawyer makes a recommendation, acting more in the role of Yente, the village matchmaker in *Fiddler on the Roof*, than online dating sites, where people go to make their own matches. Rather than a race, what Delaware usually wins is a series of one-on-one comparisons. And to an extent, the decision is clouded by the notion that Delaware is the default "other location." Most lawyers get a basic grounding in corporate law in law school. Many of those corporate law principles derive from important cases that were decided in Delaware courts, which makes sense given Delaware's outsized significance in the world of business formation. Law school graduates also generally understand that Delaware is the state where a large majority of companies incorporate. So, more often than not, the choice is not between fifty states, but between two: the state in which the company is located, and Delaware.

The result is that Delaware has a virtual monopoly in the market for out-of-state incorporations, in much the same way that Facebook has an effective monopoly over its particular type of social media. Public companies often incorporate in the state in which they are headquartered (where they're more likely to exercise political clout), but those that choose to look elsewhere invariably register in Delaware: about 95 percent of US companies that incorporate somewhere other than their home state choose Delaware.[28]

Other states, particularly Wyoming and Nevada, have tried to copy or better Delaware's corporate code, but have so far failed to tempt a significant chunk of the business-formation market away. Nothing succeeds like success. Freshly trained corporate lawyers understand Delaware's importance in the world of business incorporation. An experienced corporate lawyer may well have strong relations with lawyers in Delaware with whom they have worked in the past. Delaware benefits from these professional networks, and encourages them.

Ask officials in Delaware whether they are concerned about the prospect of competition from other states and they will say they are more troubled by the prospect of federal intervention. This need not be on the grand scale envisaged by Presidents Roosevelt, Taft, and Wilson, or even the more modest, if still sweeping proposal advanced by Cary. Rather, in recent decades the federal government has taken a variety of steps across the border between securities and corporate law, often in response to corporate scandals that have demanded regulatory action in their wake. The most obvious recent example was the 2002 Sarbanes-Oxley Act, which detailed a range of different ways in which certain members of company boards were required to be independent, required attorneys to report if their employers or clients condoned breaches of fiduciary duty, and outlawed corporate loans to executives and directors. Each of these was traditionally part of the states' purview, and Delaware took a dim view of the federal government's inability to stay in its lane. As Myron Steele, the former chief justice of the Delaware Supreme Court, noted in response to Sarbanes-Oxley:

> Prescriptive rulemaking by statute, or by devolution to regulatory power, is largely politically driven, normative decision making applicable across the board to all of those subject to it regardless of circumstance. The driving rationale is messianic populism, almost religious at its core. On the other hand, those driving in the state lane seek incremental common law building of principle-based doctrine derived from analyses of factually based controversies. I think the second better balances authority and accountability in internal corporate governance. While the first approach may well be better for addressing market fraud and disclosure issues designed to maximize transparency in the broader market, the second approach better balances authority and accountability in internal corporate governance.[29]

Delaware's real struggle, then, is to keep the jurisdictional lines clear between itself and the federal government. As Mark Roe, a professor at Harvard Law School, has observed, "When the issue is big, the federal government takes control of it or threatens to do so, or Delaware players are conscious that the federal government, even if silent, could step in if roused. . . . Thus, that which persists in Delaware is that which the federal authorities tolerate."[30]

If anything is likely to prompt the federal government to extend its jurisdiction in corporate governance, it is a corporate scandal. Scandals reinforce the sense that, at least in some areas, there has been a race to the bottom, and that the logic of that race means states cannot improve standards on their own. The argument is not just academic. For Delaware, it is about holding on to the company-registration business, the life force of its economy.

The Franchise was Delaware's salvation. As it became increasingly important to the state's economic well-being, Delaware discovered in the incorporation business a unifying system that enabled its residents to enjoy the benefits and others—consumers, taxpayers, and citizens elsewhere in the United States and around the world—to pay the price.

To understand these benefits and costs fully, we need to dig deeper into the workings of the Franchise and its effects.

3

The Delaware Loophole

Homer D. Poe is the lovable mascot of Home Depot. With his oversized head, bulbous nose, and orange baseball cap obscuring his vision, Homer can sometimes be seen schmoozing with customers among the power tools, lumber, and plumbing parts at Home Depot stores.

Homer was designed to be funny and nonintimidating, a way to show shoppers that you don't have to be an expert contractor to take on projects around the house. But he's also performed another important job for the DIY chain. He's helped it save billions of dollars on its taxes.

Bringing Homer to life was the brainchild of Doug Kincaid, who owned a St. Louis mascot-manufacturing company with his brother Bill. They approached Home Depot in 1991. Homer had actually been created ten years earlier and had been used in Home Depot ads, but the Kincaids' new idea was to create life-sized versions of the handyman character to interact with staff and customers.

At the same time that it introduced Homer into its stores, Home Depot also gave Homer his own corporate identity. The company (incorporated in Delaware) created a wholly owned subsidiary in Delaware, called it Homer TLC, and assigned to it all of its trademarks, including "The Home Depot," "Do-It-Yourself Warehouse," and "Where Low Prices Are Just the Beginning," the phrases it uses in its advertising, on its website, and all over its stores, from their facades and signs to their shopping carts and employee aprons. At the time, those trademarks were valued in an independent appraisal at $354 million.[1]

Up until this point, Home Depot itself had owned these trademarked phrases. Overnight, they were transferred to Homer. Under the new arrangement, Home Depot paid Homer TLC royalties to use the trademarks as a proportion of all its profits from its more than twelve hundred stores across the United States, as well as more than seventy in Canada and a handful in Argentina and Mexico. Home Depot originally agreed to pay Homer 1.5 percent of its gross sales, increasing that amount to 4.0 percent in 1999. In return, the hardware chain was allowed to use the trademarks—the same trademarks it had been using all along. The company was effectively paying itself to use the same intellectual property that it had created and had used up to that point.

This trick helped Home Depot slash its tax bills. Even though Homer was a subsidiary and Home Depot was effectively just transferring money around internally between departments, officially, Homer was registered as a distinct business. And, because it was a distinct business registered in Delaware while Home Depot was headquartered in Atlanta, Homer could take advantage of a quirk of Delaware law that can prove very profitable to some companies.

The relevant law, section 1902(b)(8) of Delaware's corporation income tax code, exempts companies from paying state corporation tax to the First State if their main activities are managing "intangible investments," such as patents and trademarks.[2] So companies without any real operations in Delaware don't incur any state corporate income tax there.

This is widely known as the "Delaware Loophole," although it is not so much a loophole—an unintended gap in the tax code, to be fixed on discovery—as a deliberate pitch to companies to register businesses in Delaware as a way to channel their income and avoid paying corporate taxes in other US states. "This is a time-honored sham (oops, I mean 'tax planning strategy') perpetrated by the legislature of the state of Delaware on the treasuries of its sister states," observes Sheldon Pollack, a law professor at the University of Delaware.[3] There is nothing underhanded about this. The US Constitution prohibits states from imposing their tax jurisdictions on "foreign corporations" that do not have sufficient involvement with the state. For the purpose of state taxes, companies not based in Delaware are considered "foreign."[4] Delaware is not the only state that doesn't tax companies that only hold "intangibles." Michigan, for example, has similar provisions in place. In Delaware, the measure dates back to the early 1980s, when the First State introduced it in an attempt to attract bank holding companies, as we'll see in more detail in chapter 9.

The Delaware Loophole makes the state a domestic tax haven. Like any tax haven, companies use it to avoid paying taxes elsewhere. In this case, the specific taxes that Delaware can help them avoid are state corporate income taxes. "The state of Delaware is indeed a domestic tax haven in the sense that its corporate laws appear to enable firms to significantly reduce state income tax burdens," note economists Scott Dyreng of Duke, Bradley Lindsey of Utah State, and Jake Thornock, of Brigham Young University. "This reduction comes at the expense of other states and benefits Delaware via franchise taxes and fees."[5]

Effectively, then, the Delaware Loophole replaces the corporate tax revenues collected by a variety of states with the corporate fees collected by Delaware.

There is an irony here: it was the Biden administration that in 2021 spearheaded the goal of implementing a global minimum corporate tax of at least 15 percent, an aim that was endorsed by the leaders of the G7 and the G20, the world's biggest economies. The administration also signaled that it would push for higher top rates of US tax on corporations. Yet Biden's home state had long benefited from enabling companies to lower their overall tax bills.

To be sure, the taxes that companies avoid using the loophole represent a relatively small part of a big corporation's overall tax burden, but using it can cut their state tax bills by up to 24 percent, boosting their overall profits by 1.0 to 1.5 percent, a significant amount for businesses with billions of dollars in earnings.[6] For large corporations, a lot can ride on an extra 1 percent of net income.

Like the First State itself, stock-market investors seem to like companies that exploit the Delaware Loophole, although they don't seem to like it when anyone brings attention to it. Companies that use the loophole are valued by the stock market at up to 1.9 percent more than those that do not.[7] But the day that the *Wall Street Journal* ran a front-page story about the practice in 2002, the companies mentioned in the article had an average of 2 percent wiped off the value of their shares.[8]

Regardless, the Delaware Loophole offers one more reason for companies to choose to incorporate in the First State. Of course, the loophole doesn't in itself explain the Franchise, but the First State's place as part of a low-tax strategy is clearly an important attraction.

The Delaware Loophole turned Homer TLC, a company with just four employees—a lawyer, a paralegal, and two administrative assistants—into a corporate titan with annual revenues of up to $2 billion by the early 2000s. Homer took in a total of $4.7 billion for the tax years ending in 2000, 2001, and 2002, primarily in the form of payments from Home Depot for use of trademarks and other similar items.

A decade later, when tax authorities in Arizona were auditing Home Depot's books, they found the retailer had excluded from its state tax returns the payments made to Homer, lowering Home Depot's state tax bill. The Arizona Department of Revenue asked the company to include the Homer payments. Home Depot at first protested and then decided to fight the authorities in court.

Home Depot's argument was effectively to disown its own loveable mascot. It argued that Homer and Home Depot were two separate organizations. Homer, it noted, was in the business of protecting its trademarks, while Home Depot was a retailer of home-improvement products. The chain pointed out that its stores sold one thousand different brands of products, most of which did not bear its own trademark. The trademarked phrases were therefore nothing more than an "accessory" to its main business.

The State of Arizona argued that although Home Depot and Homer were legally two separate organizations, one could not exist without the other. "Home Depot needed the intellectual property to make its sales and be able to secure repeat business in the state," argued Arizona assistant attorney general Kimberly Cygan. "And the subsidiary that held the trademark needed Home Depot, obviously, just because that's how it made its money. . . . If Home Depot were to go out of business, then the trademarks would not be worth anything."[9]

The courts sided with the state, ordering Home Depot to pay Arizona state tax on all revenues from its Arizona stores, including the payments it made to Homer. "Home Depot would not be 'Home Depot' without the trademarks that it licenses from Homer for its retail stores, advertising and website," wrote Judge Diane Johnsen of the state's court of appeals in her 2013 ruling. "It is the 'Home Depot' brand on the company's advertisements and website and throughout its retail stores that Home Depot relies on to distinguish the quality of its products, selection, and customer service from those of its competitors."[10]

But many other businesses have taken advantage of the Delaware Loophole. It is particularly useful for companies with lots of spread-out locations, like the big retail chains. In many cases, the companies have only stopped the practice after state tax authorities have fought them in court.

Like Home Depot, Toys "R" Us named its Delaware trademark-holding company after its mascot, a giraffe named Geoffrey. The parent company in 1984 transferred to the subsidiary the ownership of its trademarks and trade names, including Toys "R" Us, Kids "R" Us, Babies "R" Us, and the logo of Geoffrey himself. By 1991, Geoffrey Inc. was valued at $1.5 billion.[11] In 1993, the State of South Carolina won a landmark victory against Geoffrey, which was followed by successful legal action by Oklahoma, Louisiana, and Massachusetts. By the time of these later cases, Geoffrey had retreated from Delaware to its parent company's hometown of Wayne, New Jersey. Ironically, Toys "R" Us filed for bankruptcy in 2018, a process that only its name and logos survived, and in 2021 Macy's announced plans to revive the brand by opening four hundred Toys "R" Us concessions within its own stores.

In the 1990s, Walmart funneled revenues from its stores through a Delaware subsidiary, WNR. Walmart transferred brand names including Sam's Club into WNR, paid it for the use of those brands, and deducted them as expenses from its taxable income in other states. But after a group of states, including Louisiana and New Mexico, successfully challenged the strategy in court, WNR and Walmart merged in 1997. Walmart subsequently moved on to employ a range of other state tax-dodging strategies.

Many other big retailers have made extensive use of the Delaware Loophole, including the Gap, Ikea, Kmart, Kohl's, Bath & Body Works, Victoria's Secret, Payless Shoes, and Staples.

But it isn't only retailers. One high-profile example of a very different company that used the Delaware Loophole was WorldCom, the telecommunications company that filed for bankruptcy in 2002 amid revelations of massive financial accounting fraud. (WorldCom subsequently changed its name to MCI, which Verizon bought in 2005.) WorldCom, which at the time was based in Clinton, Mississippi, funneled nearly $20 billion through its Delaware-based subsidiary, MCI WorldCom Brands, between 1999 and 2001.[12] (Oddly, US tax authorities and regulators had not even noticed the subsidiary's existence until a group of MCI creditors alerted them.) Unusually, the company wasn't paying its subsidiary for the use of trademarks or patents, but for what its accountants called "management foresight"—the profits that the company made, supposedly because of the superior skill of its top executives.

We don't know exactly how much money is or has been funneled through Delaware-based subsidiaries and holding companies, because corporations do not have to disclose anything about what they transfer to them. The most authoritative estimate is that the loophole cost other US states somewhere between $6.6 billion and $9.5 billion in lost revenues between 1995 and 2009.[13]

The Delaware Loophole hit its height in the 1990s, but has waned since.[14] In an effort to combat tax avoidance, twenty-eight US states have mandated "combined reporting," under which multistate corporations must state in one report the profits of all subsidiaries, regardless of location.

But corporations have fought tooth and nail against combined reporting. In both New Jersey and Kentucky, the debates over bills including combined reporting (which passed in 2018) went down to the wire. In New Mexico, comprehensive legislation passed in 2019 after decades of contentious debate. Business groups and Republican politicians have argued that the requirement adds an unnecessary burden on businesses, calling it effectively a hike in corporate taxes, and have cautioned that the expected bump in revenues may fail to materialize. Kentucky's former Republican governor Matt Bevin refused to sign the bill into law—but he also refused to veto it, enabling the state legislature to enact it anyway. Tom Wolf, the Democratic governor of Pennsylvania since 2015, has been trying for many years to get his state to pass a combined-reporting bill, but Republicans who lead the state legislature have repeatedly blocked it. Similar efforts in Florida, Maryland, and Virginia have been repeatedly blocked.

The trend may be toward combined reporting, but twenty-two US states have still not enacted the measure. Two of them, South Dakota and Wyoming, levy no corporate taxes at all, so they have nothing to chase. Nevada, Ohio, and Washington levy "gross receipts taxes" instead of corporate income taxes (Delaware has both). The remaining states, which retain separate state-by-state accounting, include seven of the poorest states in the union: Alabama, Arkansas, Louisiana, Mississippi, Oklahoma, South Carolina, and Tennessee. Most of these states have "addback" rules, which try to limit corporate tax abuse by requiring corporations to add back some expenses to their state income tax filings. But there are typically lots of exceptions, so, in practice, addback statutes are generally much weaker than combined-reporting rules.

That means that the regions of the United States that most need state revenue to combat the effects of poverty are the very ones that most enable corporations to dodge local taxes. (To be fair, Delaware has also not passed combined-reporting legislation, which means that companies based in the First State could avoid state corporate taxes there by transferring their profits to holding companies, either in Delaware or elsewhere.) The failure to pass combined-reporting rules in these states speaks to the power of business lobbying. Combined reporting has come under "intense opposition from the corporate community," notes David Brunori, a senior director at RSM US, a middle-market audit, tax, and consulting firm, and a professor at the George Washington University's Law School.[15] Michael Mazerov, senior fellow at the Center on Budget and Policy Priorities, a left-leaning think tank, echoes that view: "Corporations lobbied very hard against combined reporting to preserve their tax shelters," he says.[16]

The Delaware Loophole may have shrunk somewhat, but it could regrow again as companies restructure in response to the Tax Cuts and Jobs Act, the 2017 tax-cutting law that President Trump often touted as one of his greatest achievements. One of the Trump administration's key aims was to encourage US companies to repatriate the assets they held overseas back to the United States and thereby to broaden the US tax base. With that aim in mind, the law dealt with intangible assets through two provisions, the GILTI (global intangible low taxed income) and FDII (foreign derived intangible income). These provisions essentially operate as a global minimum tax, imposing tax on the intangible income that US companies collect from overseas, at an effective rate of 10.5 percent.[17] But they may not end up expanding the tax base as much as policymakers expect, says LeAnn Luna, a professor of accounting at the University of Tennessee. Multinational corporations will look for ways to avoid GILTI and FDII, Luna predicts. As an employee of KPMG, one of the "Big Four" global accounting firms, Luna used to advise companies on how to structure their corporations to avoid taxes.[18] When Congress passed the Trump tax cuts, she advised the State of Tennessee that companies might try to get around new provisions by using the Delaware Loophole. "To reduce state tax liabilities that could result from the Trump tax cuts, many US multinational corporations can be expected to form subsidiaries," Luna wrote, "that, in turn, own the stock of subsidiary corporations operating in foreign jurisdictions. . . . Delaware is a good choice to locate such holding companies because Delaware does not tax the earnings associated with intangible activity. . . . As a separate reporting state [i.e., without combined reporting], Tennessee will be unable to share in the tax base of the Delaware corporations and, therefore, will not gain additional tax revenues from the new international federal tax provisions."[19]

The new rules came into effect in 2018. It may take several years for companies to assess how it affects them and to restructure themselves accordingly. But there is a good chance that, rather than paying the taxes, US companies will try to avoid the tax, and create even more Delaware holding companies to do so.

In 2020, Google, the search engine giant, announced it was overhauling its global tax strategy, ending its use of a complex structure dubbed the "Double Irish Dutch Sandwich," which had saved the company and other US multinationals hundreds of billions of dollars.[20] The "Double Irish" part of the structure saw companies shift taxable income from a company in the Republic of Ireland to another company registered in Ireland but operating in an offshore tax haven. In the Dutch part of the recipe, companies took advantage of a tax law that allowed them to move untaxed profits via a company based in the Netherlands to a tax haven without incurring any withholding tax. This Dutch company was used in the middle of the Irish "sandwich." The money would end up in traditional tax havens such as Bermuda, beyond the reach of US authorities. In just 2017 and 2018, for example, Google had saved more than $40 billion using the scheme.[21]

Such strategies helped US companies to park more than $1 trillion of their profits offshore by the end of 2017. But, in response to a crackdown by the Organisation for Economic Co-operation and Development against international tax avoidance, Irish authorities closed the loophole and gave the companies until 2020 to stop using it. Google was actually one of the last US companies to drop the sandwich.

Google had used that time to prepare its exit strategy, and the Delaware Loophole played a significant role in it. In 2015, the internet company had completely overhauled its structure, creating a new Delaware-registered holding company, Alphabet. "The primary purpose of the Alphabet reorganization appears to be aggressive state corporate tax avoidance," concluded Bret Bogenschneider of the

Vienna University of Economics and Business and Ruth Heilmeier of the University of Cologne, in a 2016 paper. "The Alphabet entity is designed as a Delaware intellectual property holding company designed to reduce taxation by the deduction of royalty payments as an expense," the researchers noted.[22]

Google offered proof, if it were needed, that so long as states that charge corporate taxes fail to pass combined-reporting rules, it will continue to make sense for some companies to use the Delaware Loophole.

———

Applebee's is a casual dining chain known for below-average food at below-average prices.

The restaurant definitely has its fans, otherwise it wouldn't have almost two thousand locations around the world. The Triple Chocolate Meltdown, a molten chocolate cake, and Riblets, boneless pork ribs, are cult classics among Applebee's devotees.

But when Reddit, the online discussion forum, asked its readers in 2018, "What restaurant have you sworn to never return to and why?," Applebee's came top of the list. Readers complained about finding bugs in their dishes, being served raw chicken, getting extreme food poisoning from dining there, and the chain's rude and inattentive waitstaff. Even some of the more complimentary comments were far from glowing. "I'm a 35-year-old father of two. When I want to go for a beer, I head to Applebee's," said one contributor. "No crowds, no loud music, no lines for beers or bathrooms. The food's not great, but it's cheap. If I could bring a recliner there, that would be my heaven."[23]

While the food and service may sometimes miss the mark, there is nothing slapdash about Applebee's' corporate strategy.

The chain traces its origins back to 1980, with the opening of T. J. Applebee's Edibles and Elixirs in Atlanta. By 1983, the concept was bought by a restaurant operator with the idea of creating a national franchise. The chain grew steadily, but started expanding in earnest in 1988, when it was sold to Abe Gustin, a former truck driver and an Applebee's franchisee, and the company's president, John Hamra. They opened dozens of new restaurants with amazing speed. In their first year running the company, Applebee's revenues increased by 500 percent.

Just two years earlier, Gustin had opened Kansas City's first Applebee's, near 103rd and State Line Road, the street that divides Kansas City, Kansas, from Kansas City, Missouri. The restaurant was on the Missouri side, so when Gustin and Hamra bought the company, they set up its first independent headquarters in Kansas City, Missouri. In 1990, they took the company public. By 1993, Applebee's was opening about one hundred new restaurants a year and the chain had outgrown its headquarters, so it moved to a larger building across State Line Road in nearby Overland Park, Kansas.

By 2005, the company needed an even bigger headquarters. By now it was a big local employer, with power and influence. So the company made the State of Kansas an offer, attaching a threat: it could build its new building in Kansas, or it could move back across State Line Road to Missouri. The price to stay? Applebee's wanted to pay zero property tax on its new headquarters. The State of Kansas weighed its options and pretty much gave the company what it had asked for, plus other perks—a $12 billion package in total. Two years later, Applebee's moved into its new building in Lenexa, Kansas. Around the same time, Applebee's was bought by the parent company of IHOP, the chain of breakfast restaurants with the distinctive blue roofs, once winningly known as "International House of Pancakes." The new parent company had a different strategy: instead of Applebee's continuing to own and operate some of its own restaurants, it set a goal of franchising 98 percent of its restaurants by 2013. The slimmed-down company no longer needed its 187,000 square-foot building. Because it was getting rid of staff at the head office, the State of Kansas was planning to cancel its property tax deal. After another round of negotiations with both states, Applebees's crossed State Line Road in 2011 for the last time, relocating to Kansas City, Missouri after the State of Missouri offered a $13 million incentive package.[24] But by 2015, Applebee's was on the move again. Its parent

company wanted to consolidate operations and announced it would
transfer Applebee's corporate home to its headquarters in Southern
California.

Ultimately, in this battle, part of a larger economic war of attri-
tion between Kansas and Missouri, both sides lost. But the war
for investment across the United States is relentless, as states and
local governments compete heavily to offer companies incentives
to invest in facilities and employment in their areas. There is a lot of
debate about whether these incentives, which amount to at least
$45 billion a year, and by some estimates, up to $70 billion a year, are
worth it for the states that emerge as the winners.[25] In practice, the
benefits can fall short of expectations. Sometimes, not as many jobs
end up being created as first thought. Tax revenues can fall short of
projections. As the Applebee's case illustrates, companies can always
relocate again if other states offer an even better deal.

There is little doubt that the competition among states to win
corporate headquarters is intense. There are jobs and prestige at
stake, and all states compete to some extent, whether they agree with
the logic of the system or not. Depending on your perspective, this
is either a healthy race to the top or a damaging race to the bottom.
As we saw in chapter 1, that is quite different from the market for
business registrations, in which Delaware has an effective monopoly
on out-of-state incorporations.

Delaware takes a unique approach to this war for jobs. The First
State certainly tries to compete for corporate facilities. But at the
same time, it counteracts those incentives by giving companies two
good reasons *not* to locate themselves there, at least not physically.
One is the Delaware Loophole, which offers corporations all the
benefits of being in the First State without actually creating any significant number of jobs there. The second reason is that, ironically,
the corporate income tax rate that Delaware levies on companies
located in the First State is a steep 8.7 percent, the ninth-highest
among US states, only just lower than the rate in much less business-
friendly California, which charges 8.84 percent.[26] Combine these
two disincentives and you have a good reason *not* to locate your
company physically in Delaware.

The state's political leaders still try to play the incentives game and offer economic packages for companies to locate in the First State, but the tax-dodging power of intercompany transfers makes it just as easy for companies to stay where they are, avoid any upheaval from a move, and still reap the financial benefits. Delaware is not really selling its labor force so much as its tax efficiency.

To be sure, not all companies have structures that let them exploit the Delaware Loophole, but they can still locate themselves in any of the forty-one other states that offer lower state corporate income tax rates. The collapse of Delaware's once strong manufacturing sector speaks to the challenges it has had in attracting a range of investment. In perhaps the most high-profile recent example, Delaware's then governor Jack Markell and then senator Joe Biden triumphantly announced in 2009 that the state was granting $21.5 million in economic incentives to Fisker Automotive, an early competitor to Tesla in manufacturing high-end plug-in electric cars. Fisker was planning to retool a former General Motors plant in Newport, Delaware, a project that promised to create up to 2,500 jobs. But Fisker ran into problems, the facility never opened, and the plant sat idle for another decade. The state has even had to offer big incentives to its companies to stay in Delaware. In 2016, it gave $8 million in tax breaks to Chemours, the maker of Teflon and Freon, a year after DuPont had spun it off. Chemours had been threatening to site its headquarters in Pennsylvania or New Jersey, but some tax breaks persuaded it to stay.[27]

Now out of office, Jack Markell is prepared to say out loud that the system is broken. While the Fisker grant was a bust, other incentive payments handed out by his administration did create jobs, he notes. But overall, he says what we have is "a market failure in which neither side is motivated to fix the problem," and he advocates a ruthless solution: a federal tax of 100 percent on state or local incentives directed to specific companies.[28] "I was as guilty of playing this game as anybody else," Markell told me in 2019. "It's of course a waste of time, and it would be so much better off if this money was spent on things like infrastructure, workforce development—the things that made the whole society better and more attractive. But, as long as one state is playing this game, other states feel like they have to."[29]

One unfortunate by-product of Delaware's attempts to compete in the war for investment has been to narrow its tax base, making the state even more dependent on the Franchise. This is because taxes are, of course, not the only way for states to offer incentives for companies to invest. In the late 1990s, Delaware introduced a series of measures to attract investment, including changing its accounting rules to increase the number of years companies are allowed to carry forward their losses and adopting a generous tax credit for research and development. Such policies reduced its tax base, meaning that even the high corporate income tax rate was less of a revenue raiser than it might have otherwise been. While the war for investment is heated, not all states chose to narrow their tax bases. Michigan, for example, broadened its tax base by limiting the use of accelerated depreciation in company accounts.[30]

This struggle for investment helps explain why, in spite of its high corporate income tax rate, Delaware takes in relatively little in corporate income tax, just $245 million in 2020. Delaware got more than six times as much revenue that year, $1.6 billion, from the Franchise.[31]

In one way, Delaware's dependence on the small-fee, high-volume Franchise as a cash cow is smart. US states' revenues from corporate taxes have been falling for decades, and the amount they contribute to the states' total revenues has essentially halved since the early 1980s. This drop in the state corporate tax take has affected all of us. On the one hand, it has strained the services that states provide and has threatened retirement funds for public workers such as teachers and firefighters. On the other hand, the states have increased taxes on the rest of us, who obligingly help make up the shortfalls.

This pattern has little to do with corporate profits. For example, inflation-adjusted federal corporate income taxes grew by an average of 2 percent a year from 1995 to 2000, indicating that companies were reporting increasing revenues. But state and local corporate tax revenue over the same period actually declined by 0.12 percent.[32]

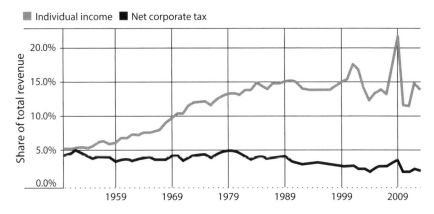

FIGURE 3. Income Tax Share of Total State Revenue.
Source: US Census Bureau Annual Survey of State Government Finances. See Mike Maciag, "How States' Dependence on Corporate Taxes Has Declined," *Governing*, January 6, 2016, https://www.governing.com/archive/gov-state-corporate-income-tax-revenues.html.

Why have state corporate tax revenues dwindled? In part it's because of how the Delaware Loophole and related strategies have enabled companies to transfer revenues to lower-tax or tax-free jurisdictions. And in part it's because, in fighting each other in the war for investment, states have lowered corporate tax rates and offered a range of incentives that have narrowed their corporate tax bases.

Individual taxpayers who have to make up for the states' decreasing revenues from corporate taxes effectively pay twice: once to corporations, in the form of incentives to attract their investment, and once more to state governments through taxes or fees, to make up for the shortfalls that they themselves helped create.

But Delaware has been able to buck the trend. By increasing its dependence on the Franchise, Delaware has seen the corporate contribution to its state revenues go in the opposite direction from almost all other states. In fact, Delaware collects more in corporate fees than forty-two US states take in corporate income tax.[33] The Delaware Loophole has helped contribute to the problem of falling corporate state income tax, and the Franchise has helped the First State insulate itself from the trend.

In that sense, Delaware has played a critical role in the rise in recent decades of the tax-planning industry, a multibillion-dollar business that has grown up to help corporations—along with wealthy individuals and their families, as I'll explain in the next chapter—avoid paying taxes. Big professional services firms such as Ernst & Young, PricewaterhouseCoopers, and KPMG have long crafted strategies to save companies billions of dollars in taxes.[34] Much of this activity has focused on helping multinational corporations avoid US federal taxes by establishing foreign subsidiaries and sending money around the world, but Delaware has certainly played its part within an overall strategy of avoiding taxes.

Tax planning gives big incumbent businesses an unfair advantage over smaller upstarts, since the more established firms can afford the best lawyers and the lobbyists to try to squash any attempt to pass rules such as combined reporting. While most individuals and small companies make do with tax software to avoid paying more than their fair share of taxes, wealthy people and corporations can hire specialized tax lawyers to help them exploit loopholes. As a result, big companies usually pay lower effective tax rates than their smaller counterparts, effectively cementing their positions and insulating them from smaller rivals with less access to complex accounting and lobbying firms. Ultimately, these elaborate lengths to avoid taxes make the US corporate system less competitive and anti-entrepreneurial. Anyone who believes in free and open markets, dynamic competition, and disruptive innovation ought to hate it. Big corporations love it.

Consider the corporate tax situation in Pennsylvania. The state corporate income tax rate is 9.99 percent, the second-highest in the United States. But thanks to tax planning, most companies located in Pennsylvania simply do not pay it. Of the 113,400 businesses that were subject to the Pennsylvania tax in 2015, 76 percent paid no tax, according to the state Department of Revenue.[35] Those that do are typically small and medium-sized companies that do not have out-of-state subsidiaries.

Tax planning makes corporations look much more profitable, but it doesn't necessarily reward the best companies—the ones adding the most value to the economy. In the words of Bill Fox, a professor of economics at the University of Tennessee, "If we find that companies have differing abilities to tax plan, what's going to happen is the returns are going to go to the tax planning and not to the efficient economic activity."[36]

Delaware bristles against suggestions that it is a tax haven like Bermuda or the Cayman Islands. "Myth: Delaware is America's onshore tax haven," reads a page on the First State's official website. "Fact: Comparisons between Delaware and sovereign nations such as the Cayman Islands are inaccurate. Delaware companies are subject to the same US tax laws as companies formed in other states."[37] Officials in Delaware sometimes cite the state's corporate income tax to argue that it is not a tax haven. Companies based in Delaware have to pay both state corporate income taxes and federal taxes, so how could it be considered a tax haven?

But simply having an official corporate income tax doesn't mean Delaware isn't a tax haven. After all, the Republic of Ireland for many years had a corporation tax rate of 12.5 percent, going up to 25 percent for "passive" (nontrading) income. Yet, because of its low effective tax rate, Ireland was frequently deemed a tax haven after at least 1981, when the US Internal Revenue Service first deemed it as such, a verdict echoed by countless reports since then.[38] (In 2021, Ireland bowed to international pressure to sign on to the Biden administration's proposal for a 15 percent global minimum corporate tax rate.)

Similarly, through its holding-company rules, Delaware has effectively lowered corporate tax rates and made itself into a domestic tax haven. The Delaware Loophole is one method (among many) that companies have used as part of their tax planning. Like the Republic of Ireland, Delaware helps companies lower their global tax rates by enabling them to avoid not federal taxes, but state corporate income taxes. That may not make the First State an international tax haven as the term is commonly understood, but Delaware is certainly part of the global tax-planning system. Corporations that use foreign tax havens are more likely to exploit the Delaware Loophole, suggesting that avoiding domestic and international taxes cannot be neatly separated.[39] As the economist Gabriel Zucman notes, "Delaware would be one step in an international tax-planning scheme."[40]

For Duke University economist Scott Dyreng, the difference between Delaware and international tax havens is one of scale, not of type. "Delaware allows companies to reduce the tax that they pay to other governments," Dyreng notes. "This is exactly what's happening with many of the tax-haven countries that you hear about in international tax planning."[41]

And while Delaware rejects the notion that it is an international tax haven, Delaware holding companies have certainly been used by multinational corporations to avoid paying taxes overseas. A case in point is Chevron, the United States' second-biggest energy company.[42] The California-based company got into a dispute with Australian tax authorities that involved its use of a shell company in Delaware, Chevron Texaco Funding Corporation, to loan $2.5 billion to its Chevron Australia unit. CTFC borrowed the money in the United States at an interest rate of 1.2 percent and lent it to Chevron Australia Holdings at a rate of 9 percent. The Australian arm got to deduct $268 million (US dollars) in interest repayments from its taxable income, while the US arm made big profits on the difference between the interest rates, without having to pay any tax on the transaction. But the Australian tax authorities took Chevron to court and won, landing the energy company with a $340 million unpaid tax bill. The case, which closed in 2017, might be just the warm-up for an even bigger case involving Chevron: the company admitted in 2015 to a similar deal, this time involving a $42 billion loan that could reduce its Australian tax bill by as much as $15 billion.[43]

It is easy to blame companies for using tax planning to shirk their responsibility to pay their fair share of public revenues. But it is governments that devise the tax regimes and put them into place. Corporations merely navigate those regimes so as to minimize their exposure, which is exactly what one would expect them to do, so long as they do so legally.

Since governments allow corporations to take advantage of the Delaware Loophole and other tax dodges, it's worth asking, does this actually provide any economic value? After all, the battle for investment creates jobs, which increases spending and boosts the local economy. Even if the costs are considerable, they can be measured against the benefits.

But in fact, the Delaware Loophole creates very little economic value. It creates very few jobs. It does not increase sales. It simply transfers revenues from one place to another. It is an accountant's sleight of hand, magically making taxable cash flow disappear. "The sole purpose is to take an extra expense from a related party," says LeAnn Luna, the University of Tennessee accounting professor. "There's no *real* activity going on."[44]

Again, Delaware is far from the only actor in this tax-planning world. Several other states also offer low-tax incentives, including Nevada, Wyoming, and South Dakota. But Delaware's critical role in corporate America has made the Delaware Loophole particularly important in helping big companies avoid taxes.

As David Brunori observes, "There's an old joke that if you're a Fortune 2000 company and you're paying corporate income taxes, you need to find a new accountant and new tax lawyers."[45]

4

Delaware Has Our Money

Delaware is home to some of the world's most valuable art.

You won't find these masterpieces among the artworks at the Delaware Art Museum in Wilmington, whose galleries feature a fine collection of British Pre-Raphaelite paintings. They are, instead, kept in an ultra-private, darkened, video-monitored, temperature-controlled facility (70 degrees Fahrenheit with 50 percent relative humidity) on the outskirts of Newark, a small city in the north-western part of the state, in a former factory that once made foam packing peanuts. Security is tight. Few people go in or out.

The art inside this nondescript white building is an ever-shifting permanent collection, not intended to be enjoyed but held as an investment. And it is brought here because its owners want to avoid paying tax on their purchases. Delaware is even-handed: it doesn't just help big corporations avoid taxes, it also helps the world's super-wealthy avoid taxes as well.

Art is an increasingly popular investment for the überrich, who have helped drive prices higher and higher. One-third of the world's wealthiest people buy and sell art, an obsession more of investment than aesthetics that helped generate $67 billion in sales in 2018.[1]

Most of the elite buy art and then don't sell it. Only 14 percent of collectors actively resell. And the frenetic pursuit of famous art is likely to continue as the global elite get wealthier. About 130,000 people around the world each have assets of more than $50 million. Between them, these "ultra-high-net-worth individuals" own more than $26 trillion, compared to the United States' pre-COVID-19 pandemic gross domestic product of around $21.5 trillion.[2] During the pandemic, as millions of people around the world slipped back into poverty, most billionaires' wealth increased dramatically. All indications are that the concentration of wealth at the very top of the global elite is set to intensify further, and so is their art buying.

Although few like to admit it publicly, two-thirds of art collectors admit privately that making money is an important reason why they purchase art, according to a Deloitte survey.[3] The really smart money is at the very top of the market. The auction market for artworks priced up to $1 million declined in value between 2007 and 2017, but sales worth more than $10 million rose by 148 percent over the same period.[4] Investment banks have hired "art advisory teams" to help the wealthy choose what to purchase. Their clients typically have collections worth hundreds of millions of dollars, or even billions.[5] Since the business is international and the stakes are so high, this has prompted concerns about tax evasion, money laundering, and fraud.

The art market is the biggest legal unregulated market in the United States. Anti–money laundering and antiterrorism financing controls don't apply to art sales—art dealers aren't required to know the identity of buyers and sales are often done using an intermediary. Americans are prohibited from selling to or buying from individuals or groups on the US Treasury's sanction list, and the biggest auction houses perform voluntary anti–money laundering checks. Yet shady dealing continues. A 2020 Senate report revealed how Russian oligarchs used art sales to evade US sanctions, buying more than $18 million of artworks using shell companies, including René Magritte's *La Poitrine* (The Chest) for $7.5 million in a private sale.[6] The report was prepared by the staff of the Senate's Permanent Subcommittee on Investigations, whose most senior Democratic member is Delaware's Tom Carper. "Criminals, terrorists and wealthy Russian oligarchs . . . are able to use an unregulated art industry . . . to hide assets, launder funds, and evade sanctions," Carper noted.[7]

The global elite's feverish quest for great art reached a crescendo in November 2017, with the auction of Leonardo da Vinci's *Salvator Mundi* at Christie's in New York. The twenty-six-inch tall painting dates to 1500. It shows an image of Jesus with flowing brown ringlets, raising his right hand in a blessing and holding a crystal orb in his left. In 1958, the painting had been sold for just £45 in an auction at Sotheby's in London to a buyer identified only as "Kuntz." It had been damaged and badly overpainted, and was attributed to Giovanni Boltraffio, who worked in da Vinci's studio. Then in 2005, Robert Simon, a New York art dealer, bought it at an estate sale in New Orleans for $10,000. In 2011, the work was authenticated as a da Vinci. Two years later, the Swiss billionaire Yves Bouvier bought the painting for $80 million and immediately resold it to Dmitry Rybolovlev, a Russian billionaire based in Monte Carlo, for $127.5 million.

So expectations were high when *Salvator Mundi* came up for auction again. Robert Simon himself anticipated that the bidding could go as high as $280 million, but when the contest came down to two bidders, they had already blown far past that.[8] The increments between bids jumped wildly, from $332 million to $350 million, and then from $370 million to $400 million. The crowd in the salesroom gasped with excitement.

Eventually, the painting sold for $450 million, making it the most expensive ever auctioned. The identity of the buyer was initially a mystery, but a month after the auction, it was revealed to be Saudi crown prince Mohammed bin Salman. The Saudi royal made it known that he intended to give it as a gift from Saudi Arabia to the United Arab Emirates, to be displayed in Abu Dhabi in the newly opened sister museum of Paris's Louvre. The art world welcomed that intention, since there had been concerns that the sale would effectively withdraw the masterpiece from public view. After all, almost no museum could compete with the art prices paid by the global elite.[9]

Yet, at the time of writing, almost four years later, the painting had not been seen since the sale. "That this work has been mysteriously off the scene since, despite being promised for exhibition at the Louvre Abu Dhabi . . . sums up the opaque workings of the multi-billion-dollar art world," the *Financial Times* noted in 2018.[10]

Could *Salvator Mundi* be in Delaware? If so, the Saudi royal family could have delayed paying New York taxes on the purchase. Delaware is one of only five US states with no sales tax, along with Alaska, Montana, New Hampshire, and Oregon, and is the only one located in the mid-Atlantic region, just 130 miles from New York, the world's most important art market, where the sales tax rate is 8.875 percent.[11] If art is purchased in New York, one way to avoid the sales tax is to ship it directly from the auction house to Delaware. By doing so, the Saudi crown prince would have saved himself a hefty $40 million.

Art buyers have been trying to avoid the sales tax in New York for decades, and international tax havens such as Switzerland, Luxembourg, and Singapore have been delighted to help them. But it's much cheaper and less bothersome to ship the art to Delaware instead. It can go in a truck, not a plane. Insurance is less expensive. You don't have to deal with customs. And storing art in Delaware costs less.

By the time Fritz Dietl took over the former foam-peanut plant in Newark, the Delaware art storage / sales tax–avoidance business was already well established. But Dietl was the first person to see that Delaware could compete for the global art-storage market. In 2015, he secured a "foreign-trade zone" designation from US Customs and Border Protection. That allows art from abroad to enter duty free to his warehouse. Among a string of art-storage facilities in Delaware, only Dietl's is certified as a foreign-trade zone, which enables purchasers of Chinese or European art to avoid paying US tariffs when they store their art with him. Dietl pays the State of Delaware a mere $10,000 a year for the privilege.[12]

Dietl, a middle-aged, bald Austrian, learned about art storage and logistics as an apprentice in Austria. He drove trucks stuffed with art, wrapped and packed artworks, and learned to negotiate complex customs and tax procedures while shipping pieces around the world. In 1988, at the age of twenty-five, he moved to New York. Three years later, in a rented room at JFK Airport and armed with just a fax machine, he started a firm specializing in shipping artwork.

The company grew steadily, fueled by collectors buying art in New York and shipping it to tax-advantaged free ports overseas such as Geneva or Luxembourg. It expanded to become the largest art logistics provider in the United States. In 2015, Dietl decided to compete with those European locales. His answer was the Delaware Freeport, which sits on an industrial zone beside the train tracks, next door to warehouses run by distributors of forklift trucks and rail siding. It has proved far more popular than expected. When we spoke in 2018, Dietl's 36,000-square-foot Newark facility was completely full and he was looking for another building.

In the early days, Dietl drove his truck every week 130 miles southwest, down Interstate 95 from Manhattan, carrying art for private buyers, museums, and other institutions. But then the New York attorney general ruled that the sellers themselves must ship the art out of state if the buyers are to avoid sales taxes. So now the art collectors open accounts in Delaware, and the New York auction houses and galleries ship directly to facilities such as Delaware Freeport. "It's like Amazon," Dietl told me. "You buy something from them, they ship it to you."[13]

Comparing sales tax–free Delaware to Amazon is interesting, since for many years Amazon was a target for the anger of US state legislatures for refusing to add state sales taxes to purchases, thereby allowing the company to underprice competitors. The company bowed to pressure to collect the tax across the United States in 2017.[14] Millions of regular American shoppers who bought items on Amazon had not been charged sales tax by the company, because Amazon did not have a physical presence in their state. When Amazon began constructing distribution centers all over the United States, giving it a physical presence in most states, it was forced to start collecting sales tax from purchasers and to remit that tax to almost every state. Millions of Americans regularly cross state, county, and municipal boundaries to avoid paying taxes on alcohol, cigarettes, gas, and many other items. (One traditional wheeze is for residents of the District of Columbia to buy cars in Delaware and register them in the First State, using their beach houses as their home addresses.) This is certainly lost revenue for the affected taxing authorities, but it is fairly low-level stuff. Avoiding millions of dollars on an art purchase is in a different league.

Delaware caters to the buyer of expensive art who is more concerned with buying art as an investment than actually displaying it, hanging it on their walls, or loaning it to a museum—that is, most art buyers. In practice, the line between investment and appreciation is blurry, since enforcement is weak. If a New York collector removes their art from Delaware and hangs it in their home, they are supposed to report it on their tax filings, but it is hard to police that system. "Enforcement is not what it could be, and people are not as honest as they could be," says Jordan Rosen, an accountant in Wilmington.[15] Some art that is supposed to be shipped to Delaware or international tax havens "really goes out the back door," notes Jack Sullivan, a tax lawyer in New York.[16] But officially, buyers are entitled to avoid sales tax as long as the art stays in Delaware—not a place that's well known for its superwealthy art buyers. And as long as the artwork stays in the First State, when it comes time to sell it, there is no tax to pay on that transaction either. So artwork worth hundreds of millions of dollars can pass between buyers without ever leaving a facility such as Delaware Freeport, and without a penny spent on sales taxes.

Sales taxes aren't the only taxes and fees that Delaware helps the superwealthy avoid. In 2018 Delaware scrapped its estate taxes, which formerly went up to 16 percent for the biggest estates. What's more, nonresidents can avoid paying estate taxes in their home states by forming trusts in Delaware, a process similar to registering an LLC. Trusts hold assets, such as cash or property, which they can "lend" to heirs tax free. In some states, trusts have a fixed life. In Delaware they can last forever. You can buy art, put it into a Delaware trust, and give it to your heirs tax free. Like the Delaware Loophole for corporations, this lets you keep the art anywhere while enjoying some of the tax benefits that Delaware offers.

Art storage is just one example of how Delaware's business-friendliness chiefly benefits the wealthy—if not necessarily actual Delaware residents. Just as the tax planners help corporations use Delaware holding companies to avoid paying corporate income tax, so LLCs help the wealthy avoid taxes, in many cases by simply reclassifying their business operations as "pass-through" companies such as partnerships, which can be registered as LLCs. Income from pass-through companies is typically taxed at less than the corporate rate. The amount of US business income going through partnerships has increased more in the past thirty years than any other type of corporate structure, enabling mostly wealthy individuals to avoid about $100 billion that they would have had to pay in tax under traditional corporate structures.[17]

The art market is also an example of how the overall economy is getting "darker" and less transparent due to the growth of private markets, where trading takes place out of the public eye in alternative investments such as private equity, private lending, venture capital, real estate, private equity, infrastructure, and direct lending. Private markets have boomed since the turn of the millennium, and they have privatized much of what was formerly public. In the year 2000, for example, there were 8,000 publicly traded US stocks. Today there are about 3,700.[18] "The fact that more capital is now being raised in private markets means that a burgeoning portion of the U.S. economy itself is going dark," notes Securities and Exchange Commissioner Allison Herren Lee. "Investors and the public are increasingly left in the dark when it comes to ever-expanding segments of the economy."[19]

By enabling tax dodging, Delaware has played its role in helping to exacerbate inequality in America, both inequality between the big corporations and the mom-and-pop shops, and the growing inequality between the top 1 percent of income earners and the rest of us. The top 1 percent of earners in the United States accounted for 8.5 percent of total income in 1970, but by 2010 they accounted for 17.4 percent.[20] At the same time, middle-class family incomes stagnated, and the wealth gap between America's richest and poorer families more than doubled from 1989 to 2016.[21] Tax policy, both at the federal and state levels, is one significant driver of inequality, and Delaware tax policy gives wealthy out-of-staters a big boost.

Just as multinational companies employ big professional services firms to help them avoid paying taxes via complicated global strategies, as seen in the last chapter, so wealthy individuals and their families have in the past half century increasingly used the help of "asset protection" or "wealth defense" experts—lawyers, boutique consultants, and other assorted experts—to help them pay lower tax rates than the rest of us. This was brought home when the *New York Times* revealed in 2020 that President Donald Trump had paid just $750 in federal income tax in 2016 and 2017, after legal credits and other allowances. Given that Trump had earned capital gains of $7.5 million and taxable interest of $6.7 million in 2017 alone, this looked like an extreme form of accounting alchemy.[22]

It's easy to pick on Trump, yet his behavior is more the norm among the very wealthy than an aberration. The twenty-five richest Americans paid an effective federal income tax rate of 3.4 percent between 2014 and 2018, according to a 2021 ProPublica investigation. Jeff Bezos, the Amazon founder, who in 2018 became the world's richest person, paid no federal income tax at all in 2007 and 2011. Elon Musk, the ostentatious entrepreneur whose empire includes electric car maker Tesla, didn't pay any federal income tax in 2018. George Soros, the controversial liberal hedge fund billionaire, enjoyed a zero federal income tax bill in 2016, 2017, and 2018.[23] All of this was perfectly legal.

And, of course, tax avoidance is a politically ambidextrous activity, enjoyed by conservatives and liberals alike.

In the two years after the Obama administration ended in January 2017, Joe Biden earned about $15.6 million, most of which he shielded from the media using two opaque "S corporations": Celtic-Capri Corp. for the former vice president (a nod, perhaps, to his Irish roots), and Giacoppa Corp. for his wife Jill. If you wanted to hire either Biden for a speaking gig, you would pay the fee—up to $234,000 per speech, according to the *Washington Post*—directly to one of the S corps.[24] The Bidens then paid themselves a relatively small portion of the income from these S corporations: a total of $245,833 in 2017 and $500,000 in 2018. Because these payments were categorized as "distributions" rather than wages, they were exempt from the 15.3 percent combined Social Security and Medicare tax.[25]

Protecting the assets of the wealthy from tax authorities is an enormous and highly specialized industry, but it is central to the global economy. "Wealth managers construct and manage large, complex international structures involving banks, tax havens, trusts and foundations, wills law and accounting, corporations share and bond portfolios, insurance products, hedge funds and more—putting them right at the heart of the machinery of global finance," notes the investigative journalist Nicholas Shaxson.[26]

No one likes to pay taxes. But by "tax dodging," I don't just mean using the tax breaks that have been provided to minimize the amount of tax you have to pay. After all, the tax software most of us use online does just that. The difference is that most of us do not turn ourselves into legal corporations and set up complex structures deliberately to exploit tax loopholes, nor do we create multiple business entities to make it harder for the authorities to calculate how much we're worth. In spite of our progressive income tax system, in reality, the rich tend to pay lower tax rates than the middle class. Warren Buffett, one of the world's wealthiest men, has repeatedly observed that he pays a lower tax rate than his own secretary.[27]

The aggregate effect of all this has transformed developed economies. As Northwestern University political scientist Jeffrey Winters has chronicled, an important dynamic fueling the increasing gap between rich and poor since the 1970s has been the growth of an entire new business sector devoted to ever more elaborate schemes to trim the tax bills of the superwealthy. Winters encapsulates the scale and reach of this operation:

> The income defense industry is comprised of lawyers, accountants, wealth management consultants, revolving-door lobbyists, think-tank debate framers and even key segments of the insurance industry whose sole purpose is income defense for America's oligarchs. The industry is wholly funded by oligarchs, and it would simply not exist if oligarchs did not have massive fortunes to defend. There is no parallel (much less countervailing) industry serving the material interests of the mass affluent, the middle class or the poor. The activities of the income defense industry extend far beyond mere "interest group" lobbying over policies. Its salaried specialists assist oligarchs in exerting a form of power that is unique to the ultra-rich: the defensive redeployment of their money and income across a global geography of jurisdictions,

banks and offshore havens through the use of tailor-made tax instruments, evasive trusts and shell corporations.[28]

Who wins and who loses when a wealthy art buyer saves tens of millions of dollars in New York sales taxes by shipping artworks to Delaware? Apart from the fees to auctioneers, New York is a big loser, but Delaware is barely a winner. The benefits to the First State are fairly paltry. The art-storage business creates few long-term jobs. The fees Dietl pays are insignificant. If the owner creates a Delaware trust, the First State collects fees, but again, those are minimal. So the only clear winner is the wealthy individual.

The race-to-the-bottom dynamics make it hard for a state like New York. The more it tries to collect sales and use taxes on art transactions, the more attractive shipping artworks to Delaware looks. You can only "win" by losing less revenue that you might otherwise have done.

The end result is that Delaware's tax policies hurt other US states, benefit the wealthy, and create little other economic value.

————

Let's return to Rehoboth Beach, the seaside resort in southern Delaware where Jack Abramoff and Michael Scanlon set up a fake think tank to fleece Native American tribes. The town, which styles itself as "the Nation's Summer Capital" has a permanent population of just 1,400 residents, but that swells to many tens of thousands in the summer months.

Most of Rehoboth Beach's property owners don't live there: about 80 percent of the town's properties are owned by nonresidents.[29] A key attraction is the very low property taxes enjoyed in Sussex County— about 0.27 percent of the property's market value, on average.[30]

Perhaps the resort's most famous nonresident is President Biden. The Bidens bought a $2.7 million, six-bedroom oceanfront house in Rehoboth Beach in 2017, after visiting the town for decades.[31] The community briefly reappears in the news when President Biden returns there, as he did in November 2020 and in June 2021.

The same year that the Bidens bought their home, Rehoboth Beach's political leaders came up with an innovative proposal: to allow LLCs to vote in elections. Under the US Constitution, companies are considered people, at least when it comes to spending money in elections and refusing to observe federal mandates due to conscience. "Corporations are people, my friend," the US senator and failed 2012 presidential candidate Mitt Romney famously told a heckler in Iowa who was haranguing him about corporate tax policy.[32] Rehoboth Beach was the first town in the United States to try to extend that concept into political voting.

Delaware is already one of the few states to allow non–US citizens the right to vote in local races. Much in the same way that Delaware does its best to draw business registrations from out of state, it is also at pains to attract nonresident property owners, and an unusual law empowers cities and towns to give these out-of-staters—including those outside the United States—the opportunity to vote in local races.[33] According to state law, once a municipality does so, it cannot reverse its decision.

In Newark, Delaware's third-biggest city, a similar rule allowed one property manager to vote thirty-one times in a local referendum in 2018, one for each of the LLCs their company owned. Although the circumstances were unusual—such referendums are rare, and the city does not allow LLCs to vote in regular elections—it prompted a backlash from residents. "I just think it's fundamentally undemocratic," Newark councilwoman Jen Wallace told the *News Journal*. "It should be one person, one vote."[34]

Rehoboth Beach was proposing to take the principle further, allowing LLCs to vote not just in referendums but also in regular elections. That idea didn't originate in Rehoboth. Several other tiny nearby beachfront communities had already implemented similar measures. But Rehoboth Beach was the first significantly sized town to try it out. The mayor of Rehoboth Beach at the time, Paul Kuhns, explained the origin of the idea to me as we sat in his office in 2018. Kuhns, a tall, rugged, earnest man with neat gray hair, was decked out in the unofficial uniform of the mayor of a seaside resort: pink t-shirt and shorts. Decades before, Kuhns recalled, the town had given nonresident property owners the right to vote, and ten years before we spoke, the town had extended that right to trusts, a measure that added no more than one hundred new voters to the rolls. Meanwhile, many nonresident owners had bought their properties using LLCs in order to limit their liability from tenants, and they had asked to have a say in local elections, so he thought it made sense to extend the voting right to LLCs also.

But the LLC measure provoked a backlash among the Rehoboth Beach community. In part, this reflected resentment toward the new money flowing in, which had jacked up real estate prices. Some of the newer owners had been installing swimming pools in their backyards, leading to complaints about the noise of screaming kids during the day and drunk adults at night. Many of the properties with new pools were being rented out on websites such as Airbnb. They were investment properties, and when the locals tried to find out who the owners were, they discovered they were LLCs controlled by investors who never came to Rehoboth Beach. Some locals had banded together and pushed through an ordinance to limit property owners' ability to build pools. But now the town was proposing to give these LLCs more political influence.

Jan Konesey was one of those who objected. Putting a property in a trust is one way to pass it on to your children, she told me, but LLCs are designed precisely to hide the identity of their owners. "A corporation or an LLC is not a person. It's a business entity. And business entities don't vote," she said. "If you look in [the documents filed with] the secretary of state's office, all you have for an LLC is a contact person. Well, that contact person could be the registered agent. It could be the owner of the LLC. It could be their next-door neighbor. It could be anybody."[35]

Konesey knows something about the issue. For one thing, she is the chair of the Delaware branch of Common Cause, the government-watchdog group. What's more, she herself sits on the board of a registered agent that helps organizations, almost all of which are not based in Delaware, to form their business entities in the state.

Konesey alerted the American Civil Liberties Union, which had successfully sued towns in Maryland in the 1980s and 1990s for removing voting rights from nonresident property owners. Ironically, had the ACLU gone to court in Delaware, Konesey herself might have been adversely affected: she is not actually a Rehoboth Beach resident, but lives in Dover, the state capital, and gained her right to vote in Rehoboth by virtue of owning property there.

In any case, it did not come to that. When the issue came up for discussion at a packed public meeting held at the town's volunteer fire company building, speaker after speaker rose to oppose the measure. Sniffing defeat, Kuhns and his allies on the town council decided to drop the idea.

The episode showed how mainstream LLCs had become in day to-day life in Delaware—not just in business, but in how decisions got made on the ground. It also highlighted how open and welcoming the state was to nonresidents, both the big corporations for which it had long been a registered home and all sorts of individuals who were using entities such as LLCs and trusts to protect their assets.

This phenomenon became clear when the COVID-19 pandemic hit the United States in 2020 and Congress's $2 trillion taxpayer-funded stimulus package in March of that year included the Paycheck Protection Program (PPP), a $669 billion fund to help companies that were struggling to continue paying their workers.

Delaware's *News Journal* dug into federal records to see which local companies had received those funds. Their meticulous investigation showed that a string of companies registered in Delaware had been granted stimulus funds ostensibly to support workers employed in the state, even though they did not actually employ anyone there. TOI Management LLC, which runs cancer clinics in the Southwest, received between $2 million and $5 million to preserve 386 jobs in Delaware, where the company in fact had no employees. TCFC Hotel Co LP also received between $2 million and $5 million, ostensibly to retain 202 jobs in Delaware, but there wasn't any evidence that the company had such a workforce there. Some companies appeared to receive funds even though they didn't actually exist. POUC LLC received between $350,000 and $1 million, but there were no records of the company with the Delaware Division of Corporations. Israel Gifts Store Inc. also received $350,000 to

$1 million to retain fifty-six Delaware employees, but there were no records of the company online or in Delaware business filings. An Isreal [*sic*] Gifts Store Inc. had been formed in 2016, but was dissolved two years later after it failed to file an annual report.[36]

The *News Journal* stressed that they were not jumping to the conclusion that these PPP claims were fraudulent, but what the investigation and the dustup in Rehoboth Beach had really highlighted was the outsized role that nonresidents and nonresident companies play in Delaware and its economy.

In many cases, what exists in Delaware is nothing more than a shell. The corporate lights are on, but no one's home.

———

In June 2016, officials from twenty-one US states gathered on the steps of the US Supreme Court. Their target was Delaware.

Ken Paxton, the Tea Party Republican attorney general of Texas, was one of the group's leaders. Paxton is known for his archconservative views on immigration (vastly inflating the number of crimes committed by undocumented residents),[37] climate change (fighting plans to cut US carbon emissions), and same-sex marriage (supporting clerks who defy the law and refuse to issue marriage licenses to same-sex couples). He is a close ally of former president Trump. For a few days in late 2020, he led a doomed, legally flimsy attempt to overturn the 2020 presidential election in favor of Trump, the losing candidate. He also spoke at the infamous January 6, 2021 rally in Washington, DC, that ended in Trump's supporters violently storming the US Capitol.

Paxton is a rough-and-tumble fighter. Tall and broad, he wanted to play football as a kid, but his Air Force father wouldn't let him, worried he might get injured. At the age of twelve, Paxton nearly lost an eye playing hide-and-seek. He kept the eye, but it is severely damaged. (Years later, playing basketball, Paxton took an elbow to the face that shattered the bones around the already-damaged right eye.) In later life, Paxton's skirmishes were more legal and political than physical: in 2015, he was indicted by a state grand jury on two counts of securities fraud and one count of failing to register with state securities regulators. (At the time of writing, more than five years later, he has still not faced trial.) In 2020, seven of his most senior staff resigned, accusing their former boss of improper influence, abuse of office, bribery, and other crimes.[38]

But on the steps of the Supreme Court in 2016, Paxton squared up for another tussle, leading the charge on behalf of twenty-one states suing Delaware in the US Supreme Court, accusing it of violating federal law by snatching up to $400 million in unclaimed checks. "The State of Delaware elected to begin playing by a different set of rules," Paxton bristled, adding that the First State's behavior was both illegal and unfair. "Delaware has our money," he told the assembled media.[39]

The case centered on "unclaimed property" such as financial accounts that have had no activity or for which the bank has had no contact with the owner for at least a year. This includes more than just savings or checking accounts. Think of stock accounts, uncashed dividends, security deposits, or tax refunds. Think also of gift cards, which have become increasingly popular presents in recent years. It's estimated that around $1 billion of the money put on gift cards every year never gets spent.[40] Retailers cannot consider the revenue from these cards as income until it's spent or declared "unused." Until then, this money sits in accounting limbo, unearned revenue that appears as a liability on companies' balance sheets. But a card sometimes has an expiration date. If the card remains unspent by then, or if five years have passed, the money is considered to be unclaimed property.

Delaware seizes the unclaimed money from companies that are registered in the First State, in a practice known as escheatment. To be fair, Delaware also operates a website where those who own the funds can try to claim them back. But Delaware has come to be dependent on the funds that consumers have failed to use, for whatever reason. Unclaimed property provided about $444 million to the state's coffers in 2020.[41] That makes escheatment Delaware's third-largest source of funds after incorporation fees and income taxes. Delaware can seize this unclaimed property because it is held on the balance sheets of companies that have registered in the First State. So unclaimed property is really part of the Franchise, a neat little side business to incorporation fees themselves. Other states such as New York also seize unclaimed property, but no other state is as dependent as Delaware on the revenue. Delaware officials dismiss the idea that they have viewed abandoned property as a means to grow state revenues. But commenting on a previous case, Supreme Court Justice Samuel Alito wrote in 2016, "Cash-strapped states undoubtedly have a real interest in taking advantage of truly abandoned property to shore up state budgets."[42]

The issue is yet another source of enmity between Delaware and the many other states that would like to seize the funds for themselves. All states have unclaimed property laws, but few are as lucrative as those of Delaware, which uses its position as the home of business formation to claim priority over other states. And, unlike Delaware, which funnels the revenue from escheatment to its general fund for spending, some other states set the money aside and do all they can to find the rightful owners. The State of Washington, for example, has a staff of thirteen people dedicated solely to seeking the people who actually own the abandoned or unclaimed property that the state seizes. Rather than spending it, as Delaware does, Washington hangs on to all unclaimed property in perpetuity until it can find the rightful owners.[43]

The 2016 case brought by the twenty-one states alleged that, for the prior four or five years, Delaware had been requiring financial institutions incorporated there to turn over unclaimed funds only to Delaware. But the other states claim that such funds rightly belong to the state in which a transaction originated. They focused on MoneyGram, the money-transfer company that is headquartered in Dallas but incorporated in Delaware—at 1209 North Orange Street in Wilmington, an infamous address that we will revisit in chapter 11 of this book. MoneyGram charges its customers a fee to purchase a check they can send to someone else. Someone in Arkansas, one of the states in the lawsuit, might have sent another person in Arkansas a $100 gift through MoneyGram. If the other person failed to cash the check, Delaware seized the funds. The litigants argued that Delaware had seized more than $150 million in unclaimed checks that originated in the other twenty-one states. Paxton said that the real figure, extrapolated to the entire United States, could be as high as $400 million. Texas alone was owed $10 million, he said.

The unclaimed property issue hasn't just brought Delaware into conflict with other states; it's also sparked legal struggles with affected companies. A few weeks after the twenty-one states sued the First State, a separate case, brought against Delaware by Temple-Inland, a corrugated packaging company based in Austin, was being heard in federal court in Wilmington. The presiding judge, US District Court Judge Gregory Sleet, wrote a damning thirty-nine-page ruling criticizing Delaware's unclaimed property actions, which he said violated due process and exploited loopholes in the statute of limitations.

"To put the matter gently, defendants have engaged in a game of 'gotcha' that shocks the conscience," Sleet observed. The way the state enforced its rules was "troubling," Sleet said, targeting large companies and, in the case of Temple-Inland, waiting twenty-two years to conduct an audit without notifying the company that it should retain its records for that long. "The court cannot help but wonder at Delaware's sense of cadence," Sleet continued. "It is true that unclaimed property should not become a windfall for holders [or companies]. But, at the same time, unclaimed property laws were never intended to be a tax mechanism whereby states can raise revenue as needed for the general welfare."[44]

Delaware proposed to audit twenty-two years of Temple-Inland's finances, but the company kept only seven years of records. Delaware law did not require the company to keep more than that, and, ironically, the state had destroyed its *own* copies of unclaimed property records, so it was unable to prove that the company had failed to file unclaimed property reports for the audit period. But because Delaware did not have the records, it assumed the company had not filed them, and that allowed the state to ignore its own three- to six-year statute of limitations. So Delaware informed Temple-Inland it was increasing its unclaimed property liability by $1.4 million, accounting for unclaimed payroll and accounts payable. Judge Sleet took a dim view of all this, plus the loose method by which Delaware had calculated Temple-Inland's unclaimed property. He ruled that the way Delaware enforced its unclaimed property laws was unconstitutional. The state promptly settled with Temple-Inland, reportedly withdrawing the $1.4 million assessment and paying all of Temple-Inland's costs.

The case opened the floodgates for other companies to take Delaware to court.[45] In a panic, the state realized that unless it reined in the bounty hunters and overhauled its unclaimed property laws, it risked damaging its business friendly reputation. The rules were quickly rewritten, limiting the search for unclaimed property to ten years and moving more to voluntary compliance, which regularly brought in small amounts of revenue rather than the big "gotcha" audits that had so peeved Judge Sleet.

But the new law didn't completely solve the problem. For one thing, it papered over some of the issues companies were concerned about. As representatives of Amazon noted in one hearing, it remained unclear how the state would handle virtual unclaimed currency such as Amazon points or video-game "money." Tension with companies was likely to persist in spite of the tighter rules, noted Pat Reynolds of the Council on State Taxation, a group representing multistate businesses. "If I was sitting in your shoes," Reynolds told Delaware's *News Journal*, "I would be wondering, 'Are we putting a little teeny Band-Aid on a large open wound?'"[46]

Moreover, the law dealt only with Delaware's aggressive auditing of companies, not with its struggle for unclaimed property that other states contended was rightfully theirs.

The Temple-Inland case highlighted Delaware's insatiable pursuit of unclaimed property, using independent auditors who scour companies' books looking for anomalies, like bounty hunters of the accounting world. The First State doesn't just sit back waiting for gift cards to be unspent—it relentlessly pursues companies that try to avoid having their abandoned gift cards seized. One of the First State's more controversial methods is to send companies a bill for unclaimed property, with the amount calculated based simply on industry averages.

In 2014, Delaware joined a whistleblower lawsuit alleging that dozens of household-name retailers, such as Netflix, California Pizza

Kitchen, Shell Oil, Skechers, Sony, Polo Ralph Lauren, and Overstock.com, had fraudulently withheld hundreds of millions of dollars in unredeemed gift cards from the First State. The dispute centered on Card Compliant, LLC, a company formerly known as CardFact, which helped the retailers set up subsidiaries outside Delaware to issue their gift cards, in states such as Ohio and Florida, where unused gift cards are not considered unclaimed property. The states argued that CardFact was the issuer and holder of the gift cards. Delaware claimed that the whole thing was a sham. CardFact, the First State alleged, was nothing more than a front, and the retailers continued to run the gift-card programs in the same way that they always had. The entire arrangement, the state said, lacked any economic substance and created a false paper trail to conceal the retailers' true role as the issuers and holders of the gift cards. (This claim sounded remarkably similar to what critics of Delaware had long said about the First State itself.) Over the years, the number of defendants in the case dwindled. Some defendants were dismissed, and about a dozen others (including CardFact itself) settled with Delaware to avoid going to trial, reportedly paying a total of $25 million to $30 million.[47] Eventually, only one retailer was left standing: Overstock, a website that sells clearance household items. After a six-day trial in September 2018, a Delaware jury took just one hour to find Overstock liable for about $3 million in unused gift cards, which, including damages and adjustments, left the company with a bill estimated at $7 million.[48]

Delaware received further confirmation of its right to pursue unclaimed property in other cases in 2017 and 2018, when federal courts ruled that the state was entitled to audit store cards issued by the Virginia-based subsidiary of Office Depot, the office-supplies chain store, and the Ohio subsidiary of Marathon Petroleum, which owns Speedway gas stations. Since both parent companies are incorporated in Delaware, the First State was allowed to conduct an audit, the courts said, although it held open the right of the companies to sue once the state completed its audits.

Apart from Delaware itself, some of the people who benefited the most from the pursuit of unclaimed property have been former senior public officials. According to an investigation by Wilmington's *News Journal*, in 2012, Secretary of State Jeff Bullock appointed Drinker Biddle & Reath, a Philadelphia-based law firm, to run a new program in which companies could get concessions on their unclaimed-property liabilities if they voluntarily disclosed to the state how much they owed. Tom McGonigle, who, as Governor Jack Markell's chief of staff, had a hand in drafting the law to create the program, had come from Drinker Biddle & Reath to work for the governor and went back to the firm months after the program was created. Geoff Sawyer, McGonigle's former deputy, also went to work for the firm, and Greg Patterson, another former deputy chief of staff to Markell, joined the firm in 2014.

The Markell administration insisted the contracts had been awarded through a competitive process, but according to state records, state officials had rated proposals from other bidding firms more highly. David Gregor, who ran Delaware's unclaimed-property program at the time, warned in his review of the bids that Drinker Biddle & Reath probably had a conflict of interest, since it represented companies affected by the program. "Practically speaking, high likelihood of conflict," Gregor noted, while also observing that the firm scored lower than other bidders on "experience and reputation," and in its financial and analytical capability.[49] Both Drinker Biddle & Reath and McGonigle have said they acted in good faith in awarding the contract. And Markell dismisses the case as the media connecting dots that should not be connected, noting that there was nothing illegal or unconventional about the incident. "It did not give me any less confidence in the people who had worked at my administration, so long as they abide by the policies that had been approved over a long period of time," he told me.[50]

Another example of officials moving on to well-paying gigs with companies in the unclaimed-property business involves Kelmar Associates, a Massachusetts-based auditing firm that specializes in unclaimed property. In 2013, Mark Udinski, a Delaware Department of Finance official in charge of the First State's unclaimed-property program, took a job at Kelmar, as did Patrick Hurley, a deputy attorney general who also worked on the program. It appeared to many to be a particularly Delawarean type of revolving door. "Here's a

guy who has been administering the program, who has hired Kelmar, who has helped Kelmar make millions of dollars," said Doug
Lindholm of the Council on State Taxation, a group representing
corporations, of Udinski. "It looks like a payout."[51]

None of this is illegal. But the issue of unclaimed property helps us
further color in a picture of Delaware as a rapacious money hunter,
enriching itself at the expense of other states.

———

In May 2013, Gloria James found herself badly in need of cash.

James was working at the time as a part-time housekeeper at the
Hotel du Pont, Delaware's fanciest hotel, a grand historic establishment on Wilmington's Rodney Square. The job paid her $11.83 an
hour, not enough for her to pay for her rent and groceries. To make
ends meet, she went to a payday lender called Loan Till Payday
and borrowed $200. James had taken out payday loans five times
before and had always managed to make the repayments on time.
The following day, while she was cleaning a toilet at the Hotel du
Pont, she broke her hand. The accident made her miss work. James
was able to make the first repayment. But after that, she simply
didn't have enough money to pay the installments and wound up
defaulting on the loan.

Even if Gloria James had not had an unfortunate accident, she
might not have been able to keep up with the repayments on the loan
this time. The total repayments on the $200 she borrowed added
up to a staggering $1,820, meaning that the annual percentage rate
worked out at more than 838 percent.

When the case wound up in Delaware's Chancery Court, Vice
Chancellor J. Travis Laster deemed that rate of interest to be "uncon-
scionable." He ruled against the lender, rescinding the loan and
concluding that Loan Till Payday's parent company had violated
the federal Truth in Lending Act. James had not fully grasped the
implications of the loan agreement she had originally signed—she
thought she would only have to pay back $260. In line with the statu-
tory remedy outlined in the Truth in Lending Act, Laster awarded
her $3,240 in damages—double the $1,620 interest on the original

$200 loan. Gloria James still owed $3 of the original $200 loan, so Laster removed the $3 from her award.

Ironically, the year before Gloria James borrowed money from Loan Till Payday, Delaware had enacted legislation to crack down on payday loans. The state passed a law that restricted borrowers from taking out more than five payday loans of $1,000 or less in any year and limited lenders to no more than four "rollovers," where a borrower takes out a loan to pay off another loan.

But the payday loan industry is nothing if not adaptable, even in states that have banned the industry outright—officially, at least— and outlawed practices such as rollovers altogether. Delaware's law had been much softer and easier to get around. It applied only to loans with a term of no more than sixty days. In response, the owners of Loan Till Payday recharacterized its payday loans as "installment loans" with longer repayment terms. James's loan was one of these. As Vice Chancellor Laster observed in his ruling, "By making this change, National sidestepped the law."

There was another aspect of payday loans that Delaware legislators declined to tackle. Unlike states such as Nebraska, New York, New Jersey, Arkansas, New Hampshire, Montana, and South Dakota, the First State does not impose any kind of interest-rate cap on small loans. This explains why there's a good chance that one of your credit cards is issued from Delaware: about half the US credit card market is based there. The First State is the home to the credit card businesses of Chase, Discover, and Barclaycard US, as well as a chunk of the credit cards offered by Bank of America and Citi.[52] It lured them there forty years ago by allowing them to charge whatever rate of interest they want and has kept them there ever since on the same basis. If Delaware now suddenly limited the amount of interest lenders can charge, it could lose jobs and corporate headquarters, which would be anathema to the state's business-friendly image. And the implications are national: Delaware's desire to attract financial services jobs has effectively neutralized interest-rate caps elsewhere. Financial institutions based in the First State only have to abide by the laws of Delaware, enabling them to issue cards in other states and bypass any local rate-cap provisions.

Delaware has not always felt that way. Like most other states, it traditionally had on its books a "usury law" that capped interest rates on loans. But in 1981, the state passed the Financial Center Development Act under the vigorous stewardship of Republican governor Pierre Samuel "Pete" du Pont IV, a scion of the du Pont family, whose chemical company was, at the time, Delaware's biggest business and chief employer. (Confusingly, the family name is du Pont, the company name DuPont.) Du Pont lived in a palatial estate named "Patterns" in Rockland, a tony community on the outskirts of Wilmington. He had enjoyed an elite upbringing, representing the United States on the Olympic sailing team and once dating Jane Fonda.[53] This princely station had effectively isolated him from the normal Delawarean, whom he derisively dubbed "Joe Six-Pack." On a trip to a Chrysler plant, du Pont had once started a conversation with one of the workers by asking, "Did you make any good cars today?"[54]

As part of his plan to attract banks to the state, du Pont put together and enthusiastically promoted a proposal to scrap the First State's usury law, freeing banks, credit card issuers, and other lenders to gouge customers as they pleased when it came to interest rates on credit cards.

The process was replete with secrecy and corporate clout, and light on oversight and democratic debate. The legislation itself was written by lawyers for Chase Manhattan and J. P. Morgan, two of Wall Street's financial giants, without any written analysis from any actual Delaware state officials. During its crafting, the bill's details were not shared with anyone who might have questioned the law—the press, the public, or state officials. When the bill was introduced, the legislature held only one hearing about it, lasting just three hours. Many Delaware lawmakers whose names were among the bill's sponsors freely admitted that they had not read it and didn't even understand it.[55]

The background featured an economic crisis. Du Pont had taken over the governorship in 1977 following many years of economic stagnation and years of undisciplined state spending. Delaware had debts of nearly $1,000 per capita, compared to an average among all states of $175. The First State had the highest top income tax rate—19.8 percent for those earning above $100,000—and a higher rate of unemployment than the US average. "Our finances border on bankruptcy," du Pont warned in his inaugural address, a statement that only made the situation worse, as two big bond-rating agencies lowered Delaware's credit rating to the lowest among the US states.[56]

The following year, the US Supreme Court ruled that credit card interest rates should be governed by the law of the state where the card was issued, regardless of where the consumer lived. This threw open the market to competition between the states for credit card issuers. At the same time, states were starting to look more seriously at allowing out-of-state banks to set up shop. In 1980, after South Dakota abolished its usury law, Citigroup rewarded the sparsely populated Great Plains state by moving its credit card operation to Sioux Falls. Governor du Pont was in a hurry to ensure that other banks transferred their operations to Delaware and not to South Dakota.

In the summer of 1980, Irving Shapiro, chairman and former CEO of DuPont and a director of both the Bank of Delaware and Citibank, organized a lunch meeting at the Wilmington Country Club between top Chase executives and Delaware officials. Shapiro, the son of Lithuanian immigrants who had run a dry-cleaning business in Minneapolis, had long been a strident advocate of corporate America. Chase was looking for a state that would mimic South Dakota and scrap its usury law, and it offered to move some of its credit card operations to whatever state that might be. Despite Chase's influence in its home state of New York, the Albany legislature had rebuffed the idea.

Pete du Pont set up a bank task force to see whether Delaware could do what Chase wanted. A key member of the task force was O. Francis "Frank" Biondi, a Wilmington lawyer who wielded tremendous influence both in business and in politics. Biondi took the lead in drafting a bill that would meet Chase's desires. The son of Italian immigrants, Biondi grew up in Wilmington and by the 1970s had become, according to the *Wilmington News Journal*, the "Godfather of the local Democratic organization."[57] Du Pont, a Republican governor facing a Democratic-dominated state legislature, wanted a heavyweight like Biondi on his side. Biondi needed little convincing.

He was eager to do the bank's bidding, both informally, as a member of the task force, and formally, when he became a paid lobbyist and attorney for Chase in Delaware a few months after joining the task force. Biondi was less than transparent about this transition, as the *New York Times* observed around the time: "Mr. Biondi's multiple roles in the drafting of the legislation, representing Chase and later Morgan as well as the Governor's task force, created some confusion, even among task force members and bankers."[58]

The governor kept the task force's existence a secret. He was running for reelection and feared the political consequences. "If this becomes an issue," he reportedly told his aides, "everyone will take positions against it because it's easy to run against New York banks."[59] It wasn't until the following January, months after he had decisively won a second term, that the governor revealed the proposed legislation to state lawmakers.

The proposal was subject to little democratic scrutiny. This was deliberate: du Pont did not want politics to derail his plans. The bill was introduced with little notice, and anyway, the legislation was not written with transparency in mind. Few legislators could grasp the details, in any case. Douglas Shachtman, a Wilmington consumer attorney and an expert on credit practices, only discovered that there was a hearing on the legislation from a newspaper reporter. He had just a few hours to read and digest the bill before addressing a committee of the Delaware House. By the time he was allowed to outline his misgivings, it was 7 P.M. and most of the representatives had left the legislature for the day. The bill then rapidly went to the state Senate, which passed it overwhelmingly without a hearing.

The whole episode left many observers confused and frustrated. "I believe we have acted too fast," said David McBride, a Democratic senator. "There was not enough public input; the legislation is too complicated." Even some of those who had supported the bill were no more enthusiastic. "I am mystified by the bill," said Harris McDowell, the majority whip for the Democratic-controlled Senate. "In fact, I'm sure it's designed to do that."[60]

Given its national implications, the legislation's velocity was also intended to prevent any intervention from outside Delaware. At the last gasp, Ralph Nader's Public Interest Research Group criticized the proposal as "one-sided" and a banker's "dream."[61] But it was too late. It had taken more than six months to draft the bill, but in just over a month, du Pont and his allies had introduced the legislation and got it through both state houses and to the governor's desk for signing into law, with barely a squeak of opposition.

Trumpeting the legislation, du Pont said it would turn Delaware into "the Luxembourg of the United States for banking and finance," taking as his standard the tiny European duchy that has been designated as an offshore financial center by both the IMF and the OECD.[62] Luxembourg attracted scores of foreign banks in the 1960s and 1970s with its business-friendly and tax-light regime. More than 120 banks have subsidiaries in the country, which is about half the size of Delaware (and one-eighth the size of Wales) and has a population about two-thirds as big as the First State.

It had been a case study in the workings of what is known as "the Delaware Way," the system of closed-door dealmaking and scant oversight that is the hallmark of First State politics. "Perhaps no other public policy better illustrates the centrality of the 'marketplace' and the primacy of big business in Delaware," wrote William Boyer, a University of Delaware professor and one of the most authoritative of Delaware historians. "It also illustrates how a small group of Delaware business executives and lawyers can prevent the public and its elected representatives from participating actively in the formulation, review and authorization of important public policy."[63]

As well as giving credit card issuers the ability to charge unlimited interest rates, the legislation also allowed them to raise interest rates retroactively, to charge variable interest rates, to levy unlimited fees for credit card use, and to foreclose on homes belonging to people who defaulted on their credit card debt. What's more, it introduced a regressive tax system on bank profits. New York banks that relocated to Delaware and had earnings of more than $30 million a year would be subject to a tax rate of 2.7 percent, compared with 8.7 percent for Delaware banks earning less than $20 million.

The only stipulation in all this was that in order to reap all these benefits, the banks locating themselves in Delaware would have to hire at least one hundred workers in the state. This was, of course, the main motivation for the First State. It proved a great success, providing tens of thousands of jobs in Delaware and making the banking sector one of the state's top employers. In turn, that made Delaware and its Washington representatives something of a lobbying group for big banks.[64]

The growth of the financial sector in Delaware seems to have altered the views of some of those involved. By 2016, Harris McDowell, the Senate majority whip who had declared himself "mystified" by the legislation, recalled the legislative process that had produced the law as a leading example of the Delaware Way, defining it as a process in which leaders "from both parties work together to get things done for the benefit of the people."[65]

There have been efforts in the Delaware legislature over the years to introduce interest-rate caps, but they have always been snuffed out. The clout of the financial sector is just too overwhelming. Delaware is not unique in this area. Wisconsin and Texas also do not cap payday-type loans. And average small-loan interest rates are higher in Idaho, South Dakota, and Nevada. But at more than 500 percent, the average cost of a small loan in Delaware remains outrageously high.[66]

That is great for the big banks, which found in Delaware a host willing to do almost anything, so long as they created jobs in return. It is good for the State of Delaware, which found a sector to create jobs just as traditional sectors such as manufacturing were shrinking.

It is less good for people such as Gloria James, the woman who cleaned toilets in the hotel where so many of the First State's elite met for power lunches. The victims of predatory lending are invariably poor and vulnerable. They are also disproportionately Black: in 2010 the federal government sued Wilmington Finance Inc. for charging higher fees on loans to Black borrowers—one-fifth of a percentage point higher than for whites, on average—and the firm was forced to pay $6.1 million compensation to victims.[67]

In a democratic society, one would want a great deal of scrutiny over lending practices by well-informed elected representatives who were given the time and space to deliberate. You might expect that lawmakers would do their utmost to consider carefully the impact of any new legislation on those who actually do the borrowing, rather than just focusing on the interests of the lenders or the state's coffers. Like so much else in the process of Delaware lawmaking, the passage of Delaware's 1981 Financial Center Development Act failed those tests.

———

Chapter 1 described Delaware's role in corporate life events. Companies are legally created there, merge and acquire each other there, and go there for bankruptcy. This last part of the life cycle is another key component of Delaware's legal-industrial complex, a billion-dollar-a-year adjunct to the state's main business. The First State's specialty is Chapter 11 filings, when struggling companies try to keep their businesses going as they restructure their debts.

Delaware's success in grabbing prime place in the race to host big bankruptcy cases was as dramatic as its victory in the incorporation business. In the 1980s, the first decade to see significant numbers of big US companies filing Chapter 11, the United States Bankruptcy Court for the District of Delaware presided over one solitary big company case. From 1991 to 1996, it drew forty-one large public company cases.

This boom was largely due to the efforts of Helen Balick, the Delaware bankruptcy court's sole judge from 1974 to 1993 (who continued as one of its judges until 1999). Balick was a phenomenon, the first and only woman attorney or judge in Delaware to have been admitted to law school without ever attending college.[68] (Her brother-in-law Sid was a mentor to Joe Biden when the future president first graduated from law school.[69])

In 1988, Balick made a bid to massively expand her court's caseload, declaring for the first time that corporations registered in Delaware should file for bankruptcy in Delaware rather than in the states where their headquarters were located—effectively touting for business among the hundreds of thousands of companies incorporated in the First State at the time. It paid off in 1990, when Balick scored the bankruptcy case of Continental Airlines, a company twenty times bigger than any corporation that had ever filed for bankruptcy in Delaware before. In the process, Balick took on and overcame the objections of the bankruptcy court in Houston, Continental's home base; American General, an insurance company and Continental's biggest creditor; and the airline's pilots. She then proceeded to make a series of unusual rulings in Continental's favor. "Once the case was firmly in her grasp, she showered the debtor with every imaginable benefit," wrote UCLA's Lynn LoPucki. "If any doubts remained that Judge Balick was seeking to attract large public company bankruptcies to Delaware, the Continental Airlines case should have put them to rest."[70] In 1992, *Businessweek* hailed her as the most "powerful woman judge in America," under the headline, "Helen Balick's Bailiwick Is a Backwater No More."[71]

The *Businessweek* profile came in the year that Delaware attracted six bankruptcy filings by big public companies, eclipsing New York as the biggest venue for such cases. By 1996, the Delaware bankruptcy court had established a near monopoly on large public company bankruptcies, hosting thirteen of the fifteen cases filed that year.[72] "The war is over and Delaware has won," stated Robert K. Rasmussen of the University of Southern California and Vanderbilt's Randall S. Thomas in 2001. "The 'Delawarization' of bankruptcy law appears complete."[73]

The competition for bankruptcy cases was enabled by a system in which companies choose where to file. There are ninety-four federal court districts in the United States, and companies can file for bankruptcy at the court nearest their headquarters, the court closest to where they have their most significant assets, or the state where they, or any of their subsidiaries, are incorporated—which makes the Wilmington, Delaware, bankruptcy court an option for most big companies. Traditionally, the closest competition Delaware has faced is New York, but the First State has in many years won this contest handily.

Like the Chancery Court, Delaware's bankruptcy court offers expertise, particularly in large Chapter 11 filings. The state's bankruptcy judges are known for their willingness to be flexible in order to get deals done. And like the speedy system of incorporation itself, bankruptcy is another example of Delaware acting with corporate-like efficiency itself: companies can file an emergency Chapter 11 within two business days.

The bankruptcy industry, then, is a lucrative by-product of the Franchise. Delaware owes its position in the bankruptcy business to its success in attracting incorporations. Large Chapter 11 cases last about sixteen months on average, but can stretch on for as much as three years (although cases in Delaware court generally get resolved about 40 percent faster than in other courts).[74] As well as the fees for local attorneys, big bankruptcies usually mean out-of-town lawyers and financial journalists flocking to the First State, providing important revenue for local hotels and restaurants. "It fuels Wilmington and [the] state economy, no question," noted Joseph J. Farnan, a former US district judge for Delaware.[75]

To the state's supporters, Delaware's ascent as a bankruptcy location in the 1990s reflected another race to the top, which Delaware won thanks to the expertise and efficiency it quickly developed. To its detractors, Delaware had succeeded in making its system as friendly as possible for incumbent corporate leaders, the ones who choose where to file. Research also suggested that companies filing for bankruptcy in Delaware were more likely to file for bankruptcy again in the future.[76] "The Delaware bankruptcy story is one of a court that took bold, decisive action to serve the parochial interests of the case-placers and quickly and decisively won a new, lucrative industry for the state," observe UCLA's LoPucki and Joseph W. Doherty. "The court broke more than a few companies along the way, but has since masked its illgotten gains with the trappings of respectability."[77]

Bankruptcy is a terrific example of Delaware's "heads I win, tails you lose" revenue model: when corporate America is doing well, the state benefits from dealmaking and business formation; when corporations are doing badly, Delaware benefits from bankruptcy filings. (As bankruptcies soared in 2020 and 2021 because of the havoc wreaked by the COVID-19 pandemic on the US economy, Delaware cashed in, hosting many more of these cases than any other state).[78] Given that hardly any of the corporations in question have real business operations in the First State, Delaware can be somewhat agnostic as to the state of their health.

But not everyone is happy with Delaware's dominance of corporate bankruptcies. Chapter 11 proceedings are ideally a legal problem-solving exercise involving the company, its creditors, and the bankruptcy court. If a company chooses to file in Delaware, the creditors most likely to turn up are those with the most money at stake. Smaller creditors are more likely to struggle to send representatives halfway across the country to sit in on the proceedings. Employees can effectively be cut out of the process by being physically far from it.

These concerns have led to several attempts in recent years to use federal legislation to unseat Delaware from its position. In 2018 and 2019, Washington lawmakers introduced bills in Congress to try to prevent companies from "forum shopping" by forcing them to file for bankruptcy wherever they have their headquarters or hold most of their assets. Delaware's congressional delegation and the business lobby cried foul, and the bills failed.

In recent years, Delaware's hold over bankruptcy cases has diminished somewhat. As well as New York, rivals such as Texas and Virginia have emerged as strong contenders for big bankruptcies. Both have succeeded by specializing. The bankruptcy court in Houston has attracted filings from energy companies by building expertise, making its deadlines more flexible, and providing easy access to judges. Richmond's bankruptcy court has made headway by focusing on retailers.

But bankruptcy continues to be an important part of Delaware's legal-industrial complex. Of the bankruptcies of companies with more than $100 million in assets, some 40 percent were filed in Delaware in 2020 and the first half of 2021. (Texas was second, with less than 30 percent.)[79] Coupled with the Franchise itself, this Leviathan funds the salaries of elite lawyers, earns the state government a big chunk of its annual revenue, and enables Delawareans to avoid paying sales and other taxes. And the process is set up to perpetuate itself.

Is that process good for the United States? As Cary observed in 1974:

With respect to public policy, the question arises whether the policy of a single state occupying a critical position should be permitted to grant management unilateral control untrammeled by other interests. Should one state set social policy in the corporate field when a cornerstone of that policy is to stay ahead of (or behind) the rest? It is understandable that Delaware would choose not to let its premier position in American corporate law go by default, but it must also be understood that the generic reason for attaining it was revenue.[80]

A key driving force behind the crafting of US corporate law, then, is not the interests of the general population, or of US business, or of some other group of stakeholders, but of the financial well-being of the State of Delaware. That is the highest aim of the Delaware Way. The system is set up in the interests not of the 327 million citizens of the United States, but the 967,000 residents of the First State—less than 0.3 percent of the national population. And the biggest financial gains from the system flow to a tiny fraction of that 0.3 percent—the lawyers who design the system, argue the cases, and collect the fees.

5

Delaware Is Everywhere

In 1989, the United States invaded Panama to overthrow Manuel Noriega, the country's leader, whom it had indicted on charges including drug smuggling and money laundering. The United States said it was invading to protect the lives of US citizens and military personnel stationed there, to defend democracy, to combat drug trafficking, and to keep the Panama Canal open for US shipping.

Noriega took refuge in the Vatican Embassy in Panama City. The general was known to love opera, and the US military soon began blasting the embassy twenty-four hours a day with irritating pop and rock, played at top volume: Rick Astley's "Never Gonna Give You Up," the Clash's version of "I Fought the Law"—and Van Halen's "Panama," naturally. The musical bombardment lasted just three days, stopping after the Vatican complained, but after ten days stuck in the embassy, Noriega surrendered.

Noriega was a colorful authoritarian ruler who reportedly wore red underwear to ward off the "evil eye." A former army officer who had seized power in 1983, he had run Panama like a gangster boss. He partnered with the Medellín drug cartel in neighboring Colombia, charging $200,000 per plane to safeguard the cartel's distribution networks. Noriega's Panama, in the words of the US Senate's Iran-Contra report, became the Western Hemisphere's "first 'narco-kleptocracy.'"[1] At the same time, Noriega had been pocketing up to $200,000 a year from the US Central Intelligence Agency for helping to funnel money and weapons to the Contra rebels in Nicaragua. These funds were channeled through accounts he maintained at the Bank of Credit and Commerce International and then cash was siphoned off into shell companies to buy, among other things, three luxury apartments in Paris.

James Henry, an American investigative reporter, had visited Panama a couple of years before the US invasion to try and untangle the labyrinthine finances surrounding Noriega. On his quest to understand what the Panamanian leader was doing with his money, Henry sought out an expert in offshore finance.

Henry was introduced to a young lawyer who, he was assured, was highly knowledgeable. The lawyer was Ramón Fonseca Mora, who had founded Mossack Fonseca a decade earlier. The firm went on to earn worldwide notoriety in 2016 as the source of the Panama Papers, the leak of 11.5 million files that showed how the global elite exploit secretive offshore tax regimes. But at the time, Mossack Fonseca was simply a large, if largely unknown, player in the world of offshore finance. Fonseca answered Henry's queries about the industry. As their interview was ending, the American asked him a more personal question. "By the way," Henry ventured, "where do you have *your* money?" Fonseca did not hesitate to answer. "Oh, in Delaware," he said. "They'll never find it. There's too many companies there."[2]

Fonseca could have found secrecy in any one of the many tax havens that he used for his clients: the British Virgin Islands, the Bahamas, or the Seychelles. But he chose Delaware, because it was the perfect place to hide in plain sight.

———

You need more identification to obtain a library card in most US states than you do to create a corporation. In Delaware, getting a library card requires you to produce a photo ID and proof of address. In all states, you have to apply for a library card in person—assuming there isn't a pandemic in progress, of course. By contrast, in Delaware, as in most states, you can officially establish a business without proof of your identity, address, or phone number, and you don't need to turn up in person to do so.[3]

Picking up a library card may not allow you to do anything much more nefarious than illegally copying a CD, but corporate names have been used for much more devastating ends: money laundering, financing terrorism (both international and domestic), buying elections, busting sanctions, acquiring weapons of mass destruction, bribery, corruption, and kleptocracy.[4]

Of course, only a tiny minority of business entities engage in such activity, but it is instructive that, in spite of the relative harm that can be caused with a corporate entity, it remains easier to form a corporation than to borrow a library book. Like many US states, Delaware is apparently more amenable to external business interests than it is to its own resident readers, even though you might reasonably think that we should encourage reading at least as much as starting a company.

Those who have argued against greater transparency in Delaware and elsewhere over the years have regularly recycled the notion that requiring more verified information from those trying to set up companies would add an undue burden on businesses, which could stifle entrepreneurship. Yet, so far as anyone can make out, the photo ID requirement has not discouraged the people of Delaware and other US states from obtaining library cards; more than 170 million US residents have registered for one.[5]

For decades, Delaware operated a system with hardly any regulation of who was behind the hundreds of thousands of LLCs and trusts that were registered in the First State. As the leading incorporating state, Delaware could have set the highest standards in corporate transparency and accountability, and depended on the expertise of its courts and lawyers to attract reputable companies. Instead, it claimed it could not raise standards alone, and that only the federal government could enforce greater transparency. But at the same time, for many years Delaware campaigned in Washington precisely against such transparency, changing its mind only after a series of high-profile scandals threatened the Franchise. In the meantime, Delaware was knowingly enabling international corruption and kleptocracy; turning a blind eye to the trafficking of children, adults, drugs, and weapons; and facilitating sanction busting. It took all the scandals outlined in the introduction to this book—and many more—to force it finally to act.

Delaware has always been at great pains to ensure the Franchise is efficient. The First State pours considerable resources into this effort. Its incorporations unit acts more like a financial-services business than a small-state bureaucracy. Delaware's Division of Corporations brags that it "exists to provide corporations and their advisors with prompt and efficient service." The office is open fifteen hours a day, until midnight, to accommodate requests for filings from different time zones around the world. And just like paying the Prime fee gets you expedited shipping on Amazon, a range of extra fees on offer can get you your new corporation in twenty-four hours, two hours, one hour, or thirty minutes. "The personnel of the Division of Corporations view themselves as employees of a service business, and the Division meets worldwide quality standards," the state's marketing copy informs. It touts its ISO 9001 certification, a designation awarded by the International Organization for Standardization in Geneva, Switzerland, for management features such as customer focus, a process approach, an expanding customer base, and increased revenue and market share.[6]

As Jack Markell, who was governor of Delaware from 2009 to 2017, told me:

> We've got a Division of Corporations that looks unlike any other state agency that you've ever seen. They're there till midnight. I remember seeing a letter from the CEO, I think it was of an airline, and they had a merger deadline, and it was snowing like crazy—a massive snow storm, but the people from the Division of Corporations heroically were able to process all the paperwork in time that the merger happened on a timely basis, and he was just unbelievably appreciative.[7]

The result is that it is easier to set up a corporation in Delaware than in many places around the world that we think of as tax havens or homes for dirty money.

Traditionally, for example, an international money launderer looking for a new location to set up a shell company might consider several locations to form the business and start laundering cash: Belize, the Cayman Islands, Panama, Bermuda, or the United States. Until very recently, the one that required the least documentation was the United States.

As the name suggests, shell companies are hollow—there's nothing underneath the name and the legal entity. Shell corporations have no real employees, no offices, and no significant assets or operations. They exist on paper only.

Not all shell companies are sketchy. Some businesses use them to protect their staff who are working in countries where they might be in danger if their true identities were known. Other companies use shells when they're developing new products and want to keep them secret from their competitors. Large corporations sometimes use shell companies to hold assets temporarily when they're involved in complex mergers and acquisitions.

But shell companies have traditionally lent themselves to illegitimate ends. "Shell companies that cannot be traced back to their real owners are one of the most common means for laundering money, giving and receiving bribes, busting sanctions, evading taxes, and financing terrorism," note three political science researchers who carried out a famous experiment in 2012: Michael Findley of the University of Texas at Austin, Daniel Nielson from Brigham Young University, and Jason Sharman of Griffith University in Australia.[8]

Shell companies have been frequently identified in investigations into illegal global activity. For example, Mexico's Sinaloa cartel, the world's most powerful drug gang, was revealed in 2015 to have used a shell company registered in New Zealand to launder millions of dollars. The Iranian government used shell companies registered in Germany, Malta, and Cyprus to evade international sanctions in 2009.

There are clear international rules against this kind of thing. In essence, they say, first, that countries should prevent money laundering and terrorist financing, and second, that there should be "adequate, accurate and timely information" on who owns and controls shell companies. The rules come from the Financial Action

Task Force on Money Laundering (FATF), set up in 1989 by the G7 (which includes the United States), and they've been endorsed by 180 countries as well as the United Nations, the G20, and the World Bank. But the United States effectively ignored the rules for more than thirty years, during which all sorts of malevolent organizations and individuals set up their legal homes in states such as Delaware.

In their experiment, Findley, Nielson, and Sharman set out on an email fishing trip to test if the FATF rules were actually being observed. FATF said that the lawyers and brokers who help people set up shell companies must collect identity documents from their customers. So the researchers sent more than 7,400 emails to about 3,700 go-betweens in 182 countries who help establish "shell" companies, to see what kind of information they ask for. What they found was that in the United States, the go-betweens didn't ask for very much.

The researchers impersonated a variety of potential customers, from legitimate users to would-be money launderers, corrupt officials, and terrorist financiers. One of their emails, for example, purported to be from a national of Lebanon (a country perceived to have a high risk of terrorist financing, according to international guidelines), living in Saudi Arabia and working for a Muslim charity (which at the time was considered another conspicuous risk factor for terrorist financing). "The combination of individuals from a country perceived to play host to terrorist groups, working for a Muslim charity, and seeking financial secrecy poses a very unsubtle terrorist financing risk," the researchers observed.

Setting up shell companies has historically been ridiculously easy. The staff of NPR's *Planet Money* podcast were amazed at how quickly and easily they could register companies in Belize (which they dubbed "Unbelizable Inc.") and in Delaware (the "Delawho?" corporation) in 2012.[9] It took Fusion reporter Natasha del Toro just five minutes to set up a shell company in Delaware for her cat Suki in 2016. She called the company She Sells Seashells LLC.[10]

But it wasn't just the ease of incorporating that Findley, Nielson, and Sharman demonstrated. They highlighted how easy it was to evade the rules on identification, even when you wave a series of large red flags.

The researchers worked out an index they dubbed the "Dodgy Shopping Count," which showed on average how many providers a particular kind of customer would have to approach before being offered an untraceable shell company. The lower the Dodgy Shopping Count, the easier it was to set up an anonymous shell corporation.

Incorporating agents in the United States turned out to be almost the dodgiest in the entire study—dodgier than those in Switzerland, Jamaica, Serbia, Ghana, Macau, Lebanon, Brazil, or dozens of other jurisdictions surveyed by the researchers. The only easier way to set up an untraceable shell company was to do so in Kenya.

Findley, Nielson, and Sharman's research confirmed what many campaigning groups had been saying for years. But even though the United States made some (albeit slow) progress in countering money laundering in the subsequent decade, many other countries cracked down on shell companies more aggressively, making the United States relatively an even easier destination for those seeking corporate secrecy.

Given the strength of the Franchise, it would be reasonable to assume that a significant proportion of the shell companies created in the United States were registered in the First State, a good place to hide under a mountain of corporate entities.

———

Recall from the introduction the case of Luka Bojović and Darko Šarić, the Serbian crime bosses. The pair used two companies registered in Delaware, Lafino Trade and Digivision LLC, to launder money from drugs and other criminal activity, according to Serbian investigators.[11] Bojović had fought during the Yugoslav wars of the 1990s as part of the Serb Volunteer Guard, a paramilitary group led by the infamous warlord Arkan that was found guilty of a string of crimes against humanity, including rape and genocide. After the conflict, Bojović murdered his way to the top of the Zemun Clan, a grouping within the Serbian mafia that was reportedly involved in plotting the 2003 assassination of Serbian prime minister Zoran Đinđić, and organized at least eleven murders of Zemun Clan opponents, according to Serbian authorities. Šarić, who started his criminal career as a salami-stealing youth, would transform himself over the decades into the Balkan "Cocaine King," overseeing a vast international narcotrafficking and money laundering empire. In 2018, Šarić's was given a fifteen-year jail term for drug smuggling. In 2020, he was sentenced by a Serbian court to nine years in prison for laundering more than €20 million, some of which passed through Lafino Trade and Digivision.[12]

Those companies can be traced to Harvard Business Services, a leading Delaware incorporating agent firm that claims to have helped form more than two hundred thousand entities since 1981. (The company is unrelated to Harvard University or Harvard Business School.) When CNN Money pressed Harvard Business Services about Bojović and Šarić, Richard Bell, the Delaware company's president, told the media outlet that their names never appeared on any paperwork filed with its firm, and that it resigned as their registered agent when alerted to the pair's possible criminal activity by the US Department of Justice. "We are as concerned as anyone about the fraudulent use of Delaware companies by a few of the people who obtain them," said Bell. "These few who misuse them threaten our existence and we come down hard on them whenever we are alerted to such cases."[13]

Bell pointed out that criminals were attracted to Delaware by the ability to hide themselves in a deluge of incorporations. "These fraudsters want to appear legitimate so they pick the premier state in the premier country to camouflage themselves," he told CNN. Bell has a point. There are shell companies hiding nefarious activity across the United States. The difference in Delaware is the scale. When you register as many businesses as Delaware does, just by the law of averages, a proportion of them are likely to be fronts for criminals.

Cassara agrees. "There's drug trafficking, money laundering, fraud—it's just odds," he says. "It's just the sheer numbers involved. Delaware registers more than 480 companies a day. The odds are, out of 480 companies a day, going back, say, ten years, there's going to be some irregular LLCs structured in Delaware."[14] (Actually, as the introduction noted, Delaware now registers on average about 683 new entities every day.)

Delaware stresses that the overwhelming majority of companies that incorporate in the First State and elsewhere in the United States are legitimate. While that may be valid, the extent of illicit uses of company formations such as LLCs has always been hidden.

The First State's formulaic "few bad apples" rejoinder was always unsatisfying. First, criminal investigators were not interested in the overwhelming majority of law-abiding shell companies. They were interested in the tiny minority of companies that engage in nefarious shell activity, and the system that did not require these companies to reveal their beneficial owners for use by criminal investigators was of little use to the lawful companies, but a huge advantage to criminals.

Second, without ownership information, it has always been impossible to know the scale of the problem. It would not be unfair to assume, given the lack of information available to law enforcement, that not all criminal shell companies were exposed and shut down. It is not clear whether the known cases were the tip of an iceberg or something bigger, but it's at least likely that they did not represent the entirety of the problem.

Third, even if Delaware had wanted to cooperate with criminal investigations, it could not produce information that wasn't collected in the first place. In Cassara's experience, when criminal investigations led to Delaware, federal authorities gave up trying to seek cooperation from the state. "We wouldn't even bother asking because it was pointless," he recalls.[15] This lack of information also hampers the most basic type of data collection about corporate activity in Delaware. For example, the state does not even know how many of the entities it registers are based in the United States or overseas.

Delaware was far from the only culprit among US states. For example, Viktor Bout, the arms trafficker we talked about in the introduction, also used shell companies based in Texas and Florida. In 2009, Los Zetas, a ruthless Mexican drug cartel, set up Tremor Enterprises, a shell company registered in Texas and California, which purchased a 140-acre Oklahoma horse ranch that served as a front for laundering millions of dollars in drug money. While Delaware has had particularly lax registration requirements, so have Nevada and Wyoming. There are some minor differences. Nevada was historically the only US state that refused to share information with the Internal Revenue Service, the federal tax-collection agency. Incorporation fees are cheaper in Wyoming than in Delaware.

A big difference, though, is scale. Delaware has long been by far the biggest incorporating state for large publicly traded companies, multinational enterprises, and "complex alternative entities," and as we've seen, the state's economy has come to depend on the Franchise. Since the ownership of public companies and many large multinationals has always been transparent, one wonders who benefited from corporate anonymity. Delaware officials repeatedly claimed that anonymity was irrelevant to companies' decision to register in the state and that the Franchise would continue to flourish without it, given its strong "brand" of fast processing and long record of corporate case law. But, if the attraction was always efficiency and predictability, why did Delaware need secrecy?

After all, it was always possible for individual US states to adhere to higher standards. A handful of US states did take steps toward greater corporate transparency, among them Alaska, Arizona, Massachusetts, Montana, and Oregon. Had Delaware—given its status as the incorporation behemoth—demanded that business owners identify themselves at the point of registering their companies, it might have single-handedly raised the bar for the whole of corporate America. States impose burdens on business all the time above what the federal government demands. Most US states, including Delaware, have set a minimum wage that is above the US federal minimum wage,[16] for example, and some states have set stricter environmental standards than the federal government.

In the private sector, many big US corporations have not waited for federal intervention on issues such as diversity, parental leave, and combating racism. Instead, the most enlightened corporations have created their own policies without waiting for a federal mandate. You do not hear them worrying that investors might go elsewhere because they might be devoting money and resources to anti-racism efforts rather than delivering shareholders the maximum returns possible. It is companies that have often set the standards on such issues—not the federal government (even if it is fair to be skeptical about how sincere these efforts are). Delaware wants to act like a company when it comes to serving its clients, but not when it comes to its stakeholders more broadly, or society at large.

This was never simply a domestic US issue. As Cassara points out, the effect was truly global. As hot money swishes across international borders, it looks for an obscure, secret corner to cool down. And traditionally, Delaware was opaque enough to be a good destination.

This means that Delaware in effect hampered the fight against international drug smuggling, illicit weapons trading, and terrorism— the very fight the US government was committed to in country after country around the world—for decades. Delaware's attractiveness, at least in some part, was as a safe haven for objectionable characters. You could even say that the State of Delaware was in some sense, and at certain times, in a proxy war with the United States itself, aiding and abetting our enemies abroad. "The efforts by Delaware's officials have effectively aided those corrupt and criminal interests that are seeking to do harm to Americans," says Clark Gascoigne of the Financial Accountability and Corporate Transparency Coalition, a nonpartisan campaign group. "It's a tragic downside of this."[17]

One of the reasons criminals were able to get away with their illicit actions was that, by being registered in the United States, shell companies have benefited from the good reputation that the federal government and most US corporations have worked hard to develop around the world. "A company in Delaware has the American flag stamped on it, so to speak, and people are going to see that company in other jurisdictions as potentially more legitimate," says Mark Hays of Global Witness, an anticorruption group. "They might ask fewer questions."[18]

After all, if you are stealing money from public coffers in a poor country with weak governance, the best place to stash it is in a country that has a strong rule of law. "Kleptocrats and arms dealers actually prefer shell companies in Delaware to places like the Bahamas because they're taking advantage of America's political stability and property rights," said Casey Michel, an expert on offshore financing.

"It's long past time people in this country understand Delaware's role as this almost cancerous role on the American body politic."[19]

Although Delaware officials always denied that terrorists were behind shell companies incorporated in their state, it was near impossible to confirm or deny such a charge, given the lack of disclosure traditionally required to register an entity in the state. The officials simply did not know what was going on in their own backyard, and most generally did not seem overly troubled to find out.

As the *Financial Times* columnist Ed Luce pointed out, this gap in diligence had serious implications for US foreign policy. The United States has expended a huge amount of energy on fighting foreign wars, but America's international aims might have been better served by focusing on the home front. "A better US foreign policy would be to close down weapons of mass incorporation in states such as Delaware and Nevada and hold their enablers in New York and Washington to account," Luce wrote in 2019.[20]

Cassara likes to tell a story that illustrates the situation. It concerns an interview with Osama bin Laden, conducted by *Ummat*, a Pakistani newspaper, and published on September 28, 2001, a few weeks after the 9/11 attacks and a week before the official start of the US invasion of Afghanistan. The interviewer asked Al-Qaida's then leader what the impact would be of the United States freezing the organization's bank accounts. Bin Laden's reply was revealing: "Freezing of accounts will not make any difference for Al-Qaida or other jihad groups," he said. "Al-Qaida comprises of such modern educated youths who are aware of the cracks inside the Western financial system as they are aware of the lines in their hands. These are the very flaws of the Western fiscal system, which are becoming a noose for it."[21]

For Cassara, corporate anonymity was an obvious example of a "crack" that terrorists and other criminals knew they could use. "Bin Laden himself knew about our vulnerabilities," he says. "That's exactly why there are very few pieces of financial intelligence filed on terrorists both in the United States and in Europe. They are aware of our vulnerabilities, like, for example, Delaware corporations."[22]

This crack was well known and widely documented, both by US government agencies and by independent and multilateral organizations. The chief multilateral was FATF, which repeatedly called out the United States on its lack of compliance with the 1989 declaration. In 2006, for example, it deemed the United States to be "non-compliant" over anti–money laundering rules. A decade later, little had changed, and FATF observed, "Lack of timely access to adequate, accurate and current beneficial ownership information remains one of the fundamental gaps in the US context. . . . Challenges in ensuring timely access to and availability of beneficial ownership . . . raise significant concerns."[23]

The US federal government's own General Accountability Office noted in 2006 that both "government and international reports indicate that shell companies have become popular tools for facilitating criminal activity in the United States and internationally and can be involved in fraud and corruption or used for illicit purposes such as laundering money, financing terrorism, hiding and shielding assets from creditors, and engaging in questionable tax practices. Such schemes can conceal money movements that range from a few thousand to many millions of dollars."[24] The GAO's concern was reiterated regularly by US law enforcement officials in subsequent years.

And in 2016, Transparency International criticized the response of officials in jurisdictions such as Delaware when they noted that most registered companies are law abiding. That response, the watchdog group said, was a bit like complaining of a leaking ceiling in a hotel room, only to have the hotel staff tell you, "I don't see what the problem is. There is clearly more roof than holes on average."[25] Or to draw a more potent US analogy, it is a bit like the argument made to protestors against police brutality that "most cops are good." That is no comfort for the families of Black men and women who have been killed by the minority of cops who were clearly not in that category.

Cassara thinks the US federal government was at least complicit in the setup. The US State Department and the Treasury regularly called out other countries and condemned them as havens for financial crime, he notes, but ignored similar havens in their own backyard. It made US officials hypocrites, he says, when they preached to other countries to act more forcefully against wrongdoing. Those countries, he says, loved to throw that hypocrisy back in the United States' face.[26]

Hypocrisy is one thing, but corporate opacity has also facilitated corruption around the world. That corruption in turn enabled abuses of power by corrupt politicians, fed a culture of impunity, and kept some of the world's most desperate people poor and powerless. "We call anonymous companies 'financial getaway cars,' because you've stolen the money and you need to find a way to get away from the scene of the crime," said Mark Hays. "By having a presence in the US, corrupt politicians gain closer access to the financial sectors and actors that they need to spend their ill-gotten funds, to launder them, and to gain access to the kind of political and social circles that are part of their strategy of maintaining power."[27]

About 75 percent of cases of grand corruption—cases involving tens of millions of dollars—involved the use of opaque corporate structures, according to a 2011 report by the Stolen Asset Recovery Initiative, a partnership between the World Bank and the United Nations.[28] Given that the United States was one of the world's biggest registrants of shell companies, there was no shortage of US-based examples, many but not all of them connected to Delaware.

For example, Pavlo Lazarenko, a former Ukrainian prime minister whom Transparency International once ranked the eighth-most corrupt official in the world, used a Wyoming shell company to control an estimated $72 million in real estate in Ukraine, purchased using stolen Ukrainian government funds. The case only came to light in 2004 because Lazarenk was sentenced to an eight-year jail term in California on money laundering and extortion charges.

In December 2008, the US Attorney's Office for the Southern District of New York seized a 40 percent stake in 650 Fifth Avenue, a thirty-six-story building on the edge of Rockefeller Center in Manhattan. It charged that one of the building's owners was Bank Melli of Iran, whose ownership violated US sanctions against Tehran. The ownership was hidden by a shell corporation. "As a former property manager of the building, we never knew exactly who we were working for," Michael T. Cohen (not the Trump fixer), who managed the building in the 1980s for Williams Real Estate, told the *New York Times*. "We knew there were people in New York to whom we reported, but beyond that we couldn't be sure of anything."[29]

Between 2004 and 2008, Teodoro Nguema Obiang Mangue, son of President Teodoro Obiang Nguema Mbasogo of Equatorial

Guinea, used a string of US shell companies to move more than $110 million in suspect funds into the United States, according to a 2010 report by the US Senate Permanent Subcommittee on Investigations. The shell companies had names such as Beautiful Vision, Unlimited Horizon, Sweetwater Malibu, Sweetwater Management, and Sweet Pink. Equatorial Guinea's president allegedly licensed foreign companies to dump toxic waste on the country's pristine Atlantic island of Annobón and, according to the testimony of former ministers, encouraged his diplomats to use their immunity to smuggle large amounts of drugs all over the world—even in the president's own baggage. Meanwhile, the younger Obiang—who is also Equatorial Guinea's vice president—used the funds to purchase a $30 million house in Malibu, on Southern California's coast, as well as a $38.5 million US-built Gulfstream jet and Michael Jackson memorabilia worth almost $2 million. In 2017, France tried the junior Obiang in absentia for embezzlement, money laundering, corruption, and abuse of trust, handing down a three-year suspended jail term. In 2020, an appeal court added a €30m fine.[30]

But perhaps the strangest case saw the US government itself paying taxpayer money directly to a corrupt politician because of its reluctance to collect beneficial ownership information. In 2017, the Government Accountability Office (GAO) found that high-security federal offices in Seattle used by the FBI and DEA were ultimately owned by the family of Abdul Taib Mahmud, former chief minister of Sarawak in Malaysia, through a web of domestic and foreign companies. In 2013, Taib had been the subject of a Global Witness undercover investigation that found he and his family used their political status to buy land and forest concessions for much less than their commercial value. The land deals resulted in the destruction of large swathes of Sarawak rainforest, and various abuses against the rightful land owners. Taib's brother used a secret Singapore company to hide profits from the land deals to avoid paying some $10 million in taxes. The FBI and DEA were able to rent offices from Mahmud because the General Services Administration (GSA), which oversees office management for the federal government, was not required to collect beneficial ownership information about the owners of the buildings it leased. Noting that it could not identify ownership information for about a third of the federal government's 1,406 high-security real estate leases across the United States, the GAO urged the GSA to determine the real owners of the space it uses for federal offices. This demand came too late to change the situation in Seattle: by the end of the US government's twenty-year lease in 2019, US taxpayers had paid the Taib family $56 million in rent.[31]

The United States' effective aiding and abetting of corrupt foreign leaders has kept wealth from spreading down to the poorest parts of society in these countries. Worse, less-developed countries typically have had much less appetite and fewer resources to pursue political wrongdoing. If anyone is equipped to aid the global fight against corruption, it would be investigators in the United States. As Cassara observes from his tours in Africa and the Middle East: "Here in the United States, as a criminal investigator, you have a whole lot of support. You have resources. You have data. You have cars. You have phones. You have everything you want, basically. When you go overseas, most law enforcement don't have the resources that we take for granted. They don't have enough money to gas up the cars. They don't have communication systems. They don't have training. What they do have is a lot of political pressure. Lots of times, I've been overseas working with counterparts, and when I would talk to them about money laundering, they'd say, 'Yeah, John, we had a big money laundering investigation, but it went to the ruling family, and we were told to stand down.'"[32]

What benefited Delaware hurt the world. Corrupt officials around the world long took the lack of transparency in the United States as an open invitation to bring their loot to the United States. In this way, the Franchise helped further impoverish some of the world's poorest and most downtrodden people.

———

History's biggest-ever data leak came in October 2021.

The "Pandora Papers" (named after the character in Greek mythology whose curiosity led her to release a string of cooped-up curses into the world) amounted to nearly 12 million financial records collected from fourteen providers of offshore services. The documents, obtained by the International Consortium of Investigative Journalists, revealed a global system operating in the shadows, in which celebrities, politicians, and business elites from more than two hundred countries shifted their money around the world to avoid tax and legal claims.

The scale of the document hoard was vast, and its impact will be felt for years to come. It identified some twenty-nine thousand offshore accounts owned by more than one hundred billionaires, thirty current and former leaders, and three hundred public officials. It named sixteen serving heads of state or government from Europe, the Middle East, and Latin America: the king of Jordan; the emirs of Qatar and Dubai; the presidents of Ukraine, Azerbaijan, Montenegro, Cyprus, Chile, Ecuador, the Dominican Republic, Congo, Gabon, and Kenya; and the prime ministers of the Czech Republic, Lebanon, and the Ivory Coast. It also revealed some of the financial holdings of celebrities such as Elton John, Ringo Starr, Shakira, Claudia Schiffer, and Julio Iglesias, and sports personalities including Luís Suarez, Guy Forget, Carlo Ancelotti, and Sachin Tendulkar.

The Pandora Papers highlighted the importance of South Dakota in the world of trusts, often used by the superwealthy to shelter their fortunes from inheritance taxes. Recall from the last chapter how Delaware and South Dakota competed in the 1980s to attract credit card companies, a race in which Delaware came out ahead. South Dakota's revenge was to pivot its financial services industry to become the top spot for the world's richest people looking to park their personal money in the United States. In 1983, South Dakota became the first state to abolish rules against perpetuities, a restriction inherited from English common law that prevented trusts from lasting more than three generations.[33] In the context of the competition between the two states for the credit card industry, South Dakota's move sent shivers up Delawarean spines. Delaware's general assembly fretted that the repeal had given the Mount Rushmore State "a competitive advantage over Delaware in attracting assets held in trusts created for estate planning purposes."[34] In 1985,

Delaware followed by allowing perpetuities, with many other states joining in the subsequent years; some allowed perpetuities, others capped them at 365, 500, or 1,000 years (a measure that recalled the old joke in which the convicted criminal has received a 400-year sentence but says he is confident that on appeal, he can cut it in half). But South Dakota retained its first-mover advantage. By 2020, its trust companies held more than $367 billion. "We're the Cayman Islands of the prairie," one South Dakotan remarked as the Pandora Papers started to make headlines.[35] Delaware, however, was not left empty-handed: while South Dakota was home to eighty-one trust companies identified in the Pandora Papers, Delaware had thirty-three, behind Florida with thirty-seven. And in any case, the trust industry did not prove to be the boon that the incorporation industry was. In spite of their size, South Dakota trust companies pay paltry fees that add up to less than 1 percent of the state's annual revenues, and are not great job creators.[36] The trust industry turned out to be more a status symbol than a real revenue-generator.

You might've thought that the revelations in the Pandora Papers would bring protestors onto the streets, demanding transparency and moves against tax avoidance, but the response was somewhat muted. In part, this was because the news came during the COVID-19 pandemic. But it was also because the Pandora Papers felt like the umpteenth release of masses of information that demonstrated how the global elite operate under different financial rules than the rest of us.

Five years earlier, the world had been rocked by the "Panama Papers," some 11.5 million files from the database of Mossack Fonseca, the world's fourth-biggest offshore law firm at the time (it closed its doors in 2018) that had showed how the global elite—including 12 serving or former national leaders and 143 politicians—hid their wealth offshore. Sigmundur Davíð Gunnlaugsson, the prime minister of Iceland, was forced to resign in the wake of the revelations. Again, there had been a long list of famous people identified in the documents, including the filmmakers Pedro Almodóvar and Stanley Kubrick and the actors Emilio Estevez, Jackie Chan, and Emma Watson.

The vast majority of the activities exposed in both the Pandora and Panama Papers were not illegal. There were relatively few cases of criminal tax evasion; it was not until 2020 that a US resident was sent to jail for crimes uncovered by the Panama Papers leak.

But the extent of the global elite's involvement in extraordinary (if legal) tax-avoidance schemes was shocking and laid bare the emptiness of their public pronouncements on the issue. Just six months before the release of the Panama Papers, David Cameron, the serving UK prime minister, had claimed he had "taken the lead" in fighting for corporate transparency. When the documents came to light, he was forced to admit that he had been a shareholder in an offshore trust set up by his father in Panama.

The Panama Papers arguably added to the sense among the general population that the global economy is run for the benefit of a small elite, a sentiment that boosted the UK vote in favor of Brexit in June 2016 and helped Donald Trump win the US presidency that November.

Like many a good scandal that we've already discussed, in 2019 the story of the activity unveiled by the Panama Papers was made into a Hollywood movie, *The Laundromat*, a fictionalized version of the tale, narrated by the Panamanian law firm's eponymous partners. Gary Oldman played Jürgen Mossack. Antonio Banderas portrayed Ramón Fonseca. The real Mossack and Fonseca unsuccessfully sued to halt the film's release, saying it would interfere with their right to a fair trial in the United States, where they were under investigation by the FBI. "Once the cat is out of the bag, it is impossible to put it back without the consequence of tainting a verdict," the duo observed in the legal documents. "This is especially true where the cat is named 'Laundromat' and the charges would include money laundering."[37]

The Pandora and Panama Papers likely only scratched the surface of the problem. An estimated $21 trillion to $32 trillion of private financial wealth is held in what the Tax Justice Network terms "secrecy jurisdictions," which have historically used anonymity to attract illicit and illegitimate money. To get a sense of the scale, the size of the US economy was about $21 trillion in 2019.

But although the Biden and Obama administrations tried to clamp down on tax avoidance, the United States continued to be one of the world's most successful offshore centers, second behind the Cayman Islands, and ahead of Switzerland, Hong Kong, Singapore, Panama, and the Bahamas in terms of secrecy and the scale of offshore financial activities, according to the Tax Justice Network's 2020 Financial Secrecy Index.[38] As we'll discuss later, new rules should help tackle the issue, but only after decades in which the United States' offshore role had damaging consequences worldwide.

In response to the Panama Papers, Obama honed in on one revelation: that Ugland House, a five-story building in the Cayman Islands, was the registered address of more than eighteen thousand companies. Ugland, Obama said, was "either the biggest building in the world, or the biggest tax scam on record." Yet Delaware has a much smaller building that is the registered home of at least fifteen times more companies: the Corporation Trust Center at 1209 North Orange Street in Wilmington. At least 285,000 companies identify the nondescript single-story building as their official address because its owner is their agent, CT Corporation, a subsidiary of Wolters Kluwer, a global professional services firm based in the Netherlands. Almost all of CTC's clients are out-of-state organizations whose headquarters are elsewhere, and who often have little to no physical presence in Delaware. They include big corporate names such as Apple, American Airlines, Coca-Cola, Walmart, and dozens of others on the Fortune 500 list of America's biggest companies. They also include Donald Trump, as well as Hillary Clinton—who, of course, worked closely with Barack Obama and Joe Biden as US secretary of state.

Obama's comment revealed an old-fashioned way of thinking about offshore finance: that it happens overseas somewhere and that cracking down on it means bringing transparency to small islands and far-flung destinations.

But offshore is less a location and more a way of behaving, a set of practices that enables secrecy. Shell companies can be set up offshore or onshore. Findley, Nielson, and Sharman (the researchers we met in the last chapter who developed the "Dodgy Shopping Count") note that "while most companies formed offshore are shell companies, the majority of shell companies are probably formed in *on*shore jurisdictions."[39] In any case, such distinctions are largely in the eye of the beholder. Panama, Bermuda, and the British Virgin Islands don't consider themselves offshore tax havens. However it is classified, Delaware was surely a huge contributor to the United States' high ranking as an offshore center.

That means that Delaware has been a critical part of an international system that has diverted revenues from some of the poorest countries in the world. The developing world loses at least $160 billion a year in tax revenue from tax evasion, according to a 2008 report by Christian Aid.[40] That dwarfs the annual amount the United States spends on foreign aid, which is about $50 billion.

Corporate anonymity clearly made it an exceedingly difficult task to tackle this problem. But even when the owners of individual companies can be identified, those companies are often entangled in webs of complex corporate structures that are impossible to disentangle. If you can avoid transparency with one corporate entity, it doesn't take much imagination to grasp that you can avoid more transparency with more entities.

As the US Treasury pointed out in a 2020 report, bad actors love to combine corporate complexity and anonymity:

> Money launderers and others involved in commercial activity intentionally conduct transactions through corporate structures in order to evade detection, and may layer such structures, much like Matryoshka dolls, across various secretive jurisdictions. In many instances, each time an investigator obtains ownership records for a domestic or foreign entity, the newly identified entity is yet another corporate entity, necessitating a repeat of the same process. While some federal law enforcement agencies may have the resources required to undertake complex (and costly) investigations, the same is often not true for state, local, and tribal law enforcement.[41]

The aim is beautifully illustrated by a document buried in the mound of Panama Papers, a message from a Mossack Fonseca lawyer to a Hong Kong banker, asking for help with setting up bank accounts for one of the firm's top clients, William R. Ponsoldt, a Florida hedge fund manager. "This is a very special client of ours," the lawyer wrote, explaining that Mossack Fonseca was trying to create a labyrinth of companies so complex that it "leaves us in the position to legally argue that our client is NOT the owner of the structure."[42]

This, then, is what truly distinguishes the superrich from the rest of us. The middle class struggle to own things. The überwealthy ensure they "own" as little as possible. More specifically, the wealthy want to retain control while giving the appearance of owning nothing. This means that the real owners of shell companies—the beneficial owners—are often obscured in a multilayered structure in which companies appear to be owned by other companies which are themselves owned by other legal entities, a complexity that the University of Chicago sociologist Kimberly Kay Hoang has dubbed "spiderweb capitalism."[43]

To be sure, complex ownership structures are not in themselves illegal. Global companies often use them to simplify business transactions across international jurisdictions and currencies. And just being complex doesn't necessarily make them opaque, should the owners wish to identify themselves.

In some cases, companies use complex structures to avoid liability spreading between their different businesses. Real estate businesses, for example, often use so-called series LLCs, which create legal walls protecting each property from claims against the others. A series LLC is an umbrella company, and each individual property acts like a subsidiary.

But corporate complexity is not necessarily good for business. In fact, having a simple, transparent corporate structure is considered optimal for credit quality. Investors ideally want clear and transparent financial statements that spell out the company's fundamental dynamics and risk profile. It is hard to assess the performance of a business if it hides its investments in a complex web of opaque holding companies.

Complex structures, then, are often rightly seen as a red flag. As the Financial Action Task Force noted in a 2018 report, "A key method used to disguise beneficial ownership involves the use of legal persons and arrangements to distance the beneficial owner from an asset through complex chains of ownership. Adding numerous layers of ownership between an asset and the beneficial owner in different jurisdictions, and using different types of legal structures, can prevent detection and frustrate investigations."[44]

Clearly, complexity has frequently been used to hide owners' identities, dodge taxes, launder dirty money, and conceal fortunes, in a variety of ways and for multiple purposes. The FATF reckons that most international cases of tax evasion and fraud make use of complex structures. President Biden has fretted that "sophisticated adversaries like Russia and China know how to bypass the ban on foreign funding by exploiting loopholes in the system and using layers of proxies to mask their activities, making it difficult for the FEC, the FBI, and the Treasury Department's Financial Crimes Enforcement Network to follow the money."[45] So it is not just anonymity that frustrates the fight against criminals, but complexity too.

Complex corporate structures can even be useful for hiding money from your spouse. When Robert Oesterlund, a Finnish businessman, and his British wife Sarah Pursglove began a bitter, multiyear divorce process in 2014, he attempted to hide from her the $400 million fortune they had made together, by using multiple corporations with complex ownership structures. Oesterlund and Pursglove made their money in internet advertising and had lived the life of the international business superelite. In 2011, they bought a C$30 million penthouse at the Toronto Four Seasons, then decided while it was being renovated that they would buy a 165-foot yacht (their second), which they named *Déjà Vu*. They spent a year sailing around the world with their two daughters and a twelve-member crew and staff, including personal tutors they had hired for their girls' education. But within a few years, Pursglove filed for divorce after discovering her husband was having an affair.

Oesterlund claimed he was worth only a few million dollars, but Pursglove discovered he had spent a good deal of time and effort concealing the true extent of their fortune—not just from the tax authorities, but from her. To take just one example, he had transferred ownership of their Toronto penthouse to a Delaware corporation, but that Delaware corporation was in turn owned by a corporation in Nevis, a small Caribbean island, which had in turn been deposited into one of several trusts controlled by Oesterlund and located in the Cook Islands, a South Pacific country made up of fifteen tiny islands. Cook Islands trusts are known to be difficult to crack. The courts in the Cook Islands usually do not recognize court orders from the United States, such as divorce judgments. And if you want to sue a Cook trust, you have to do so in person in the Cook Islands. In a deposition, Pursglove's lawyer asked Oesterlund how the property ended up being in such a remote trust. The business-man's memory appeared hazy, as he described the arrangement as part of "a transaction between me and my attorney." Which attor-ney?, her lawyer prodded. "I can't remember," Oesterlund replied. "I have too many."[46] It took Pursglove years of legal battles and in-depth investigations to secure the money she argued she was owed.

The case highlighted how Delaware corporations are used as part of an international network of financial arrangements the superrich use to hide their wealth, whether from tax authorities, regulators, law enforcement, or spouses. Delaware's defense has often been that it was not the only location where nefarious activity happens. But it has clearly been a critical part of a global network used to avoid transparency and accountability.

Companies can also use corporate complexity to avoid their cred-itors. Many individual contractors set up LLCs to establish a legal wall between their personal finances and their business dealings, but companies can also set up multiple such walls to avoid account-ability. A 2018 rule enabled Delaware LLCs to divide themselves into two or more separate companies and allocate assets and liabilities between them, enabling companies to move assets beyond the reach of creditors.[47]

Some companies use complex corporate structures to evade lia-bility. Trucking companies, for example, sometimes set up strings of shell companies to deter potential lawsuits. One company might be the carrier itself, which leases trucks, trailers, and property from one or more other businesses, all ultimately owned by the same person. The carrier then pledges its revenues to the other companies to pay for the various leases. This makes the carrier nothing more than a dispatcher with a phone and no actual assets, which enables it to secure the cheapest and lowest level of insurance possible. If the truck has an accident and the carrier gets sued, this structure can help limit any judgments against it to the cap specified in the stripped-down insurance policy—currently just $1 million for interstate trucking companies.[48]

It is difficult to gauge the extent of corporate complexity in the United States, but the exponential increase in business formation suggests it is increasing. As far as the State of Delaware is concerned, the more the merrier. More complex structures means more business entities, which means more fees for the First State. It all feeds the Franchise.

PART II

How the Delaware Way Became the Delaware Way

6

Colonial Origins

Return Day is a wonderful opportunity for dressing up.

Every other year, two days after election day, Georgetown, a small town in central southern Delaware, hosts this festival whose highlight is a parade featuring horse-drawn carriages bearing both the winning and the losing candidates from the elections. The losers are seated backwards so as to make sure the spotlight is on the successful candidates.

At the culmination of the parade, representatives of both political parties join a ceremony in which they bury a two-bladed ax in a tub of sand brought fifteen miles from the beach at Lewes, site of the first colony in Delaware, founded by Dutch whalers and traders in 1631, and originally known as Zwaanendael. (Within a couple of years, the original settlement had been destroyed by a Native American attack and the Dutch removed their colonists to New Amsterdam, which was to become New York.)

With the actual hatchet duly buried, the town crier reads the results of the local elections. It's a tired cliché to observe that all politics is local, but at Return Day, it's hyperlocal. The results only include votes cast in Sussex County, an area of less than one thousand square miles of land, with a population of just over 220,000. Sussex is the southernmost of Delaware's three counties, and the most conservative. This can lead to some odd-sounding election tallies, since you can easily win statewide office in Delaware but still lose the popular vote in Sussex County. In 2018, Senator Tom Carper, a Democrat, was reelected with an eighty thousand–vote majority, but in Sussex County, his Republican opponent beat him by nearly ten thousand votes.

Many of the organizers wear olde worlde costumes, which adds to the sense of tradition and continuity. The festivities trace their roots to the 1790s, when it took two days for the election results to arrive from the state capital, Dover, about forty-five miles to the north of Georgetown. Throughout the nineteenth century, farmers flocked to the county seat, eager to find out the names of their newly elected representatives.

These days, the town crier reads the election results into a microphone standing on the narrow porch at the county courthouse.

Return Day marks the end of America's interminable political season and the start of its interminable holiday season. By early November, it's getting cold in Delaware. The folks in the crowd keep themselves warm with copious amounts of beer and, by tradition, the day ends with everyone munching on roast beef sandwiches.

To those concerned about political polarization and ideological rancor in America, Return Day might seem like a new model for peaceful coexistence and respectful debate. "This provides a moderating effect, a civilizing effect on the tone of the debate," Senator Carper observed in 2018.[1] "You know . . . on Return Day, you're going to be in Georgetown, maybe riding in a carriage with your opponent and your opponent's family, and I think it tends to tone down, to temper the nature of the debate, and I think it sets a tone that says, 'The election's over, whether we're Democrats or Republicans, whether we won or lost, it's our state. It's an important state. We have important roles to play. Let's figure out how to work together.'"[2]

This desire to work together is the positive side of the "Delaware Way." It is often portrayed as a noble effort, aimed at healing by focusing on acting in the best interests of the state's population. Following Joe Biden's victory in the 2020 presidential election campaign, the media gushed about how the Delaware Way had given the president-elect a solid grounding in dealmaking, moderation, and compromise.[3] "Biden, with his unshakable faith that personal relationships prevail over partisanship," the *Los Angeles Times* observed in 2020, "is the Delaware Way on steroids."[4]

But beneath the civility, the Delaware Way has a darker side. As we saw in chapter four, the deals the state is so proud of striking have often been forged behind closed doors, with little or no effective oversight. Delaware has a history of crafting policy in private and avoiding scrutiny. Instead of transparency, the Delaware Way has fostered a sense of clubbiness and exclusivity which is at best a kind of benign paternalism and at worst a form of government by cabal.

Delaware's miniscule size has traditionally meant that the state's small number of power brokers could be quickly assembled. Delaware's leaders tend to enjoy political longevity. Biden represented the state in the US Senate for thirty-six years. When the young Democrat arrived in Washington in 1973, his senior partner in the Senate was William Roth, a Republican who occupied his seat for thirty years. Roth's successor, Democrat Tom Carper, has been in office twenty years. Coupled with the state's small population, this has produced particularly long and deep relationships between Delaware's elites and their US senators. They're very accessible—everyone in Delaware has their own Joe Biden story.

The flip side of the focus on collegiality and compromise is the state's deep aversion to division and dissent, a tendency formed from Delaware's unique past.

History is formative. It weighs on the present, shaping behavior and influencing decisions. The Franchise, and Delaware's protective attitude toward it, reflects the state's historical background. So to understand what happens in Delaware—and by extension, in corporate America—it is important to dig deep into the historical context to find the origins of the Delaware Way.

The Franchise, and the system that supports it, has been shaped by a history that may appear to be unrelated to corporations, to mergers and acquisitions, and to the relationship between shareholders and CEOs. But current economic and business policies cannot be properly understood without analyzing how we arrived here. And economic history cannot be viewed in isolation from cultural and political histories, which mold economic attitudes. Key aspects of the Franchise are uniquely Delawarean, and the state's historical legacy echoes within the system, evident in the clubby world that produces the corporate code by which the world's biggest companies are governed.

The history of Delaware paints a picture of a state with a profound psychological desire to cover up any appearance of disagreement, which is prepared to curb liberty, bypass democracy, and rewrite history to ensure that no cracks are visible in the appearance of unity. This aversion to division was the product of trauma—political conflict, and racial violence and strife—that fueled the need for Delaware Way politics, with its predictability, caution, and consistency.

To understand the Franchise, you have to understand the Delaware Way. And to understand the Delaware Way, you have to understand its evolution. As the enduring appeal of Return Day suggests, the origins of Delaware's particular approach to democracy, debate, and division can be traced back to the colonial period. It was subsequently fashioned by the state's experience during the Civil War. In the century that followed, racial strife and tension played a particularly important role in forming the Delaware Way. Each of these episodes highlighted to the First State's leaders the dangers of dissent and disunity. Collectively, they helped to mold a mindset that abides to this day.

———

At the Second Continental Congress in Philadelphia in 1775 and 1776—the assembly that passed the US Declaration of Independence—the delegation representing what is now Delaware was split.

Under British rule, Delaware did not exist as a distinct colony. But in the first few years of the eighteenth century, Pennsylvania had developed two colonial assemblies. What we now know as Pennsylvania was known as the "Upper Counties," while another assembly represented the "Lower Counties on the Delaware"—New Castle, Kent, and Sussex. These three "Lower Counties" had their own representatives at the Congress: Thomas McKean, George Read, and Caesar Rodney. Relations between the three were mistrustful and tense.

McKean was opinionated and argumentative, impetuous and driven, stern and sanctimonious, a self-made man guided by fervor and principle. Born in Pennsylvania, he had moved to Delaware as a teenager to study law and rose rapidly to become an important figure on the local political and legal scene. At the age of thirty-one, he became the youngest representative at the First Congress of the American Colonies, the "Stamp Act Congress" held in New York City in 1765. Passionate and fiery, McKean was an outspoken advocate of independence from Britain. When Timothy Ruggles, a delegate from Massachusetts, refused to sign documents from the Congress addressed to the king and the British Houses of Parliament, he and McKean got into a heated discussion, which Ruggles proposed they settle with a duel. (The duel never took place, and Ruggles remained loyal to the Crown, eventually leaving the United States after the issuance of the Declaration of Independence, with a pension from London of ten thousand acres of land in Wilmot, Nova Scotia.)

McKean created an important legacy at the Stamp Act Congress, one that would have immense influence on the United States, and on Delaware and other small states in particular. The young politician proposed a procedure for voting that was later adopted by the Congress of the Articles of Confederation, the legislature that established the American political system: each colony was to have one vote, regardless of size or population. That decision set a precedent, establishing the principle of state equality that continues in the composition of our current US Senate: every state, whatever its number of citizens, has two US senators. This system, aimed at preventing the tyranny of the majority, also enables states with small populations to punch above their weight. It allowed, for example, Republicans to keep control of the Senate in the 2018 elections, by overweighting the political power of underpopulated rural, GOP-loyal states such as Wyoming (the least populated state in the union) and North Dakota (forty-seventh in terms of population.) A voter in Delaware has thirty-nine times more influence over the composition of the US Senate than a citizen of California—thanks to the abiding influence of Thomas McKean.

In spite of this enduring gift to Delaware, McKean was not a dyed-in-the-wool Delawarean. While serving, briefly, as Delaware's second governor (or president, as the role was then known) and as a congressional representative from Delaware, he also held the title of chief justice of the Pennsylvania Supreme Court. McKean also went on to serve as Pennsylvania's second governor, from 1799 to 1808. In any case, his primary residence had always been in Pennsylvania. Fittingly, the most enduring monument to his memory is the county that bears his name in rural northern Pennsylvania.

As pro-independence as he was, McKean missed the original signing of the Declaration of Independence on August 2, 1776. But he had a good and patriotic excuse: he was busy fighting alongside George Washington in defense of New York City. McKean actually holds the distinction of being the last person to sign the document, perhaps as late as 1781. In that year, McKean also served briefly as president of the Continental Congress, overseeing proceedings at the time that the British forces surrendered at Yorktown, signaling the end of the War of Independence.

The musical *1776*—the 1970s equivalent of the 2010s smash hit *Hamilton*—portrays McKean as a gun-toting, bad-tempered old Scot who cannot stand George Read, the rich, conservative landowner. His argumentative nature is no fiction, and although born in America, McKean certainly had Scottish roots. Both his tavern-keeper father and his mother were Ulster Scots—Irish Protestants from Ballymoney in County Antrim. As an ardent advocate for independence, McKean was very much in the camp of Delaware's Country Party, a grouping largely made up of Ulster Scots whose stronghold was New Castle, the northernmost of the three Lower Counties.

But although it only had three counties, tiny Delaware was bitterly split. While the independence-minded Ulster Scots predominated in New Castle County, the largely Anglican residents of Kent and Sussex Counties, the lower of the Lower Counties, generally wanted to reconcile with the British government and formed themselves into a rival grouping, the Court Party.

The leader of the Court Party was George Read, the second of the Lower Counties' representatives at the Continental Congress. Read was a very different character from the swashbuckling and self-righteous McKean. Tall, slight, and refined, Read lacked McKean's charisma and fire in the belly. "His legal abilities are said to be very great, but his powers of oratory are fatiguing and tiresome to the last degree," observed one fellow delegate to the Constitutional Convention of 1787. "His voice is feeble and his articulation so bad that few can have patience to attend him."[5]

Like McKean, Read traced his roots back to Ireland, but his was a very different sort of Irish ancestry. His father, John, had been born in Dublin into a wealthy English family. On his arrival in America, he had bought a large estate in Maryland, where George was born. A few years later, the family relocated to New Castle County, where John Read purchased a plantation. While McKean spent his childhood in his father's tavern, Read enjoyed a more genteel existence as a child of the landed gentry.

Read and McKean had first met as teenagers in the Reverend Francis Allison's Academy at New London, Pennsylvania, but unlike McKean, Read was a true Lower Counties man. As soon as possible after his studies, he returned to New Castle County and married Gertrude Ross Till, daughter of the Anglican rector of Immanuel Church in New Castle. At the age of thirty, he was made attorney general for the three Delaware counties.

Where McKean was strident, Read was cautious. He did not favor outright independence from Britain, and although he was elected to the Second Continental Congress, he rarely actually attended the gathering, apparently preferring the life of a wealthy landowner in the Lower Counties to the rabble-rousing rhetoric in Philadelphia.

The Delaware delegation was therefore split on the question of the American colonies' relationship with the British Crown. McKean and the New Castle County Ulster Scots of the Country Party favored independence. Read and the Kent and Sussex Counties Anglicans of the Court Party opposed outright independence.

This division was not by accident. McKean and Read had been selected precisely to represent the diversity of opinion in Delaware, where the Court Party was in the majority. Other colonies did likewise. Pennsylvania, for example, included in its delegation both the pro-independence Benjamin Franklin and the vehemently loyalist John Dickinson. (Dickinson, known as the "Penman of the Revolution" for his writings, owned a slave plantation near Dover, the capital of Delaware.)[6]

It was Dickinson who presented McKean and Read with their biggest headache. Seeking to prevent a breakaway, Dickinson had proposed a motion that independence should not happen unless all colonies were unanimous in their support. Congressional president John Hancock had ruled in favor of Dickinson's motion, meaning that Delaware needed to take a stand, one way or the other. The future of the entire country was at stake. It was not only Delaware that stood in the way of American independence. Nine colonies—Connecticut, Georgia, Maryland, Massachusetts, New Hampshire, New Jersey, North Carolina, Rhode Island, and Virginia—supported independence. Two colonies, Pennsylvania and South Carolina, were opposed. In the absence of clear instructions from its legislature, New York abstained. But Delaware was the only colony whose loyalty appeared to be in the balance.

The issue came to a head in the final days of June 1776, when the assembly convened to vote on a proposal for independence from Great Britain. Both Read and McKean were in Philadelphia to cast their votes. Read's opposition to breaking with Britain apparently surprised many of the assembled delegates, perhaps because he had been unable to express much of his skepticism due to his repeated absences from the assembly. McKean's vote, of course, was strongly in favor of the Declaration.

Fortunately for McKean, the third member of the delegation, Caesar Rodney, was also an advocate of independence. He was known as a skilled politician, a man of generous and patient spirit—not a firebrand like McKean, but a thoughtful, considered gentleman. Rodney was a listener, someone who could build consensus, perhaps even between political foes such as McKean and Read.

Rodney was the only one of the three who had actually been born in the Lower Counties, on his family's eight hundred–acre farm in

Kent County. His grandfather had first arrived in the area in the 1680s. Like Read, then, Rodney was raised among landed gentry on a plantation worked by slaves. Like Read, he was an Anglican, with a pedigree that stretched back hundreds of years: one of his ancestors was the brother of Jane Seymour, Henry VIII's third wife.

Rodney was a sickly child who grew into a sickly man. He suffered badly from asthma from his early years. As an adult, he developed a cancerous tumor on his face and underwent a series of expensive, tortuous, and ultimately futile treatments. "Caesar Rodney is the oddest looking man in the world," John Adams wrote in his diary in September 1774, on first meeting the son of Delaware. "He is tall, thin and slender as a reed, pale; his face is not bigger than a large apple, yet there is sense and fire, spirit, wit and humor in his countenance."[7]

Rodney was apparently self-conscious about how the tumor had disfigured his face. He never allowed his portrait to be painted, and wore a green silk scarf to hide the tumor. He wooed several ladies in Delaware, but apparently unsuccessfully. He never married nor had children.

A lack of family life meant Rodney was unhindered in embracing public service. He became sheriff of Kent County at twenty-seven, was elected to the colonial legislature at thirty, went as a delegate to the Stamp Act Congress at thirty-seven, joined the Delaware Superior Court at forty-one, and the Continental Congress at forty-seven. Like McKean, Rodney went on to serve as president of the State of Delaware.

Along the way, Rodney also served several times as Speaker of the Lower Counties' legislature. In one such stint, on June 15, 1776, he oversaw a vote in the assembly that officially gave birth to Delaware, which became the first American colony to declare itself free and independent from Great Britain. By this point, Rodney had become a strong champion for independence.

Two weeks later, the Second Continental Congress was taking its critical vote on independence. With McKean and Read gridlocked, they needed Caesar Rodney to break the tie. But Rodney was back in Delaware, where he was serving as brigadier general of the Delaware militia—another public role he had picked up along the way.

Rodney was also trying to deal with the state's loyalist majority, upset at Delaware's break with Britain and the news from Philadelphia. Rodney may also have been suffering from the pain of his tumor. All these had kept him in the newly declared state of Delaware rather than Philadelphia.

McKean dispatched a rider to notify Rodney of the situation, with the message that he was desperately needed to cast his vote for independence. McKean's messenger reached Rodney near midnight on July 1, 1776. According to the story known by every Delawarean, Rodney immediately saddled his horse and rode the eighty miles to Philadelphia. (Coin collectors may also know the story of Rodney's long gallop to Philadelphia, which is depicted on Delaware's state quarter, minted in 1999 as the first in a decade-long series of special quarters to honor each of the fifty US states.) Rodney's brother later revealed that the journey may actually have been in a carriage, but regardless, the trip was dramatic—eighteen hours through a torrential storm that took its toll on an ill man. He arrived at the Congress at 9 P.M. on July 2, just before the doors of the chamber were to have been closed, soaking wet and splattered in mud, but "booted and spurred" and ready to vote in favor of independence.[8]

Rodney's dramatic arrival and vote proved decisive: internal wrangling had moved the Pennsylvania delegation in favor of independence, and South Carolina did not wish to be the only colony standing in the way. Since New York was abstaining rather than opposing the proposal, unanimity was deemed to have been reached on July 2, 1776.

According to one version of the story, Rodney had heard word of a physician in London who could treat his cancer. By voting for independence, Rodney made himself a traitor to the Crown, thereby ensuring he could not visit this doctor for treatment. Rodney may have forgone his own health for the sake of independence.

Rodney himself downplayed both his ride and his vote. In a letter to his brother Thomas, he wrote: "I arrived in Congress (tho detained by thunder and rain) time enough to give my voice in the matter of independence. . . . We have now got through the whole of the declaration and ordered it to be printed so that you will soon have the pleasure of seeing it."[9]

This swashbuckling Delawarean version of Paul Revere's Midnight Ride was memorialized in a statue of Rodney galloping on horseback, which, until 2020, sat in downtown Wilmington, in the square that bears his name, amidst Delaware's power brokers of today. (Like many historical commemoratives across the United States, Rodney's statue came down in the summer of 2020 as Wilmington's city government responded to widespread protests led by the Black Lives Matter movement.) The offices of Richards, Layton & Finger, one of the state's most powerful law firms, are on the southeast corner, where King Street meets Tenth Street. Young Conaway Stargatt & Taylor, another Delaware legal titan, is located a few doors further down King Street. On the square's northwest corner, at Market and Eleventh, is the Hotel du Pont, whose opulent Green Room restaurant hosts many a working lunch or dinner of the political, legal, and corporate elite.

Rodney may have been considered by many a hero until recently, but his contemporaries in Delaware did not necessarily see it that way. The new state still had a sizeable and committed loyalist contingent, and on McKean and Rodney's return from Philadelphia, the Delaware General Assembly refused to reelect them to the Continental Congress in October 1776. Within Kent County, loyalist sentiment remained strong. Rodney lost his bid to be a delegate to the state constitutional convention, and failed to rejoin the state legislature.

But it was in Sussex County, where allegiance to the Court Party had been strongest, that loyalism ran strongest. The same anti-independence forces that had kept Rodney in Delaware when he should have been in Philadelphia were now threatening to side with the enemy of the newly born United States. Delaware was not the only place where such sentiment persisted—next-door Maryland was another—but it was certainly a hotbed of loyalist activity.

The Continental Congress was so concerned that it passed several resolutions attempting to deal with the problem. In February 1777, the body voted to send troops to seize the leaders and weapons of the resistance movement: "Resolved, That a Battalion be ordered to the County of Sussex, on Delaware with positive Instructions to the Commanding officer.—to disarm all such Persons of whom it may be proven that they are disaffected to the American Cause, and to apprehend such as have been or are their Leaders."[10]

That resolution apparently failed to quell the situation, however. Two months later, the Continental Congress warned of an "imminent danger of an insurrection" in Maryland, and expressed concern "that the insurgents may be joined by disaffected persons in the county of Sussex, in the state of Delaware."

But ultimately it was the British themselves who may have dampened down the loyalist cause. Following the British victory at the Battle of Brandywine in September 1777, British troops occupied Wilmington until the following year, the first of three military occupations of the city that would leave a mark on Delaware. Resentment of this occupation may have helped turn sentiment against the loyalist cause: it at least persuaded the Delaware legislature to return Rodney and McKean to the Continental Congress in 1777.

In the subsequent election of 1783, Delaware elected to the Continental Congress Gunning Bedford Jr., a fiery, impulsive, and obese man who would leave his mark on history by threatening other framers of the Constitution that if small states such as his did not receive equal representation in the US Congress, they would ally themselves with a foreign power. The threat worked, permanently handing Delaware and other small states massive overrepresentation in Washington. Bedford then helped lead the effort to make Delaware the first state to ratify the Constitution in December 1787, a move that enabled it to dub itself "the First State," a name that stuck.

The Delaware vote to approve the Constitution was unanimous, yet Delaware had produced some of the most forthright advocates for American independence, as well as some of it most violent opponents. It was a foretaste of the political schisms to come.

———

Like many of the founding fathers, Caesar Rodney was a slave owner. By the time he became Speaker of the Delaware Assembly, his family plantation had expanded to one thousand acres, and Rodney owned two hundred slaves. Nevertheless, in 1766 he introduced into the legislature a bill proposing to prohibit importing enslaved people into Delaware. The proposal failed, but the state's 1776 constitution did ban the importation of enslaved people. (Legislation to halt the export of slaves passed only in 1797.) The issue clearly continued to gnaw at Rodney: before dying aged fifty-five in 1784, he stipulated that his slaves should be freed on his death.

The contradiction of a slave owner opposing the slave trade found echoes in Delaware eight decades later in the Civil War of 1861 to 1865, the second time that Delaware's political divisions threatened to bubble over. Today, many Delawareans like to say that opinions within their state about slavery were a microcosm of the United States itself. That is a nice way of saying that Delaware was a northern slave-owning state whose slave owners were deeply committed to keeping their slaves.

If this history seems irrelevant to the Delaware Way and the Franchise, consider that former slave states and Jim Crow states tend to be more conservative, free market–oriented, and business-friendly. To take one example discussed in chapter 3, there is a strong overlap between former slave states and the failure to pass combined-reporting laws. While Delaware is solidly Democratic and socially more moderate these days, its extremely accommodative approach to corporate interests betrays its history of leaning toward the southern states.

The number of enslaved people in Delaware fell in the decades leading up to the Civil War. The 1790 census recorded that 15 percent of Delaware's population was Black, 70 percent of them enslaved. By 1810, 75 percent of Delaware's Black population was free, and 87 percent by 1840.[11] By the time of the Civil War, the state's free Black population numbered about 20,000, and its slave population about 1,800—more than 1,300 in Sussex County, and a few hundred in each of the other two Delaware counties.[12]

Not that this trend necessarily indicated a strong sense of enlightenment washing over Delaware. Rather, it was cheaper for farmers in Delaware to hire free Black laborers than to keep people enslaved. And since exporting enslaved people had been made illegal after independence, there was no commercial point to breeding slaves, as owners did in states such as Virginia.

And "free" was, of course, a relative term. Black people could not vote. They could not testify in court against whites. They needed passes signed by white men to leave the state, and were not allowed to return if they were absent more than six months. Free Black people from other states were prohibited from moving to Delaware. Since 1829, Delaware had supported public education, but its schools were open to whites only. The state had a handful of schools for Black students, all funded by charitable donations. After a slave rebellion in southern Virginia in 1831 left about sixty people dead, the slave owners of Sussex County pressured the Delaware legislature to ban Black people from owning weapons or from assembling in groups larger than twelve people.

The Sussex County landowners had the majority in the Delaware General Assembly, but the debates in the years leading up to the start of the Civil War in 1861 were increasingly rancorous and heated. There was strong support in Delaware for slave owners and states' rights, particularly in the southern part of the state, where most of the population was concentrated. But there was also a vibrant abolitionist faction in New Castle County. Their representatives introduced a series of abolition bills in the state legislature, some of which were defeated by just a single vote. President Abraham Lincoln even offered Delaware slave owners a slave buyout: a federal reimbursement of $500 per slave, much more than their market value, if the state would abolish slavery. Little Delaware, Lincoln thought, was the ideal location for an experiment in compensated emancipation as a way to end slavery across America. Lincoln worked with two local politicians to draw up the compensation plan, which aimed to abolish slavery completely in the state by 1872. But the state legislature was unmoved, and refused Lincoln's generous offer. The majority in the state were not enamored of the president: Delaware voted against both Lincoln's presidential election in 1860 and his reelection in 1864.

As America slid toward civil war, the situation in Delaware turned tense. Factions supporting both the North and the South began to build stockpiles of weapons and train themselves. Again, and as with the question of independence, Delaware was geographically divided: more urban New Castle County leaned more toward the Republicans and their allies, the Delaware People's Party, and favored the Union; the South found its supporters chiefly in more agrarian Kent and Sussex Counties, natural territory for the Democratic Party of the day, which dominated the state legislature.

Governor William Burton, a Democrat and an opponent of Lincoln, was acutely aware of the dangers of civil war breaking out in Delaware itself, and he prevaricated over how to proceed. He initially asked the pro-Confederacy groups to disarm, but then thought better of it and withdrew the request. When the federal government called for soldiers, he refused to turn over the Delaware militia, while at the same time encouraging Delawareans to enlist.

If anyone did prevent violence in Delaware, it might have been Henry du Pont, president of the DuPont chemical company, whom Burton appointed to lead the state militia. Du Pont ensured that arms sent from the federal government did not fall into the wrong hands, and also had a strong interest in protecting his company's powder mills, which supplied more than half of the gunpowder used by the Union army.

In some cases, the authorities disarmed southern sympathizers. In the town of Seaford, in Sussex County, Edward Livingston Martin, one of Delaware's Democratic US congressmen, had organized a militia, the Seaford Cavalry. In 1861, rumors spread that Martin had been assembling arms for shipment to Virginia to supply the Confederate army. In October that year, a company of the Second Delaware Regiment arrived in Seaford, confiscated weapons from Martin's men, and forced him to swear allegiance publicly to the federal government.[13]

But the fact that Delaware averted outright conflict meant that it never dealt with its proslavery factions. So although Delaware fought for the Union—in fact, its population was overrepresented in the Union army—much of its citizenry continued to harbor Confederate sympathies during the war. Tensions between the two sides were so heated that in 1862, the federal government had to send in troops to occupy polling stations in Delaware during state and federal elections because of complaints of voters being intimidated and the possibility of unrest.

Amid the heightened tensions, one of Delaware's own senators, the intemperate Willard Saulsbury, even pulled a gun on the US Senate floor. Saulsbury, first elected to the Senate in 1859, was a firm opponent of Abraham Lincoln and a heavy drinker. These two cardinal traits proved to be a poor combination. During a debate in 1863, Democrats were attempting to filibuster a vote approving of the president's executive order suspending habeas corpus. Senator Saulsbury rose to speak on the Senate floor, visibly the worse for booze. He launched a vicious attack on Lincoln, using what Lincoln's young aide John Hay—secretary of state decades later for Presidents William McKinley and Theodore Roosevelt—termed "language fit only for a drunken fishwife." Lincoln, Saulsbury thundered, was a "weak and imbecile man" and "the weakest man ever placed in a high office." This was too much for Vice President Hannibal Hamlin, who ordered Saulsbury to sit down. When the senator refused, Hamlin instructed the sergeant at arms to "take the senator in charge." Saulsbury did not respond well. "Let him do so at his expense!" he warned, dramatically drawing a pistol, pointing it at the officer and threatening to shoot.[14] Saulsbury was disarmed, and apologized a few days later under threat of expulsion.

Some of Delaware's Confederate sympathizers did more than just grumble—they volunteered to fight for the South. William T. Cooper may have seemed an unlikely candidate. He was the only son of Delaware's thirty-second governor, William Barkley Cooper, a Whig politician from Sussex County. Two decades after he left office, his son went to fight for the South, joining a cavalry battalion in Maryland as a private. Ironically, William T. Cooper was captured at Romney, Virginia, and returned as a prisoner of war to Delaware, where he was jailed at Fort Delaware, a prison for captured Confederate soldiers about fifteen miles downriver from Wilmington. But he later escaped and returned to Confederate service.

Others supplied information. While Henry du Pont was busy protecting his company's gunpowder stores, his relative Charles du Pont Bird was busy telling the enemy how to sabotage them. Du Pont Bird, a Confederate sympathizer from Dover, Delaware's capital, was a student at Loyola College in Maryland when the war broke out. He sent a letter to the governor of Virginia that was forwarded to Confederate general Robert E. Lee, in which he gave details of DuPont's gunpowder factories in Delaware and suggested how they could be taken by secessionists and destroyed. Du Pont Bird remarked that "a strong feeling in the two lower counties of Delaware is aroused in favor of Delaware joining the Southern Confederacy."[15]

Such activities were not limited to those no longer in Delaware. Scores of southern sympathizers were active within the state, which apprehended and imprisoned some of them for their treachery. One such was William Bright, a real estate developer and grocery store owner in Wilmington, whose support for the Confederacy was no secret. In 1863, General Lee's army invaded Pennsylvania, prompting rumors that the Confederate army would attack Wilmington next. Bright was delighted, and disappointed at the news of the Union's victory at Gettysburg. A rumor went around that Bright had been hoarding supplies in order to turn them over to the Confederate army should it capture Wilmington. He was roused from his bed, arrested, and held without bail or trial at Fort Delaware. Bright was one of a few hundred political prisoners held at the fort among tens of thousands of Confederate prisoners of war. It later turned out that the people who had been whispering against Bright were motivated as much by the prospect of grabbing a piece of Bright's business as by their devotion to the Union cause. But at the time, locking up Confederate-sympathizing troublemakers was seen as vitally important to the war effort. The commanding officer for the district of Delaware was Brigadier General Daniel P. Tyler IV, one of the first Union army generals of the Civil War, who led a large division at the First Battle of Bull Run, the war's first big battle, in July 1861. There had been widespread expectation in the North of an easy victory, so much so that congressmen and their families came to Virginia to watch the battle while they picnicked. In the event, it was an ugly spectacle: the Union army was forced into a disorderly retreat, abandoning key pieces of artillery while hundreds of Union soldiers were taken prisoner. As one of the commanding officers, Tyler was deemed largely responsible for this shock defeat.

Two years later, Tyler was in Delaware, rebuilding his reputation by reporting small victories on the home front. "During the week, I have sent 2 men to Fort Delaware for treasonable language," Tyler reported, "one of them, William Bright, of Wilmington, a man of some position; and thus making an example is undoubtedly doing good to the community. I think political asperity is wearing away here, and another victory will make Delaware a very loyal state."[16] Bright was detained in the prison until he agreed to swear an oath of allegiance to the Union. He refused. But after a few months in the smallpox-ridden jail, he agreed to do so, and was released. The experience does not seem to have inflicted any long-term damage to Bright's health or reputation. After the war, he was elected to Wilmington's city council, and within a year or two, became its president. In 1874 he even ran unsuccessfully for governor. But Bright's enduring legacy in Delaware was the creation of Rehoboth Beach, the resort in the south of Delaware that we visited in earlier chapters. Bright was president of the Rehoboth Beach Association and built the town's first two hotels.

Just as with the struggle for American independence, during the Civil War Delaware produced heroes as well as villains. Thomas Garrett, a Quaker businessman from Wilmington, was a prominent and outspoken stationmaster on the Underground Railroad—the secret network of safe houses for runaway slaves—and a friend of Harriet Tubman, the abolitionist and rescuer, to whom he periodically gave money. (Their collaboration is memorialized today in Wilmington's Tubman-Garrett Riverfront Park.)

There was nothing underground about Garrett's activities: he worked in the open, speaking out as one of the leaders of the Delaware Abolition Society. In 1848, two slave owners sued him in federal court in New Castle, for the crime of helping a family of eight slaves to escape. Garrett proudly told the court that he had helped more than 1,400 enslaved people escape. None other than Roger Taney, chief justice of the US Supreme Court, was presiding over the case. Taney found Garrett guilty of violating the 1793 Fugitive Slave Act and fined him $4,500—about $140,000 in today's money. Garrett was unrepentant. "Judge," he told Taney, "thou has left me not a dollar, but I wish to say to thee and to all in this courtroom that if any-one knows a fugitive who wants a shelter and a friend, send him to Thomas Garrett and he will befriend him."[17] Although the fine was later reduced to $1,500, it ruined Garrett. Yet he continued his work on the Underground Railroad.

When the Fifteenth Amendment passed in 1870, giving Black men the right to vote, the Black community of Wilmington led Garrett through the streets in a four-wheeled horse-drawn carriage that bore the sign "Our Moses." Taney went on to write the majority decision in the *Dred Scott v. Sanford* case of 1857, declaring that no Black person, whether enslaved or free, could ever be considered a citizen, and that Congress could not prohibit slavery.

Although Delaware was still a slave state when the Civil War broke out, there was little question of it seceding, despite the pleas of a delegation sent by the Confederacy to try to persuade the Dela-ware General Assembly otherwise. This was perhaps less because of any ideological differences with the South and more because of the mechanics of the issue: the state had close economic ties to Phila-delphia, and was geographically separated from the Confederacy. Instead, Delaware was one of five slave states to remain in the Union. But Delaware was unique in that the other four—Kentucky, Mary-land, Missouri, and West Virginia—were all "border states," which neighbored Confederate states. As Joe Biden joked in 2006, the only reason Delaware had fought with the North in the Civil War was "because we couldn't figure out how to get to the South. There were a couple of states in the way."[18]

Lincoln treated the border states very delicately. His 1863 Eman-cipation Proclamation abolished slavery in the Confederacy, but allowed it to continue in the border states. Even after the Civil War, Delaware was reluctant to get rid of the scourge of slavery. The state refused to ratify the Thirteenth Amendment abolishing slavery when most other states did in 1865. In 1866, the Delaware legislature resolved that Black people were not the political or social equal of whites. In 1867, the state refused to ratify the Fourteenth Amend-ment, ensuring equal protection of the laws. Two years later, it voted against the Fifteenth Amendment, prohibiting states from denying the right to vote based on race. Delaware ratified these civil rights amendments only in 1901, becoming one of the last states to do so.

There was some belated progress. Traditionally, there had been a dual system of justice in Delaware for Black people and whites. Black people were much more likely to receive corporal punishment, such as the whipping post, if convicted. Their sentences were often longer, their fines for the same crimes larger. But in 1867, the state legislature passed a bill equalizing punishments across races. "This measure was a difficult pill for the Democrats to swallow," the *Smyrna Times* noted, "but the demands of the advanced age and the example set by several of the legislatures of Southern States has caused them at last to put upon the statutes this important measure."[19]

During the postwar Reconstruction period, schools for Black people began to open in Delaware—not funded by the state, but by philanthropy and federal funds. But, even when the state reluctantly took on the responsibility of maintaining the schools in 1875, it stipulated that it would do so exclusively with taxes paid by Black taxpayers. That same year, the Delaware General Assembly passed a "Jim Crow" law, essentially making Black Delawareans second-class citizens. The law would only be repealed in 1963.

Delaware had been riven by the independence issue, the Civil War, and by race—all issues that would feed into the desire for unity and dealmaking that became the Delaware Way.

In the twentieth century, racial tensions continued to simmer in Delaware. And it was race that was to heat the state to another boiling point, a boiling point that shaped the conscience of a young Joe Biden.

7

A Very Delawarean Lynching

On the afternoon of June 22, 1903, a large crowd started assembling at Price's Corner, about four miles west of Wilmington, Delaware. Men and boys from the city and from small towns to the south streamed in to join them. Some were armed with pistols and shotguns. Others carried cruder weapons. By nightfall, the crowd had swelled to more than four thousand people.[1]

The crowd was preparing for a lynching.

Eight days earlier, Helen Bishop, a seventeen-year-old girl, had been on her way home from Wilmington High School. She normally rode the trolley car from school to Price's Corner and then walked the remaining three-quarters of a mile home along Centre Road. Helen was from a well-respected local family. Her father was the Rev. Dr. E. A. Bishop, the superintendent of Ferris School, a technical college for wayward juveniles.[2]

Around 5 P.M., a farmer working in a field nearby Price's Corner saw a young woman stagger and fall in the road. She got up, fell again, and tried to crawl. By the time the farmer and his sons reached her, she was lying unconscious. Helen Bishop had been stabbed three times in the throat. She was badly scratched all over, and her clothes were torn. In one hand, she was clutching the small penknife she used at school to sharpen pencils, suggesting that she had tried to resist. Helen never regained consciousness, and died the following afternoon.

The horrific nature of the crime spurred an immediate hunt for the assailant. Inquiries quickly led to George White, an unemployed Black man who had recently left the workhouse and sometimes worked as a laborer on a farm owned by Edward Woodward, near where Helen was attacked. That night, White was hauled from his bed and taken into custody. He denied all knowledge of the crime, but three Black witnesses said they had seen him in the area that day, apparently following a white girl. A knife that Woodward identified as his own was found near the crime scene. The police first took White to Wilmington, before determining that he would be safer from violence in the county workhouse.

The crowd at Price's Corner was angry. There was talk of the slowness of the law and the need for quick revenge. Hours before the crowd gathered, the verdict of the jury at the coroner's inquest was that Helen had died "from the effects of an assault committed upon her by one George White, a negro." But when Delaware's attorney general, Herbert H. Ward, had introduced the case into the county court two days after Helen died, the court had refused to be rushed and set a trial date for September.

Almost as soon as White was arrested, there had been whispers of a lynching, and they had been getting louder all week. The authorities had not dared take White from the workhouse to the coroner's court, for fear that he would be harmed. Two smaller crowds had tried to get to White the prior night, but had been dispersed. This crowd was bigger and better prepared.

Around 10 P.M., the crowd began the mile-long trek to the workhouse. After the attempt the previous evening, the chief warden and his guards were prepared for them. They had secured a series of heavy steel doors, but the crowd fashioned a crude battering ram and knocked down each door in turn. The guards opened fire on the crowd, and people in the crowd shot back. Four people were injured, including a seventeen-year-old boy. Trying to avoid further casualties, the warden turned a fire hose on the crowd, which held it back momentarily. But very quickly, the crowd was inside the workhouse.

This was an extraordinarily well-organized lynching. The crowd quickly found White, cowering in his cell. Blacksmiths were on hand to open the door, and a confession was ready for White to sign. A noose was placed around his neck, and, guided by burning torches, the swelling crowd dragged White to the spot where Helen had been assaulted. A reporter for the *Morning News* observed:

> The crowd was remarkable in many respects. It was composed of men from various workshops in the city, farmers from the surrounding country and a number of women. There was not a masked man in the entire crowd, and the men in it did not appear ashamed of the part which they took in the work of the night. They talked freely of the event and expressed satisfaction that they had taken part in it. The crowd was bent on wreaking vengeance on the man White and they did it about as orderly as it would have been possible for such an act to be performed. There was not a drunken man in the entire crowd. There was not so much as might be expected from such a gathering. It was largely a calm, determined crowd.[3]

Photographs also reveal a well-dressed crowd, with many men and women in fashionable clothes carrying umbrellas. At the execution spot, the crowd had already set up a wooden stake, with dry underbrush, soaked with oil, at its base. When the victim was chained to the stake, he asked to say a final prayer. Then, as George White was burned to death, the crowd cheered.

Even in an age when lynchings were not uncommon, the murder of George White caught the country's attention. For one thing, lynchings were rare in Delaware. And this had not taken place in Sussex County, the old Confederate-sympathizing agricultural part of the state, but in relatively cosmopolitan Wilmington. The following day's front page of Wilmington's *Every Evening* newspaper screamed:

THE NEGRO BURNED AT THE STAKE

George White, colored, Taken from the Workhouse and Killed
AT 1:30 THIS MORNING

After He Had Confessed to Assaulting Miss Bishop
5,000 PEOPLE AT THE WORKHOUSE
Heavy Doors Battered Down With Railroad Ties
BOY SHOT AND SERIOUSLY HURT[4]

The gruesome method of execution garnered attention across the United States. A minister wrote to the *New York Times* condemning Delaware as "a community corrupted in civic ideals and void in civic and moral virility." When he heard about the lynching, President Theodore Roosevelt said, "Whoever in any part of our country has taken part in lawlessly putting to death a criminal by fire must forever have the awful spectacle of his own handiwork seared into his brain and soul. He can never again be the same man." A cartoon in the *Literary Digest* referred to anti-Jewish pogroms that had taken place in Russia two months earlier. It depicted a tearful Czar Nicholas II rejecting a petition of protest from B'nai B'rith, a Jewish organization. "Excuse me," the cartoon czar said. "I'm busy weeping over this Delaware affair."[5]

Both public officials and private citizens in Delaware did not enjoy the attention, and much of the initial reaction within the First State expressed concern not about the lawlessness and cruel violence but at the prospect that the incident might sully the state's reputation. Perhaps for this reason, locals told the Associated Press that the crowd had been led by "a Virginian." Conveniently enough, the agency's reporter was unable to track this character down, noting that his "identity in the confusion and excitement could not be learned."[6] The *Morning News* picked up on the same theme, dubbing the shadowy figure "the Avenging Cowboy."[7]

Instead, the police arrested Arthur Cornell, a Baltimore man purported to be one of the ringleaders. Colonel James McComb, one of the richest men in Wilmington, offered to pay $5,000 in bail for Cornell's release, but was denied. A crowd started to gather at city hall demanding Cornell be freed. Within hours, the crowd had grown into a gathering seven thousand strong, in a city with a population of just eleven thousand. Cornell was released, but the crowd's anger was not sated. They swept through the streets of Wilmington, on the hunt for Black people, dragging dozens of innocent people from trolley cars and beating them.

Nowadays, George White's lynching is usually portrayed as an anomaly, blamed on the agitations of the Reverend Robert Elwood, the firebrand conservative minister of Olivet Presbyterian Church in Wilmington. In his sermon the night before the lynching, Elwood said that in light of the delay in bringing White to trial, citizens "should arise in their might and execute the criminal, and thus uphold the majesty of the law." He showed his congregation blood-stained leaves, supposedly from the site of Helen's assault, and asked for swift justice. "Should the murderer be lynched?" Elwood rhetorically asked his congregation.[8]

This account traces its way back to the Black poet Alice Dunbar-Nelson, who moved to Wilmington the year before the lynching. In a 1924 article in the *Messenger*, Dunbar-Nelson wrote: "There are few states where the relations between the two races is more amicable, and the commonwealth still shudders with horror when it recalls its one lynching, for which it punished the inciter of the deed, a Presbyterian clergyman, who suggested the lynching in a fiery sermon, by expelling him from its borders."[9]

Dunbar-Nelson's account has informed many subsequent retellings of the White lynching. It was a convenient version of events. Much like the legend of "the Virginian," the idea that a rogue cleric had whipped into a state of frenzy a community of reasonable Delawareans, who had then dealt with him by banishing him from the state, served as a neat conclusion to the ugly episode, placing the blame on someone no longer in the First State and therefore putting the entire matter to rest. The crime was not the fault of ordinary Delawareans, but of manipulative and foreign infiltrators, the proverbial "few bad apples" who were no longer in the state.

But the University of St. Thomas historian Yohuru R. Williams highlights two problems with this narrative: it meshes poorly with accounts of the lynching, and it is incorrect about what happened to Elwood.[10]

As for the lynching, descriptions of the event itself hardly speak to a crowd overcome with emotion and righteous indignation. Rather, the meticulous planning suggests a very Delawarean lynching, with a good-natured gentility among the crowd that contrasts with the brutality of their actions. This was a crowd, but not a mob. Even at the scene of the lynching itself, good order reigned. Some men in the crowd wanted to shoot at White, but the organizers objected, saying they could only fire in the air. It was not until White's body was completely consumed, and the crowd had started to disperse, that they were permitted to step forward and discharge rounds into the charred corpse. When the women present complained that they did not have a good view of the execution, the men were asked to stand back to give them a better perspective. Helen Bishop's older sister was given a special vantage point nearest the fire. (Their father, by contrast, had consistently appealed to the people of Wilmington not to avenge his daughter's death by breaking the law.) The *Morning News* described an atmosphere more of festivity than righteous anger, noting that "there was the best of feeling between the members of the crowd" and that "about Price's Corner it looked as though there had been a picnic of some kind."[11]

The idea that the good folk of Wilmington temporarily took leave of their senses also doesn't chime with the behavior of most of the city's residents following Cornell's arrest. In fact, according to contemporary accounts, most citizens supported the lynching. Two days after White's murder, the *Philadelphia Evening Telegraph* reported that George Black, Wilmington's chief of police, estimated that 90 percent of the local community approved of the lynching.[12]

And as for Reverend Elwood, far from being shamed and expelled, his sermon urging people to lynch White earned him celebrity, and he ended up leaving Delaware in triumph. When Elwood initially refused to condemn the lynching, his congregation adopted a resolution of loyal support, noting the "unjust criticism made upon our beloved Pastor, the Rev. Robert Elwood. . . . We express our firm belief in our pastor's honesty, integrity, and Christian character."[13] A special Presbyterian committee of ministers and elders that convened the next month, in July 1903, exonerated Elwood. A subsequent church trial found the unrepentant preacher guilty of violating the church constitution by publishing opinions "contrary to the known principles of Christianity," undermining respect for constitutional authority, and endorsing and advocating lynching.[14] But there were only narrow majorities for these verdicts, and Elwood was acquitted on three other charges. The verdict also distinguished Elwood the man from his speech, and recognized both his good intentions and the febrile atmosphere in Wilmington that week.

For his part, Elwood expressed no regret whatsoever, calling the verdict "a complete vindication."[15] He promptly arranged a series of public speaking engagements at the local opera house to exploit his newfound celebrity.

Elwood also was not expelled from Delaware; he remained in his post at Olivet Presbyterian for more than two years after the lynching, only leaving when offered the pastorate of the larger and more prominent First Presbyterian Church in Leavenworth, Kansas—a town that had infamously carried out its own lynching of a Black man in 1901. Elwood left Delaware with the good wishes and prayers of the Olivet congregation.

Although the prison authorities had tried to prevent the crowd from getting into the workhouse, local law enforcement had largely stood by as an unconvicted man was publicly executed. The police said they had not used their firearms to control or deter the crowd because many of them were friends with people in the lynching crowd. And no one was ever held responsible for the criminal act of burning George White alive.

Delaware told itself it had put behind it the scourge of violent racism. But the authorities were alert to the possibility of an angry Black response to the lynching of George White and the violence following the Cornell incident. When groups of Black men gathered on street corners to defend themselves, the police dispersed them. The police closed saloons after hearing rumors that Black patrons had vowed to "load up" and "hunt trouble." When the Black community tried to organize a public meeting to discuss the situation, George Black, the chief of police, told the organizers they could not discuss the lynching, nor any of the recent racial violence in Wilmington. "Chief of Police George Black has been assured that only respectable colored people will be present and there will be no allusion made to the recent events which excited this city," the *Morning News* told its readers on July 6.[16] The police denied permission to several prominent Black individuals to carry revolvers for protection. The *New York Times* reported that "the officials realize that if a colored man and a white man should engage in a fight even over a trifling matter their quarrel could under present conditions easily grown into a riot."[17]

Delaware had long been sensitive to the possibility that racial tensions could lead to social violence, but this had not always resulted in more restrictions on the Black community. In 1915, the National Association for the Advancement of Colored People established a chapter in Wilmington. Its first success was in persuading the city council to take the unusual step of banning the screening of moving pictures that were deemed "likely to stir up bad feelings between the races," backed up with a $50 fine. Under this ordinance, the city refused to screen D. W. Griffith's *The Birth of a Nation*, a historical dramatization of the Reconstruction era that presented Black people unfavorably and lionized the Ku Klux Klan. Thanks to the ban, Wilmington was able to avoid the protests that accompanied the film's screening in cities such as Boston.[18]

Either way, the authorities' instincts were to prepare to snuff out any more racial violence. The Saturday following the George White lynching, Delaware governor John Hunn dispatched four companies of the National Guard to the armory in Wilmington, presaging another occupation of the city that would take place sixty-five years later.

Racial tensions in Delaware had been suppressed, but not addressed.

————

Like Delaware's colonial past, its troubled history of race relations might seem irrelevant to the Franchise and the context in which it operates. But the First State's past reveals two important intertwining trends that help explain the Delaware Way and the Franchise. One is that the state was historically riven by deep divisions—political, social, and racial. The second is that, as a result, its leaders developed a strong desire to paper over those differences, for fear of what would happen if they were allowed to be exposed. Part of that papering over is the dealmaking at the heart of the Delaware Way. As well as helping us to understand the First State's perspective on the Franchise, that dealmaking instinct also helps explain President Joe Biden's fundamental approach to politics.

In the twentieth century, the struggle over race in Delaware became focused on education. The issue would project the First State onto the national stage time and again, revealing Delaware's resistance to social change. For a time, it even turned the man who would one day become the state's first US president into an opponent of desegregation efforts and an ally of his racist southern colleagues.

Educational opportunities for Black people slowly improved following the mixed successes of the Reconstruction era. In 1890, the US Congress passed an expanded Morrill Act, which spurred the creation of land-grant colleges for Black students in states with segregated educational facilities. The following year, Delaware purchased a ninety-five–acre plot north of Dover, the state capital, to establish the Delaware College for Colored Students, which its second president William C. Jason called "an instrument for the upgrading of the Negro in Delaware."[19]

But the name led to confusion. It was easily shortened to "Delaware College," which upset the sensibilities of the administration at the white-only private institution named Delaware College in Newark, Delaware—the school that would later become the University of Delaware. The new college therefore changed its name in 1893 to the State College for Colored Students. In 1947 it changed again, to Delaware State College, and in 1993, to Delaware State University. The road to recognition as a full-fledged university had been a long one. By contrast, Delaware College became the University of Delaware in 1921. Today, Delaware State is recognized as one of the United States' leading historically Black colleges and universities.

Originally, the college offered five baccalaureate degrees: agricultural, chemical, classical, engineering, and scientific. It started a teacher's certificate program in 1897, and the range of subjects gradually expanded. By 1932, it was offering four-year curricula in the arts and sciences, elementary education, home economics, agriculture, and industrial arts. But in a severe blow to its prestige, the

Middle States Commission on Higher Education in 1949 revoked the college's accreditation, withholding it for eight years.

The University of Delaware opened its doors to women in 1945, but still largely excluded Black students, following a legal path under the "separate but equal" doctrine established in the *Plessy v. Ferguson* Supreme Court decision of 1896. The university made minor exceptions for Black residents of Delaware who wanted to pursue graduate study and those considered qualified for an undergraduate major not available at Delaware State College.

But in 1948, the university's board of trustees adopted a resolution that appeared to open its doors to Black students:

> Any colored resident of this State who is able to meet the established requirements for admission to the University of Delaware may be admitted to pursue a course of study of his choosing leading to a certain degree for which a course of study leading to the same degree is not furnished in any educational institution provided by this State within this State for the education of bona fide colored residents of this State.[20]

Of course, the trustees approved the measure knowing full well that they could point to Delaware State as a higher educational institution designed for Black students, thereby enabling them to keep their university virtually whites only.

After Delaware State failed to win accreditation in 1949, ten of its former students requested the following January that the University of Delaware give them application forms so that they could apply for admission. The university refused, citing the 1948 resolution in its rejection letter to several of the students, while blocking two others for failing to specify what courses of study they wished to pursue. One student, Daniel Moody, received a letter simply saying he was ineligible to apply "as a colored person."[21]

It was clear that, aside from the matter of accreditation, the two institutions were indeed separate but far from equal. The quality of education at Delaware State fell "short of acceptable standards" and the school's "education services were poorly articulated and coordinated," according to a 1949 report by the Commission on

Institutions of Higher Education of the Middle States Association of Colleges and Secondary Schools. "The present financial resources of the college do not permit the college to meet its presently stated educational objectives," the report noted.[22]

Brooks Parker, one of the rejected students, approached Louis Redding, Delaware's only Black lawyer at the time, who was playing a leading role in desegregating the state's educational institutions. Redding, who grew up a block from Rodney Square in Wilmington, had become the state's sole Black attorney when he returned to Delaware in 1929, having graduated from Harvard Law School the prior year, and he remained the state's only Black lawyer until 1954.

Redding wrote to Judge Hugh M. Morris, chair of the board of trustees, noting the inferior education offered at Delaware State College, outlining all the advantages that the University of Delaware had over the Black school. The university then had forty-four tenured full professors and thirty-three associate professors, while the college had just four full professors, none of whom enjoyed tenure. The university library housed 140,000 books, the college library just 16,000. The university had extensive athletic facilities, including a swimming pool and gym, which the college lacked. The State of Delaware created thirty-three scholarships and prizes at the university, but just one at the college.

The university should therefore properly reconsider the applicants, Redding wrote. Morris replied that he would look into it, and Redding asked him to do so promptly. After several weeks, the board met to discuss the issue, and rebuffed the students a second time, again referring to the 1948 resolution.

It was clear that Redding would now have to resort to suing the university. He teamed up with Jack Greenberg, who a year earlier had become the only white legal counselor for the NAACP Legal Defense and Educational Fund. The two came to admire each other greatly. Redding, said Greenberg, "was the one man in a whole state actually standing up and doing something with decency." Redding said of Greenberg, "Jack is not a man to spill his guts over what's inside him. He's a private individual but there has never been any question about his genuineness about the Negro cause."[23]

The two filed a class action lawsuit against the university on behalf of the students, who were grouped together as *Parker et al.* Since the University of Delaware was a state institution, it was represented by Delaware's attorney general, Albert W. James, whose name lives on in Morris James, a prominent Wilmington law firm.

As a clear matter of equity rather than damages, the case was a natural fit for Delaware's Chancery Court, which assigned Vice Chancellor Collins J. Seitz to hear the case. When Seitz had been appointed to the Court of Chancery in 1946 he was just thirty-five, the youngest judge in Delaware's history. Redding and Greenberg were lucky to get Seitz, who, as it turned out, was uncomfortable with segregation. He had only been assigned the case because the Chancery Court judge who should have heard it was also a university trustee. (Seitz's son, Collins J. Seitz Jr., is the current chief justice of the Delaware Supreme Court.)

The proceedings in *Parker v. University of Delaware* took three days, with Redding and Greenberg successfully focusing the arguments on the issue of whether the quality of education at both schools was indeed equal. They argued that as a segregated school, the college by definition could not be equal, and that in any case, it was markedly inferior.

Seitz was reluctant to be drawn on the first argument because of the "separate but equal" precedent of *Plessy v. Ferguson.* The Supreme Court had applied the same principle in two cases just two months before *Parker v. University of Delaware.* "I do not believe I am entitled to conclude that segregation alone violates the [equal protection] clause," Seitz noted in his ruling.

But, having visited both campuses as part of the case, Seitz had a clear view on the two institutions' relative status. "One came away from the College with the feeling that here was an institution which, even without comparison, was a most inadequate institution for higher learning," he noted.[24]

Seitz ruled in favor of the students and ordered the University of Delaware to desegregate. The university trustees briefly considered another appeal, but decided to comply. The university became the

United States' first state-funded undergraduate institution to desegregate by court order.

At the University of Delaware, the case is now institutionalized at the school. Both Redding and Greenberg have residence halls named after them. The library is named for Morris, the board chairman who twice refused to allow the Black students to apply.

Yet one gets a sense that the university is still grappling with the narrative of its past. When I visited in the spring of 2018, a timeline at the entrance to the library described Morris as "a prominent Wilmington judge who fought for the desegregation of this campus." But if Morris had fought for anything, the record suggests, it was the exact opposite.

After the student newspaper ran an article about the sign in November 2018, the timeline was removed from the library entrance.[25]

———

Sarah Bulah didn't want to take on the issue of segregation in America. All she wanted was an easier way to get her daughter Shirley to school.

The local white children who attended School No. 29 traveled to school on a bus arranged by the state of Delaware, but there was no bus service for Black children to their school, Hockessin School No. 107, about seven miles west of Wilmington and two miles from the Bulahs' home.

Shirley was due to start at School No. 107 in the fall of 1950, about a month after the *Parker v. University of Delaware* decision. Fred Bulah and his wife, who ran a vegetable stand together at the corner of Valley and Limestone Roads, were discussing how to get their daughter to school. In the absence of public transport, Sarah Bulah would have to drive her, and on the days when she could not, Shirley would have to walk the whole way—even though the School No. 29 bus drove right past their farm twice a day, and its route took it close to School No. 107.

Bulah decided to start writing letters requesting transportation. School officials repeatedly denied her requests to arrange a bus for

School No. 107 pupils, but then she came up with what seemed like an efficient compromise: since the No. 29 bus already passed their home anyway, it could pick Shirley up and drop her at the post office, two blocks from School No. 107. "To take my child to school would not reroute the bus at all," she noted. "Put her off at the post office and pick her up at the post office and bring her right back to my door. The bus is not full. So that isn't an excuse."

But school officials rebuffed her again, citing the state constitution, which mandated segregated education under Article X, Section 2, which required that "separate schools for white and colored children shall be maintained" while specifying that "no distinction shall be made on account of race or color."

Delaware was one of seventeen states with a segregated school system. In this sense, the state betrayed its southern leanings: the Jim Crow states that required segregation were clumped together in the southeastern United States. Segregation was banned in Delaware's neighbors to the north, Pennsylvania and New Jersey.

Louis Redding wasn't interested in helping young Shirley Bulah get on the bus, either. He had his eye on a bigger prize. "He said he wouldn't help me get a Jim Crow bus to take my girl to any Jim Crow School," Sarah Bulah told reporters, "but if I was interested in sending her to an integrated school, why, then maybe he'd help."[26]

Bulah took the help. On Redding's advice, she continued writing the letters, this time requesting that Shirley not only be allowed to board the No. 29 bus, but also be admitted to the all-white school. In one letter to the Delaware State Board of Education, she wrote:

> We believe that our citizenship entitles us to have for our child everything that the State Board of Education considers an "integral part of a school program." Moreover, all the facilities at School No. 29 are better than those at School No. 107 at Hockessin. Therefore . . . we are requesting that our seven year old daughter Shirley Bulah be admitted as a pupil at Hockessin School No. 29.[27]

Again, the board of education denied her request. This time, with Redding's help, Bulah filed suit on behalf of her daughter against the Delaware Board of Education. Fresh from his victory against the University of Delaware, Redding was also helping four other groups of Black parents in challenging Delaware's segregated secondary education system. They too filed suits against the Delaware Board of Education.

Not only were Delaware's public schools strictly segregated, but the funding system put in place in the late nineteenth century persisted: property taxes paid by whites in Delaware funded white-only schools, and those paid by Black taxpayers, Black-only schools. Because Black households had persistently lower incomes than whites, the system ensured that this inequality would be replicated in public education. In the 1910s, Pierre Samuel du Pont, who was president of DuPont, had personally given millions of dollars for the construction and maintenance of schools for Black students, a move that effectively shamed the state legislature into improving school facilities for white students as well. But even with du Pont's support, Black schools in Delaware were mostly poorly built, shabby and dilapidated, with few facilities. White schools typically offered classes that were not available at Black schools. When it came to high school, there was only one option in the entire state for Black children: Howard High School in Wilmington. Black students seeking a high school degree either had to travel to Wilmington—a heavy burden, even in such a small state—or board in the city.

Shirley Bulah's inconvenient commute to school was shorter than the ones that many Black high schoolers faced. Ethel Louise Belton, a Black high school student from Claymont, a community about seven miles north of Wilmington, was forced to travel two hours every day to get to Howard High School. Like the Bulahs, her parents had asked school officials to admit Ethel Louise to the all-white schools in their local community. Like the Bulahs, when they were refused, they filed suit, along with the families of nine other Howard students.

The two cases named the state board of education as the principal defendant, specifically charging the board's members. Since the first name listed among the members was one Francis B. Gebhart, the cases became known as *Bulah v. Gebhart* and *Belton v. Gebhart*. For the trial, they were consolidated as *Gebhart v. Belton*.

Redding and Greenberg teamed up again. Redding argued the cases pro bono and the Wilmington NAACP paid the court costs. Fresh from their *Parker* win, the two lawyers were confident. The case was highly significant, taking place near the Mason-Dixon Line in a state with a dark history of slavery. The judge hearing the case, once again, was Collins Seitz.

Seitz had apparently been emboldened by the experience of *Parker*. In June 1951, in between the *Parker* and *Gebhart* cases, Seitz delivered a commencement address at Salesianum School, a Catholic school in Wilmington, in which he focused on "a subject that was one of Delaware's great taboos—the subjugated state of its Negroes. How can we say that we deeply revere the principles of our Declaration [of Independence] and our Constitution and yet refuse to recognize these principles when they are applied to the American Negro in a down-to-earth fashion?" Seitz was taking a considerable professional risk in delivering such remarks: they were "more than rhetoric," noted Richard Kluger, the Pulitzer Prize–winning author, who has studied school desegregation in America.[28]

As he had in the *Parker* case, Seitz found that the plaintiffs' schools were not equal to the white schools and ordered the white schools to admit the Black children. It was the first time a US court had found racial segregation in public schools to be unconstitutional. But again, Seitz noted that he was not the person to overturn the principle of "separate but equal," clarifying that he was ruling strictly that existing conditions were demonstrably *not* equal. So Seitz's decision did not strike down educational segregation in Delaware, but he did call time on the standard of *Plessy v. Ferguson*. "I believe the 'separate but equal' doctrine in education should be rejected," he said pointedly, "but I also believe its rejection must come from [the Supreme] [C]ourt."[29]

Thurgood Marshall, the future Supreme Court justice who was then head of the NAACP Legal Defense Fund, greeted Seitz's verdict as "the first real victory in our campaign to destroy segregation of American pupils in elementary and high schools."[30] Marshall was soon to have intimate knowledge of the case, as the case wended its way through the US court system. The state appealed to the Delaware Supreme Court, which upheld Seitz's decision. When the state then appealed to the US Supreme Court, *Gebhart* was consolidated with four other cases into *Brown v. Board of Education*, which was argued by Marshall and Greenberg. In 1954, the Supreme Court ruled that segregated schools were inherently unequal, overturning *Plessy v. Ferguson* and upholding Seitz's original decision, the only one that was affirmed.

The case had been settled in court. But on the ground, things were far from settled.

———

On October 7, 1957, Komla Agbedi Gbedemah, the finance minister of the newly independent West African country of Ghana, was traveling with a small group of aides from New York to Washington, DC, to meet with US officials. As night fell, they decided to take a break, and stopped at the Howard Johnson's restaurant in Dover, Delaware's state capital.

Gbedemah and one of his aides, both smartly dressed in business suits, ordered two glasses of orange juice, listed on the menu at thirty cents each. The waitress brought them the juices, still in their bottles, and wrapped them up in paper bags for the men to carry out. They could not sit inside, she explained. "She told me colored people were not allowed to eat in the restaurant," Gbedemah later told reporters. "I paid 60 cents for the orange juice, left it there, and went away."[31]

Gbedemah asked to see the manager, and then showed him a card that identified him as the finance minister of Ghana, the first country in West Africa to have gained its independence from the United Kingdom. "The [white] people here are of a lower social status than I am but they can drink here and we can't," Gbedemah told him. "You can keep the orange juice and the change"—from the dollar bill that he had paid—"but this is not the last you have heard of this."[32]

Shocked and humiliated, the finance minister told the *Delaware State News,* "I intend to demand an apology from the Howard Johnson's chain."[33] Howard Cook, who actually owned the Dover Howard Johnson's, later told the media that there was no official rule against Black customers, but that his employees had behaved in line with what was more of "an unwritten community custom." Had he been in the restaurant that day, he certainly would have served the men, Cook added.

The incident could have caused shockwaves across the United States and around the world. Two weeks earlier, President Dwight D. Eisenhower had ordered troops from the Army's 101st Airborne Division from their base in Fort Campbell, Kentucky, to Little Rock, Arkansas, to escort nine Black students into the Little Rock Central High School, after a baying mob of more than one thousand anti-integration activists had forced their removal from the school the previous day. The Soviet Union was trying to exploit such incidents in order to expand its influence in Africa.

Eisenhower rapidly offered to host Gbedemah at a breakfast meeting at the White House with himself and Vice President Richard Nixon. Afterward, all three beamed for the cameras to show there were no hard feelings. "The president expressed personal apologies for all that was done in Delaware," Gbedemah explained, adding that he now considered the incident closed.[34]

The Gbedemah incident was just one of a series in which African diplomats were humiliated in the United States, but it also highlighted how racial dynamics continued to work in Delaware. The state still had on its statute books an "innkeeper's law," which allowed business owners to refuse service to anyone they deemed "objectionable." In 1962, a group of seven white and Black students attempted to test the law at the Hollywood Diner in Dover. They were told the restaurant did not serve "coloreds,"[35] and when they refused to leave, they were arrested for trespassing. A few months later, they went to trial. Their defense lawyer was Louis Redding, who had been looking for a case to test the innkeeper's law. The seven were acquitted of trespassing, and a few weeks later, the Delaware General Assembly approved an equal-accommodations law.

But on the ground, discrimination continued, and white supremacists were increasingly showing their presence in Delaware. The Ku Klux Klan had never had much of a presence in the state, but they held cross burnings in the Delaware towns of Bear in 1965 and Millsboro the following year.

While these were dramatic episodes, most racism was less dramatic and more structural. After the *Brown* decision, Delaware desegregated its schools only slowly and sporadically, while socioeconomic inequality between races persisted.

There were riots in the town of Milford, in southern Delaware, when the state began to integrate schools following the *Brown* decision. Louis Redding had recruited eleven Black students to test the state's commitment to desegregation by enrolling in the town's all-white high school. The first couple of days passed somewhat uneventfully. But then crowds of hundreds of white people began to gather to protest, hurling abuse at the "Milford Eleven" as they entered the school building.[36] The local police refused to intervene, so Redding called on the Delaware State Police to escort the Black students to school. But the protests only grew, and then white students began to stay home. The situation seemed unsustainable. When the case came before the Delaware Supreme Court, the justices ruled that the school district had acted legally, but had moved too quickly to integrate its schools. Delaware's first big attempt to honor the *Brown* ruling had lasted just twenty-eight days.

But Milford was unusual. In general, integration did not lead to much social friction—chiefly because in practice, Delaware schools remained highly segregated. In 1956, Black students in Clayton, in central Delaware, sued their local school district for refusing to admit them. In response, the US District Court ordered the Delaware State Board of Education to submit and implement a statewide desegregation plan.

But a decade after the *Brown* decision, Delaware still had seventeen Black-only school districts. In Wilmington, many middle-class white families responded to integration by moving to the suburbs. White flight in the city dramatically and rapidly changed its demographic makeup: Wilmington went from 73 percent white in 1954 to 79 percent Black by 1971. The city was so concerned that it placed restrictions on placing "For Sale" signs outside homes. By 1967, the board of education had officially broken up the remaining Black school districts, and the federal Office of Civil Rights commended Delaware as the first southern or border state to formally end its dual-school system. But, the following year, the Delaware General Assembly passed the Educational Advancement Act, which cut the number of school districts in the state from forty-nine to twenty-six and specified that the school system's boundaries must be the same as the city limits, effectively opening the door to resegregation.

The halting progress in overcoming persistent disparities in education was mirrored in the labor market. Although the situation improved over the course of the twentieth century, Black workers still had limited economic mobility. In 1940, 70 percent of all employed Black people were either laborers or domestic servants, compared with 12 percent of the white workforce, and Black workers held three-quarters of all menial jobs in Delaware. One important reason was that historically, labor unions were segregated. Being a member of a union was the main way to get a job in northern Delaware's growing industrial facilities, but many unions barred Black workers from being members or entering union-sponsored apprentice programs. That led to massive Black underemployment. During the Second World War, a shortage of labor enabled Black workers to secure factory jobs in Delaware, but as the educator and civil rights activist Pauline Young observed, "After V-J Day, the removal of Negroes from the war industries was faster and more complete in Delaware than in any of the other states."[37] Black workers typically settled for unskilled, low-wage, and low-status positions, effectively leaving them with two work options in Delaware: either as professionals within the Black community, such as doctors or clergymen, or as laborers and domestic servants. This left a legacy of labor inequality in Delaware that, along with education, bled into other issues such as housing, a subject on which the Delaware General Assembly had held lengthy debates but had passed no legislation as of 1967.

It was in this context that Delaware entered the "long, hot summer" of 1967. Nationally, tensions were rising over the Vietnam War and civil rights. Riots broke out in July in Black neighborhoods in Wilmington, as they did in Detroit, Newark (New Jersey), Chicago, Minneapolis, Birmingham, and dozens of other cities. In Wilmington, for two days there was looting and firebombing, mainly of Black property. Wilmington mayor John Babiarz called in the state police to help. But that was not good enough for the governor, Charles Layman Terry, a portly, southern-style Democrat from Dover. Terry demanded that the Delaware General Assembly grant him the authority to declare a state of emergency with crowd-control powers, and established an official riot commission. He immediately declared martial law, imposed a curfew, and banned liquor sales. Warning of the dangers of violence by minority groups, he placed 1,500 National Guardsmen on standby at the Wilmington airport and canceled leave for all state police. The violence ended after a week with no serious injuries reported, but Terry insisted that the state of emergency continue for another month. The Delaware National Guard prepared for future incidents with riot crowd-control training.

When Martin Luther King Jr. was assassinated on April 4, 1968, riots broke out across the United States. Terry was prepared to use everything he had at his command to keep the peace in Delaware. Four days after King's murder, hundreds of Wilmington residents gathered in Rodney Square to memorialize the slain civil rights leader. As the day wore on, the older folk in attendance drifted home, leaving a group of mainly teenage boys. The situation turned ugly, and by nightfall, a riot had taken hold of the Valley, a neighborhood on Wilmington's west side. But this was not like the riots that devastated swathes of Chicago, Baltimore, and Washington, DC. Wilmington's two days of riots resulted in far less destruction, either human or property, with about twenty small businesses in the Valley burned or looted, and about forty people injured. The historian Carol Hoffecker describes it as "a small, short-lived affair that did relatively little damage."[38]

But an early report of sniper fire spooked Babiarz, who asked Terry for help. The governor needed little encouragement. He ordered the entire National Guard contingent in Delaware, 2,800 troops, to occupy Wilmington and patrol the streets. After a week, when the situation had calmed, Babiarz asked Terry to withdraw the troops. Terry refused. "The Guard is going to stay in Wilmington until we're sure people and property owners are adequately protected," he said.[39] Even though Babiarz publicly and repeatedly called for the National Guard to be withdrawn, Terry refused to do so. In fact, he expanded their remit, ordering troops deployed at Rehoboth Beach and at the campus of Delaware State College, which was predominantly Black.

The occupation of Wilmington would last nine months, making it the longest peacetime takeover of a city by state armed forces in US history. Initially, residents were comforted by the troops, but as time wore on, resentment against the occupation grew. Convoys of state troopers and National Guardsmen patrolled Wilmington's streets. These were known locally as "rat patrols," after the name of a popular TV series at the time about the adventures of four Allied soldiers fighting in North Africa during World War II. Many of the National Guardsmen had no experience in urban policing, particularly in the city's narrow residential streets. A Guardsman accidentally killed a young man during an attempted robbery. So the only death attributed to the Wilmington riots had nothing to do with civil unrest.

(One of Delaware's most famous residents ever may have been in the city at the time. Type "Bob Marley Delaware" into Google, and you'll see a torn and scratched photo of the future music legend as a young man in Wilmington, wearing a tracksuit top, sneakers, and jeans, one foot resting on a soccer ball, with his toddler son Stephen standing nearby. Music historians believe Cedella Marley moved to Wilmington in the early 1960s from Kingston, Jamaica, after her husband had died and she had remarried. It was the first place that her son, the future Jamaican reggae legend Bob Marley, had lived outside his home country. Cedella ran a Jamaican music shop on Market Street called Roots, and Bob and his wife Rita lived nearby. Bob Marley returned to Jamaica for a time, but he called Wilmington home on and off between 1965 and 1977. Stephen Marley was born in Wilmington in 1972. To support his family, Marley worked for a while as a lab assistant at DuPont, under the name "Donald Marley." He also worked briefly at the local Chrysler plant, reportedly working the night shift as a forklift operator, an experience that may have inspired his 1976 song "Night Shift.")

As resentment of the occupation grew, Governor Terry withstood enormous pressure to withdraw the troops, from critics both within

Delaware and nationally. The Delaware corporate community, ever watchful of the state's reputation, said that the rat patrols "create an aura of police state repression which is drastically reducing the effectiveness of long-time programs aimed at correcting the urban conditions that cause riots."[40] But Terry was unmoved, facing down his opponents at home with a ruthless determination that earned him the nickname "The Great Divider." When students heckled the governor during a speech at Delaware State, he responded by closing down the predominantly Black school for a month.

The military occupation only ended when Terry lost the subsequent election. Even then, he kept the troops in place until the day he left office. In a sign that many Delawareans approved of the occupation, and that the state was as divided as ever, he lost reelection by just 2,115 votes, about 1 percent of the total votes cast. Russell Peterson, the new Republican governor, pulled the troops out practically the moment he took office.

Terry had undoubtedly overreacted to the public safety threat posed by the riot. But in a way, his was a very Delawarean response. Racial tensions had always had the potential to bring to the fore the divisions that had riven the state since its creation. Shutting down, forcefully and definitively, anything that might disrupt social order was a version of the Delaware Way, of getting things done, of avoiding division and focusing on what was needed. It had revealed a dark side of the Delaware Way, one with its roots in Delaware's divided past—the struggles over independence, the splits over the Civil War, the racial tension that periodically boiled up—whose impulse was to shut down dissent and disagreement. It is an impulse that continues to shape the Delaware Way today.

———

The year following Terry's military occupation of Wilmington, Joe Biden won his first elected office, a seat on the New Castle County Council. His campaign was powered by more than 150 loyal (one might even say fanatical) high school student volunteers, whom Biden dubbed his "Children's Crusade." The twenty-six-year-old candidate described himself as a liberal Democrat. He ran against industrial development on green spaces. He supported small, economically integrated public housing projects. He called for a drug treatment center in New Castle County.

The Biden family had moved from Scranton, Pennsylvania, to Delaware in 1953, the year before the *Brown* decision. Joe Biden turned eleven years old that year, and as he grew up, he was able to witness white flight turning Wilmington into a majority-Black city. Although he attended a private Roman Catholic school, Biden's own social circle was racially diverse. He worked as a lifeguard in a Black neighborhood. As a young lawyer, he joined civil rights protests on occasion, although some of those who were there remember him borrowing signs rather than bringing them, and he would later be called out for exaggerating his involvement. He was a frequent visitor to Delaware State, where he would converse with faculty, staff, and students.[41]

But in a 1970 interview, Biden shared some interesting views on race that presaged his later political career:

> I have some friends on the far left, and they can justify to me the murder of a white deaf mute for a nickel by five colored guys. They say the black men had been oppressed and so on. But they can't justify some Alabama farmers tar-and-feathering an old colored woman. I suspect the ACLU would leap to defend the five black guys. But no one would go down to help the "rednecks." They are both products of an environment. The truth is somewhere between the two poles. And "rednecks" are usually people who lack the education and skills to express themselves quietly and articulately.[42]

It is instructive that Biden was already seeking to distance himself from the American Civil Liberties Union. The ACLU would find itself butting heads with Biden before he even won a seat in the US Senate in 1972. The issue was busing, and it would not only pit Biden against his more liberal supporters and colleagues but also propel him into close collaboration with some of the most powerful defenders of the tar-and-feather brigade.

The episode was sparked by the US Supreme Court's 1971 decision in *Swann v. Charlotte-Mecklenburg Board of Education*, which allowed busing in order to achieve integration in schools. The court specified that its ruling applied only to the de jure segregation of southern states, which stemmed from policies designed to separate races, and not to the de facto segregation of the North, which had more to do with housing patterns. As a state with a history of segregation laws, Delaware was a de jure state.

Louis Redding was ready again. Working with the ACLU and Black parents, he revived a lawsuit first filed in the 1950s, arguing that the Wilmington schools had never been desegregated despite *Brown*. The campaigning lawyer argued that ending segregation in schools now required dispersing students throughout the city of Wilmington and its suburbs, using busing.

Some local Black leaders were unsure, concerned that the issue could spark more racial violence. Among them was Howard Brown, a candidate for the Wilmington mayorship in 1972. Their fears later appeared well founded: when buses brought Black students to schools in white areas of Boston in 1974, angry white crowds pelted them with bricks and rocks.

That same year, Biden was called on to cast a critical Senate vote on the issue. Edward Gurney, a conservative Republican senator from Florida and a close ally of the embattled President Richard Nixon, tried to attach to an education bill an amendment to scrap court-imposed busing. Biden voted against, and the amendment failed by a single vote. It was a decision that Biden would later point to in order to defend his record on the issue. But at the time, Biden expressed his views very clearly. "I oppose busing," he said. "It's an asinine concept, the utility of which has never been proven to me. . . . I've gotten to the point where I think our only recourse to eliminate busing may be a constitutional amendment." He had voted against the amendment, he said, not because he supported busing but because Gurney's proposal was too wide ranging and "would have created havoc in our court system." But Biden was at pains to make clear where he stood on the topic:

> We've lost our bearings since the 1954 "Brown vs. School Board" desegregation case. To "desegregate" is different than to "integrate." . . . The new integration plans being offered are really just

quota-systems to assure a certain number of blacks, Chicanos, or whatever in each school. That, to me, is the most racist concept you can come up with: what it says is, "in order for your child with curly black hair, brown eyes, and dark skin to be able to learn anything, he needs to sit next to my blond-haired, blue-eyed son." That's racist! Who the hell do we think we are, that the only way a black man or woman can learn is if they rub shoulders with my white child? [43]

Biden insisted subsequently that he always supported busing to eliminate intentional de jure segregation, but not de facto segregation. He would support voluntary busing, but not busing ordered by a court, although some critics say Biden's comments at the time reflected a much more general hostility to the practice.[44]

Yet Biden's robust defense of his position did little initially to win him friends back home. Shortly after the Gurney vote, Biden attended a meeting at a school in predominantly white Newport, Delaware. It was an ambush: the event had been advertised as organized by the local civic association, but instead, it had been called by the Neighborhood Schools Association, an anti-busing group, which had rallied more than two hundred people to attend, distributing flyers that accused Biden of betraying his "pledges to oppose forced busing." Redding's lawsuit on desegregation, and the hot summer night, turned the atmosphere febrile. The audience heckled Biden, interrupting him almost constantly as he tried to speak. "If you think I'm in trouble with you people," Biden said, smiling weakly, "you ought to hear what my liberal friends are telling me."[45]

As he had with the 1970 interview, Biden was trying to cast himself as a centrist, Delaware Way–type politician. But the event appeared to strengthen Biden's resolve on the issue. Over the following decade, he became the Democrats' chief anti-busing figure, cheerleading nearly a dozen bills seeking to limit the authority of the federal government and courts to mandate busing. "No issue has consumed more of my time and energies," he said at a 1981 Senate hearing. "We want to stop court-ordered busing." Desegregating public schools, he argued, was better achieved via housing integration. While many civil rights activists supported housing integration, it was a much slower policy response, and not so much a replacement for busing as a complement to it.

The US Third Circuit Court ruled on Redding's case in March 1975 to impose a desegregation plan on New Castle County. Two judges on the three-judge panel voted to merge the school district for majority Black Wilmington with ten suburban districts whose demographics were whiter. The ruling overturned the Delaware General Assembly's 1968 law, which had identified the boundaries of the school system as the city limits. The court's desegregation plan depended on busing as a key tool.

In spite of his public pronouncements, Biden had largely kept his powder dry while the court had been deliberating, but once the judgment went against him, he ramped up his efforts in Washington to stop busing. In the fall of 1975, he joined forces with Jesse Helms, the prosegregation Republican senator from North Carolina, on an anti-busing amendment. The following year, Biden introduced a bill preventing the Justice Department from pursuing desegregation cases that could lead to court-ordered busing. In 1978, Biden voted for several bills to limit federal judges' ability to issue busing orders. None of these measures passed into law. But Biden had established himself as a leader on the issue, forging strategic alliances with segregationist senators such as Helms, Strom Thurmond of South Carolina, and James Eastland of Mississippi. As a young, self-described liberal, Biden had also made it easier for more mainstream Democrats to come out against busing. "I've made it—if not respectable—I've made it reasonable for long-standing liberals to begin to raise the questions I've been the first to raise in the liberal community here on the [Senate] floor," Biden told the *Washington Post* in 1975.[46]

This stance, and his alliance with senators who had racist voting records, earned him the enmity of many civil rights activists, some of whom were suspicious of his defense that he was only opposed to a certain type of busing: the type that affected Delaware. The only Black senator at the time, Republican Edward Brooke of Massachusetts, said of Biden: "He can be against busing, but can he be against the Constitution?"[47]

Throughout, Biden publicly fretted that imposed busing would lead to a race war. He blamed busing for prompting further white flight and called the policy "a liberal train wreck" in his 2007 memoir.[48] The evidence is mixed. William Taylor, a civil rights lawyer who advised the Wilmington school board, told a Senate hearing in 1981:

> I am sorry Senator Biden is not here, but I would say specifically as someone who has been involved in Wilmington that despite all the dire predictions that were made before that plan was implemented, it has gone very well. It has gone peacefully. There have been achievement gains in the schools. . . . I would say Wilmington is one of the success stories. I would love to discuss with Senator Biden the evidence on which he believes desegregation has not been a success in Wilmington.[49]

But although Black students performed better in desegregated schools, they still underperformed their white peers.

Wilmington was released from the busing requirement in 1995, and many schools resegregated in the following years, according to a 2014 study.[50] In 2018, the Delaware branch of the NAACP sued state and county education officials, claiming that students in the First State had become resegregated by race and class. J. Travis Laster, vice chancellor of the Chancery Court, agreed, noting that high-need schools had many more students of color than wealthier schools, and that Delaware had provided more state funds to wealthier districts.[51]

Busing and its legacy continue to divide opinion in Delaware. Some Black leaders in Delaware agree that busing fundamentally failed in its aims. In spite of resegregation in schools, racial tensions in the state have eased somewhat. In 2016, Lisa Blunt Rochester won the election for Delaware's lone seat in the US House of Representatives, becoming the first woman and Black politician to represent the state in Congress. The protests against racial injustice and police brutality that rocked the United States in 2020 led to some rapid and positive change. In June 2020, Wilmington officials removed statues of Christopher Columbus and Caesar Rodney.[52] The following month, Delaware officials removed the state's last whipping post, an eight-foot-tall concrete structure that stood next to the Sussex

County court house, "in recognition of the violence and racial discrimination that its display signified to many Delawareans."[53] Delaware was the last state to abolish the use of whipping posts in state
punishments, officially ending the practice only in 1972. Also in
July 2020, New Castle County joined forces with a nonprofit group
to turn the derelict former Hockessin Colored School No. 107—the
only school in the area that Black children could attend until the
1954 *Brown* decision—into a "place of social impact, diversity and
educational innovation."[54]

But Biden found it hard to shake off his record on busing.[55] As he
ran for the White House in the 2020 presidential race, the issue—and
Biden's attempt to project the Delaware Way onto the national political stage—came back to haunt him. At a June 2019 campaign event
in New York, Biden cited his relationships with segregationist senators as an example of the type of "civility" that had disappeared from
Congress. (Biden had delivered Thurmond's eulogy in 2003, waxing
lyrical about their friendship.) The comments earned him attacks
from New York City mayor Bill de Blasio and New Jersey senator
Cory Booker, two of Biden's many rivals for the Democratic Party
nomination for president. A few weeks later, then senator Kamala
Harris of California, who Biden would go on to pick as his running
mate, confronted him, calling the comments "hurtful." Senator Harris also raised her future boss's record on busing. "There was a little
girl in California who was part of the second class to integrate her
public schools, and she was bused to school every day, and that little
girl was me," Harris said, a comment that was perhaps the highlight
of her failed bid for the Democratic nomination. "Do you agree today
that you were wrong to oppose busing in America?" she asked Biden.
The former vice president was clearly rattled. "I did not oppose busing in America," he fired back. "What I opposed is busing ordered
by the Department of Education."[56]

To be clear, Biden has more than played his part in addressing
racial injustice. He supported the Equal Rights Amendment. He
served as the number two to the United States' first Black president,
and he selected a Black woman as his own vice president. After his
election as president, he acknowledged that it was Black voters who

had done the most to propel him to the White House. In office, he recruited a diverse administration.

But the Delaware Way helps explain how Biden could both oppose racial injustice while simultaneously doing deals with out-and-out racists. In much the same way, the First State itself at times compromised with and accommodated racism. That is the state's history. Delaware's legacy of racial strife has prompted its leaders to project unity as an end in itself, even if that meant working with those who would seek to push back social progress. That desire for social unity still echoes in the state's economic and political agenda, where the Delaware Way has often led to backroom dealing and avoiding transparency in the name of compromise and moderation.

PART III

Politics and Reform

8

The Process

HOW THE CORPORATE CODE IS MADE

America's corporate code is not written in Washington, DC, by either the federal government or Congress. It is not crafted by a group of elected representatives, or experts appointed by them. The debates surrounding it are not open to the public or the media.

Instead, it is written every year by a group of twenty-seven unelected lawyers who meet in private over several months in Wilmington, Delaware, before sending their recommendations to the Delaware legislature for changes to the code. More often than not there is next to no debate, and the state legislators, who sit an hour downstate in Dover, the capital, effectively rubber-stamp the proposals, which then go to the governor for signing.

In its marketing materials, the State of Delaware touts as one of its critical advantages "a legislature willing to work with Delaware's corporate bar."[1] That is quite an understatement. What actually happens is that the legislature does whatever the twenty-seven lawyers tell it to do. In this way, when it comes to corporate law, Delaware has effectively eliminated political uncertainty.

The group of twenty-seven is officially known as the Delaware State Bar Association's Section of Corporation Law, but is more usually referred to as the Corporation Law Council. It is made up of twenty-six members selected from among the senior ranks of the state's fourteen top law firms, plus Lawrence Hamermesh, a law professor from Widener University in Wilmington.[2] The chief deputy secretary of state for Delaware is also part of the committee, but only as a nonvoting, ex officio member.

The Corporation Law Council has been writing Delaware's—and therefore America's—corporate code for at least the past fifty years.[3] Its recommendations almost always become law. It is almost unheard of for the state legislature to challenge it. The council's deliberations are private. Its website features an annual memo to the executive committee of the Delaware State Bar Association. The memo does not offer much by way of transparency, focusing on the mechanics of how the council came up with its recommendations, rather than the themes of the proposed legislative changes or any arguments, debates, or dissents put forward as part of the council's internal discussions.

This lack of transparency is important, since the laws that this group writes outline the responsibilities that business leaders owe the shareholders of the companies they run. And because so much corporate litigation takes place in Delaware, the corporate law of the state is de facto the law of the land. What is written in Delaware is applied across the United States and beyond. As the *New York Times* observed about Delaware in 1988, "The state has become to business law the precedent setter that Iowa and New Hampshire are to the Presidential primaries."[4]

More than half of all Americans own stocks.[5] That means an unelected group of practicing lawyers beyond public scrutiny are the ones who craft the rules and responsibilities that corporate leaders have toward their shareholders—that majority of Americans who have entrusted those companies with their savings and investments. This area of public lawmaking is effectively a black box.

The system works. It is highly efficient and highly effective at ensuring smooth corporate governance. It is not, however, transparent or democratic. When the Corporation Law Council comes up against elected representatives, the lawyers win.

A small but instructive example of unelected versus elected lawmaking in action came in June 2017 at a meeting of the Judiciary Committee of the Delaware House of Representatives. Representative John Kowalko, who was not on the committee, appeared before the panel to introduce HB57, a piece of legislation requiring agents in Delaware who register new companies (or annually re-register existing ones) to check that those companies are reputable. The bill proposed that the agents should check the companies they register against a list maintained by the US Treasury's Office of Foreign Assets Control. This list names individuals and companies controlled by, owned by, or acting on behalf of countries deemed to be acting against US foreign policy and national security goals. The list also includes individuals and groups such as terrorists and drug traffickers who are not tied to any particular countries.

One might think that such a proposal would not be controversial. After all, if the federal government bothers to maintain a list of unsavory types, wouldn't any US state want to make sure it wasn't doing business with those named? What's more, the following year, the State of Delaware actually adopted the very requirement that Kowalko had been asking for, which suggests there was nothing the authorities found objectionable in their commitment to keeping the First State business-friendly.

It's important at this point to know a little bit about John Kowalko. A former union leader with a shock of white hair and a rumpled sense of style, Kowalko styles himself "the Bernie Sanders of Delaware." He is a self-described radical liberal, likes to ask awkward questions, and does not practice the Delaware Way. That combination of traits has earned Kowalko the enmity of not only most of his fellow lawmakers in the Delaware legislature, but even occasionally some local union members, who have accused him of behavior that might deter investment and create jobs. In Delaware's 2014 Labor Day parade, one local from the Building and Construction Trades Council marched with one of those giant inflatable rats that striking workers often use on picket lines. On the rat's belly, they had plastered a huge photo of Kowalko.[6]

In the 2017 Judiciary Committee meeting, the response to Kowalko's proposal was revealing. Melanie George Smith, a fellow Democrat who was then the vice chair of the committee, asked him if the bill had gone through the Corporation Law Council. Kowalko responded that it had not. The minutes of the meeting then record:

> Vice-Chair Smith said she was concerned about this because the correct process was not followed. She said that when the General Assembly wants to take up legislation dealing with corporations, it takes the recommendations of the Section of Corporation Law. This organization is comprised of some of the state's best lawyers who vet all legislation that goes through it. She added that this process sends a message of stability across the world. She concluded by saying that she cannot support HB57.

That exchange effectively killed Kowalko's bill. Smith was one of the most powerful members of the Delaware state house on corporate issues at the time. Shortly after her interjection, the committee voted to shelve the bill. More importantly, it also revealed how the decision-making process works in Delaware. In the First State, elected officials don't really have the right to introduce laws to change the corporate code. Only unelected lawyers—the very lawyers who argue the cases in court that depend on that code—have that right. The gist of Smith's response is that only private lawyers, not public representatives, are entitled to make the laws in Delaware regarding corporate behavior. As with the passage of the 1981 Financial Center Development Act, effective democratic deliberation is considered a hindrance to crafting effective, business-friendly legislation.

When it comes to the most important rules about the governance of corporations—Delaware's primary source of government revenue—the First State's legislature is a rule taker, not a rule maker. Its elected lawmakers effectively lack the power to make law in this area. That power resides exclusively with the unelected, unaccountable corporate bar. To be clear, the Corporation Law Council does not consult with the legislature before making its proposals. On the contrary, it guards its privacy jealously. Melanie George Smith, the Judiciary Committee vice chair who rebuffed Kowalko's proposal, was at the time not only a state representative but also an attorney for Richards, Layton, and Finger, one of Delaware's most powerful law firms. She was also a regular and reliable sponsor of the legislation that introduced the changes proposed by the Corporation Law Council. Yet, even as one of the council's principal cheerleaders in the legislature, when she once had the temerity to ask if she could attend one of its meetings, she was refused.[7]

In Smith's parlance, this is "the process"—a process that effectively eliminates democratic decision making. There is nothing necessarily wrong with the state's lawyers proposing annual amendments to the corporate code. There is something wrong, however, in a system in which they are typically accepted without question.

For sure, the process is not unique in US rulemaking. Federal criminal sentencing guidelines, for example, are also written by elite lawyers, academics, and judges. Bankruptcy rules are largely crafted by elite bankruptcy lawyers.

And there have been times when elected officials have actually challenged the council's initial recommendations. In 1988, the council proposed legislation to make it tougher to launch hostile takeovers, in which one company tries to buy a majority stake in another without getting the agreement of the target company's board. Usually, the buyer tries to get around this intransigence by buying shares on the stock market and building up a big stock position. The council proposed that a hostile bidder that acquired more than 15 percent of a target company's stock could not complete a takeover for three years unless it bought more than 85 percent of the outstanding stock at the same time. This proposal proved hugely controversial. For one thing, several hostile takeovers were already underway: both Campeau, a Canadian real estate company, and Black & Decker, the US maker of power tools, were trying to buy companies incorporated in Delaware, and they were worried they might get snarled in the new law. And the proposal came as Carl Icahn, the activist investor, was threatening to take over Texaco, another Delaware corporation. Along with potential acquirers, investment bankers also hated the idea, and they warned that the law would harm investors.[8] Some challenged the proposal's constitutionality, and have continued to question it.[9] Aware of the controversy, Delaware took the unusual step of asking for public comment on the change. The result was a battle of newspaper and radio ads, and comprehensive legislative hearings with a variety of experts testifying. Along the way to becoming law, legislators managed to tweak the proposal to accommodate some of the concerns—an unusual degree of intervention in corporate lawmaking from actual, elected lawmakers.

In 2014, the council encountered another rare case of resistance as they went about their annual law-changing exercise. The group had proposed to prevent companies registered in Delaware from forcing shareholders to pay legal fees if the shareholders sued the companies and lost. Worried about a potential wave of frivolous lawsuits, the measure drew fierce opposition from DuPont, the First State's most storied corporation, and the US Chamber of Commerce, the main lobbying group for US companies.[10] This time, they lobbied hard enough to force the hand of the Delaware legislature, which shelved the proposal. The following year, the council came back with effectively the same proposal, but it overcame opposition, in part by adding a section to Delaware's General Corporation Law allowing Delaware-registered corporations to stipulate that any shareholder claims against them must be filed exclusively in the First State. So claims against companies could go right ahead as long as the Delaware lawyers earned their fees along the way. The First State thus further cemented its position as the home of corporate litigation.

But these cases of opposition to council proposals, debate, and scrutiny are rare, and a departure from the usual process of corporate lawmaking in Delaware. Lawrence Hamermesh, the sole law professor on the Corporation Law Council, observes that the 1988 debate "represents Delaware corporate lawmaking at the margin, not at the core. It is an aberration, and must be and has been explained not as an outcome of ordinary Delaware lawmaking, but as an aberrational response to an unusual confluence of competitive pressures."[11]

To Delaware's boosters—including Hamermesh—these are the exceptions that prove the rule. Where there is opposition to its proposals, they say, the council takes account of that opposition. But most of the time, they argue, there is no opposition because what the council proposes is so eminently sensible and logical that no one could reasonably object. It is a highly technical and complex area, best left to experts, they say. There is usually no public debate because no debate is necessary, just as there is no public debate over how NASA designs its rockets, even if it uses public funds to do so.

Yet, without any real debate, there is effectively no democratic oversight of lawmaking in the very area that is so critical to the State of Delaware. The system appears to have a democratic form, but it has a very weak pulse, without all the checks and balances that you might expect for legislation with such national and international significance.

Advocates for Delaware consider this objection naïve given the national context. You cannot object to the democratic deficit in Delaware without examining what happens in other US states, the argument goes, and it compares favorably to the way law gets made in most states, where changes to corporate law come about only when a company has a specific aim and lobbies the statehouse accordingly.

In 2010, for example, Michigan passed a law whose sole aim was to prevent the owner of Steak 'n Shake, the casual-restaurant chain that famously does not have steak on its menu, from taking over Fremont Michigan InsuraCorp, a small insurance company with seventy-five employees located in the west of the state near Lake Michigan. The law was crafted specifically to kill the acquisition by Steak 'n Shake's owner, San Antonio–based Biglari Holdings, run by internet millionaire whizz kid Sardar Biglari. The concern in Michigan was that Biglari would dismantle Fremont or move jobs out of the state.

These worries prompted Michigan to pass a bill requiring a two-thirds supermajority of shareholders to approve a company's sale if its current board of directors opposed it. The kicker was that the legislation specifically applied exclusively to a "domestic (Michigan-based) insurer with 200 employees or fewer."

So to protect seventy-five people, Michigan changed its entire corporate law, and without provoking a great deal of agonized debate. There was little disagreement in the legislature about the need to protect Michigan jobs and a Michigan company, especially from a marauding Texan invader. There was no in-depth public debate analyzing both sides of the argument and attempting to arrive at a considered, rational solution. Rather, political considerations produced a form of state protectionism that compelled elected state representatives to shield a small local company with a new law.

That is how the corporate code gets changed much of the time in states across America. It is an idiosyncratic, ad hoc, politically charged process that protects special interests and produces uncertain outcomes. Compared to Delaware, it looks informal and chaotic, while Delaware's cozy corporate-code arrangements seem efficient and effective. "Although the law-making process around corporate governance and securities regulation issues outside Delaware is sometimes subject to partisan squabbling, hasty and scandal-driven action, and lobbying by special interests, Delaware's statute is an island of stability, with changes being made only after careful study and reflection," according to the First State's marketing material.[12] When I interviewed the legendary Delaware judge Leo Strine in 2018, the then chief justice of the First State's Supreme Court made a similar point. Delaware is home to so many companies, Strine observed, that it cannot afford to play favorites.

To be sure, the system in Michigan is pretty awful. The state came in last among all fifty states in a 2015 ranking of executive, legislative, and judicial accountability conducted by the Center for Public Integrity, an investigative journalism nonprofit.[13]

But the stakes are so much higher in Delaware. Michigan crafts corporate code only for itself and it has to live with the consequences. But the corporate laws passed in Delaware apply effectively to the entire United States, and the body that really writes them is not only not accountable to most US voters, it's not even accountable to voters in Delaware. In the Center for Public Integrity's 2015 ranking, Delaware came in forty-eighth among US states, only two notches above Michigan.[14]

George Stigler, the great University of Chicago economist and Nobel laureate, is credited with introducing the political-economic idea of capture—the notion that interest groups come to control lawmaking and regulation of their own sectors. Delaware has perfected the model by institutionalizing capture within its model of governance. The lawyers don't need to lobby the legislature to change the corporate code, they just write it themselves.

The result is a system that is efficient and effective. So what's the problem? Aren't legal experts the best people to make these decisions? Would some form of technocracy be preferable to democracy? It's an appealing view, one that might seem a particular relief in the age of political leaders who put their faith in cable TV channels and "alternative facts." Perhaps lawmaking and governance is too tricky to be left to elected politicians. Perhaps experts would do a better job. After all, the US Federal Reserve, like many other central banks, enjoys some autonomy and protection from the winds of political change. That insulation enables the Fed's economists to focus on its mandate of keeping unemployment down and prices stable, without undue political interference.

But the Fed is a bad analogy for several reasons. First, the Fed doesn't make law; the council effectively does. Second, although the Fed is independent, it still comes under rigorous scrutiny from Congress. The Fed chair must submit to US lawmakers a semiannual report on monetary policy and appears frequently on Capitol Hill to respond to politicians' questions. There is nothing similar for members of the council. Third, the Fed was granted independence by Congress in 1913 and its continued autonomy is an oft-debated issue, whereas the council's power evolved without any public debate or discussion. Fourth, there is little sense that decision makers at the Fed benefit personally from their decisions. Yet, as we'll see, there is at least the danger of conflicts of interest for the attorneys who sit on the corporation council. And finally, although the Fed faces calls for more transparency (such as US senator Rand Paul's demand to "audit the Fed"), it has taken strides to share more about, for example, the voting decisions of individual members of the interest rate–setting Open Markets Committee. The council's deliberations, by contrast, remain as secret as ever.

Supporters of the Delaware system sometimes hit back with an interest-group theory of their own: that there is a balance within the Corporation Law Council between lawyers who represent corporations and those who represent shareholders. Thus the two main constituencies chiefly affected by the corporate code are both represented at the table, if filtered through the very narrow window of the handful of lawyers who sit on the council. The process, Strine stressed to me, was a lot more balanced than some other areas of lawmaking.

This is representation of a sort, but it is not representation of the democratic kind. It is opaque. It lacks the transparency and oversight one would expect from a representative democracy. Brian Quinn, a law professor at Boston College, calls it "open-ish—the ish is important."[15]

Some observers argue that if anything went awry with the legislative changes proposed by the Corporation Law Council, local politicians would be forced to scrutinize their suggestions more carefully. In the words of Francis Pileggi, a top Delaware lawyer and widely read blogger: "If the proposals for amendments to the DGCL [Delaware's General Corporation Law] ever backfired on the legislators—as a political matter, not necessarily a legal matter, then the next proposed bill to amend the DGCL would not pass as easily the following year. That risk, however, has not come to pass for many decades, if ever."[16]

One problem with this argument is that it suggests that the voters are watching what happens. They aren't. The Delaware public isn't clamoring for a greater say over the state's corporate code. "It's a fairly narrow area. It doesn't have a lot of broad public inspection," says Jeff Bullock, Delaware's secretary of state. "Maybe there should be more but there isn't. Because I think it's very esoteric to most people who live in the state, and that's not a knock on them, it just doesn't involve them. It doesn't touch their lives in any direct way."[17]

But if the majority of Americans are shareholders, borrowers, and credit card holders, Delaware corporate law *does* affect them. And just because it's too complex for most to grasp its nuances or get excited about, that doesn't mean there shouldn't still be rigorous democratic oversight. Democracy isn't just for policymaking that resonates widely with the general public. As the University of Chicago economist Raghuram Rajan notes, "Except for the rare occasion when they are influenced by a popular national wave, for the most part voters do not really care about public policy."[18]

There are always many areas of legislation that do not excite the public's attention, from financial regulation to the details of trade policy. Yet we do not simply hand these issues off to interest groups just to decide them for themselves. The level of public interest is not an indication of whether an issue should be debated publicly.

Pileggi's other argument is that if there were anything wrong with the amendments to the corporate code proposed by the Delaware bar, the state legislature would challenge them. This idea places an incredibly high level of trust in the ability of lawmakers in a tiny state who sit in a part-time assembly and are paid an annual salary of $45,291 to analyze a highly complex area of law. As currently constituted, the Delaware legislature is not well equipped to assess the changes being proposed. It is only in session for six months of the year. It is the least well educated statehouse in the United States—21 percent of its lawmakers lack a bachelor's degree, more than any other state, according to the Pew Charitable Trusts, even in a state with one of the better-educated populations.[19] Only four of its sixty-two legislators are lawyers, as of 2020. If we were to form a group to scrutinize US corporate law, we would invite few if any of these people.[20]

It is disingenuous, then, to suggest that the Delaware legislature acts as any kind of a check or balance on the Corporation Law Council. In the words of Larry Ribstein, a widely respected corporate-law professor, "Delaware lawyers, in essence, *are* the Delaware legislature, at least insofar as corporate law is concerned . . . virtually all of Delaware corporate law is proposed by the Delaware bar, and the bar's proposals invariably pass through the legislature."[21]

Another argument you sometimes hear from those defending the system is that all the Delaware corporate code does is simply mediate the relationship between investors and managers. As long as those constituencies are content, the argument runs, it is not much of anyone else's business. But the corporate code is law and there are many instances in which laws that do not affect most citizens still get duly debated. And, for example, the laws on marriage and divorce (governed by state law) are also designed to mediate the private relationships between people, yet over the years they have certainly come under vigorous democratic debate.

The idea that the only constituencies that matter are the two sides that might end up in court is also questionable. The rise of the idea of corporate social responsibility—the notion that companies have a duty to society, the environment, and future generations—leaves the Delaware process looking somewhat anachronistic. If CEOs are responsible to not only their shareholders but society at large, what justification can there be to maintain the country club secrecy of the Corporation Law Council?

———

Delaware's current system depends on the most traditional interpretation of the purpose of a corporation, as outlined by Milton Friedman, the legendary University of Chicago economist and Nobel laureate. In his lifetime, Friedman, a fierce advocate for free-market capitalism, argued powerfully against the idea of corporate social responsibility. "There is one and only one social responsibility of business," he argued, which is "to use its resources and engage in activities designed to increase its profits."[22] Delaware took that view and enshrined it in the corporate code. As Kent Greenfield, a law professor at Boston College, wrote in 2016:

> The corporate mantra of "shareholder value" has been blamed for everything from the global financial crisis and the BP oil spill to heartless dependence on sweatshops in Bangladesh. And what is the source of "shareholder value" as a corporate obligation? Delaware.
>
> Scholars disagree on whether the state's rules provide more protection for shareholders or managers. But one thing is absolutely clear: Delaware corporate law cares not at all about employees, communities, customers, or other stakeholders, except insofar as shareholders also gain. If there is a conflict, shareholders must win.[23]

But in recent years the tide has started to turn against that view. In 2019, the Business Roundtable, which includes billionaire CEOs such as Amazon's Jeff Bezos, Apple's Tim Cook, and JPMorgan Chase's Jamie Dimon, issued a "Statement on the Purpose of a

Corporation." In it, they committed themselves to look after "stake-holders" as much as shareholders, pledging to treat their employees well, deal fairly with suppliers, and support their local communities. While many saw this as mere window dressing, on its face it is a significant shift. As the University of Chicago's Rajan points out, investing in training employees, for example, may actually mean that shareholders lose some profits—the value of the investment.[24] The Business Roundtable statement came a year after Larry Fink, the CEO of BlackRock, one of the world's biggest investment-management firms, sent a letter to his fellow CEOs arguing that "to prosper over time, every company must not only deliver financial performance, but also show how it makes a positive contribution to society."[25] And Fink's letter came a year after two eminent economists—Harvard's Oliver Hart, a Nobel laureate, and Luigi Zingales of the University of Chicago—wrote that Friedman may have been right that managers were responsible primarily to shareholders, but that shareholders themselves care about more than just profits. Hart and Zingales noted:

> It is too narrow to identify shareholder welfare with market value. The ultimate shareholders of a company . . . are ordinary people who in their daily lives are concerned about money, but not just about money. . . . Someone might buy an electric car rather than a gas guzzler because he or she is concerned about pollution or global warming; she might use less water in her house or garden than is privately optimal because water is a scarce good; she might buy fair trade coffee even though it is more expensive and no better than regular coffee; she might buy chicken from a free range farm rather than from a factory farm. . . . Many owners of privately-held firms appear to care about the welfare of their workers beyond what profit maximization would require. . . . If consumers and owners of private companies take social factors into account . . . in their own behavior, why would they not want the public companies they invest in to do the same? To put it another way, if a consumer is willing to spend $100 to reduce pollution by $120, why would that consumer not want a company he or she holds shares in to do this too?[26]

The social protests that erupted in the United States in 2020 against racial injustice and inequality, coming as the COVID-19 pandemic gripped the world, prompted dozens of US corporations to move further toward the vague goal of "stakeholder capitalism." Big companies weighed in on social issues like never before, donating money to organizations focused on combating racism, making public statements condemning police brutality, and opposing voter-restriction measures.

Even among the legal elite in Delaware, these views were starting to permeate. When I asked Strine about the shareholder/stakeholder issue in 2018, he took the traditional line. "I am very careful to talk about the dimensions of what our law covers and what it doesn't," he told me. "I'm not afraid to say I'm a person of the left, and I care about workers and I care about the environment. But that's really not what our corporate law is about. . . . To just say to directors, 'You are elected only by these folks, but you should do all great and good things on behalf of other constituencies'—that just doesn't make any freaking sense to me." Strine tested me on the line from the Eddie Cochran song "Summertime Blues":

> Well, I called my congressman
> And he said, quote:
> "I'd like to help you, son
> But you're too young to vote."

The only people in the corporate world with votes, he told me, are the shareholders.[27] Yet, the following year, as he was stepping down from his role as chief justice of Delaware's Supreme Court, Strine changed his tune. He said publicly that US corporations *should* do more to look after workers, not just shareholders. He also backed the idea of companies hiring directors specifically tasked with protecting the interests of the workforce, and supported a bill put forward by Elizabeth Warren, the progressive US senator from Massachusetts, to expand corporate directors' purview to include the impact of their decisions on workers, consumers, communities, the environment, and the United States at large.[28] In a 2020 article, Strine argued for a significant limitation on business judgment, arguing that corporate leaders should no longer be given discretion to act in the best interests of all stakeholders, but that they should be legally obligated to do so.

Those stances markedly contrast with the criteria by which Strine had judged US corporations when he was in the Chancery Court and the Delaware Supreme Court. In 2008, as a vice chancellor on the Delaware Chancery Court, Strine noted:

> Milton Friedman's vision of the appropriate focus of corporate management has won out where it really counts, in the marketplace. . . . Friedman's view regarding the obligation of corporate management—i.e., to maximize profits for stockholders—has won a sweeping victory. . . . The realities of the marketplace and the power of institutional investors will guarantee that corporations are governed for the primary purpose of increasing returns to equity.[29]

But by 2020, Strine had undergone a dramatic change of opinion, arguing, "Fifty years ago, Milton Friedman said that the social responsibility of business is to increase its profits. He was wrong, and the consequences of the mistaken thesis have been mounting environmental and social problems around the world. Remedying this mistake requires that environmental and social policies be combined with changes to corporate law that place corporate purpose beyond profit at its heart."[30]

A fascinating piece of Delaware corporate history illustrates the consequences Strine has come to acknowledge—consequences that happen when companies consider only their own shareholders and ignore societal effects. The story once again involves DuPont, that most Delawarean of Delaware corporations, and one of its most famous products: Teflon. DuPont developed the nonstick coating in 1938, and for many years manufactured it using perfluorooctanoic acid, or PFOA, a chemical that made the final product less lumpy. In the mid-1990s, farmers in West Virginia noticed their cattle were dying after drinking water from a creek close to a landfill where DuPont dumped waste from its local plant. An independent panel would establish that 3,500 people living near the DuPont plant had suffered diseases related to PFOA, and in 2017, DuPont settled all the cases against it for $670 million. Internal memos reveal that DuPont executives in Wilmington had known as early as 1984, and possibly earlier, that PFOA was toxic. Yet they had actually increased their use of the chemical. To explain why, the University of Chicago's Luigi Zingales and Roy Shapira of IDC Herzliya analyzed company documents to understand the choice facing the executives.[31] Replacing or dropping PFOA would have cost DuPont $100 million to $200 million every year, the equivalent of about $1.1 billion today, Zingales and Shapira calculate. By contrast, the researchers reckon the legal liabilities amounted to only around $100 million in 1984 dollars, so rationally, if they were purely considering shareholder value, it made sense for DuPont to continue to pollute. What was good for the company and its shareholders was damaging for the rest of society: the societal health costs totaled $350 million, according to Shapira and Zingales. The traditional view is that such issues are best left purely to environmental regulators, but the cost-benefit analysis demonstrates that by acting in what it assumed were the best interests of its shareholders, the company ended up poisoning a community next to its facility, doing nothing to stop or remedy this situation until it was too late.

This case neatly illustrates the limits of the representation that the Corporation Law Council offers. The views of corporations are represented. The views of shareholders are represented. But the interests of society more generally are overlooked. Normally, this is where democracy would step in. Elected representatives should have broader interests in mind than simply whether corporations can keep making profits. But the system in Delaware is designed to treat democratic oversight as something of an afterthought, rather than an integral part of the corporate policymaking process.

Government by experts might lead to better outcomes for some, but democratic societies have taken the choice to place power in the hand of elected leaders, even if the outcomes are slightly less optimal. As George Stigler, Friedman's great friend, observed in 1981,

If I and my likes could design the American economy, it would have a national income larger by possibly 10 to 20 percent, without forfeiting any social goals that are widely desired. If I employed Milton Friedman as an independent contractor—that's the only kind he ever is—we would also do a good job on inflation. But notice: these good things come only because you turned dictatorial powers over to me.[32]

America's choice was to pay the cost of having a democratic system, even if an authoritarian leader could provide more optimal outcomes. And most Americans, in spite of our dysfunctional and polarized political system, would likely still prefer the current system over a dictatorship that gives them a few more dollars in their pockets.

The process in Delaware is not broken. On the contrary, it works smoothly and efficiently. But it does not work transparently. Democracy is often messy and inefficient, but that is the system under which our laws—including the laws that stipulate the responsibilities of our business leaders to their shareholders—are supposed to be written.

The process in Delaware is deeply flawed in two ways. It is antidemocratic, entrusting the role of lawmaking to a shadowy group of unelected policy experts. And it has repeatedly failed to hold companies responsible for the societal effects of their actions. The process encapsulates the perfection of the Delaware Way and its consequences.

9

Don't Screw It Up

If the system of corporate law in other states works to the benefit of individual corporations, who benefits from the Delaware system—institutionalized capture?

The system depends on working lawyers. And working lawyers are almost bound to make recommendations aligned with their particular interests and those of their clients. They define conflicts that only they can resolve, creating ever-more opportunities to line their pockets in long legal battles. In that sense, they are a special-interest lobby group with its own priorities. A system in which the recommendations of such a group are cut and pasted into law seems far from ideal, particularly when the impact of that law is so far reaching. Delaware lawyers advocate for the interests of Delaware lawyers, but they effectively make law for the United States.

The system is not completely grubby. It isn't exclusively the pursuit of exorbitant legal fees that drives the process. Another instinct among the clubby legal elites who write the rules may well be to make Delawarean law technocratically excellent and efficient. They are aware of the importance of their recommendations and are no doubt guided in part by a sense of public service.

But conversely, it would be naïve to argue that the benefit of Delaware and Delaware lawyers is not a key motivation. The most obvious example is that any case brought in a Delaware court must be argued by a Delaware lawyer. When America's biggest corporations come to court in the second-smallest US state, they must use local counsel. "Delaware's general approach to stockholder litigation . . . is to make it easy to sue the executives of Delaware corporations, no matter where they reside or the corporation does business, so long as the suit is in Delaware courts, and conducted by Delaware counsel," observed Yale law scholar Joseph W. Bishop Jr.[1] There are far more lawyers in Wilmington than the State of Delaware could ever support, so this is a wonderful way of keeping lawyers employed. We can draw this picture more precisely. The twenty-six working lawyers on the Corporation Law Council are all partners (one is a former partner) in elite firms. So their interests are narrow. In the words of law professors Jonathan R. Macey of Yale and NYU's Geoffrey P. Miller, "The rules that Delaware supplies often can be viewed as attempts to maximize revenues to the bar, and more particularly to an elite cadre of Wilmington lawyers who practice corporate law in the state." Delaware has an effective monopoly on out-of-state business registrations, and one traditional concern about monopolies is that they will exploit their market power to price-gouge. As we discussed in chapter 2, Delaware's relatively affordable incorporation fees might appear to allay that concern. But legal fees do reflect more than the First State's effective monopoly. As Macey and Miller write:

> First, the higher fees that Delaware is able to charge to corporations because of its advantage in the jurisdictional competition for corporate charters are not spread evenly or randomly throughout the state. Rather, these gains are apportioned to those special interest groups that compete most effectively within the political process. Second, the nature of the fee structure by which Delaware charges for the privilege of incorporating within the state reflects this interest group dynamic. The fee structure includes not only direct taxes to incorporating firms, but also indirect charges which come in the form of expected fees to Delaware lawyers. This last point is of particular interest because it affords Delaware lawyers an opportunity to exploit the comparative

advantage that they enjoy over other interest groups within the state. Because of their preexisting knowledge of the legal system and their low cost access to the law reform process, Delaware lawyers are able to craft the set of legal rules that maximizes the total demand for their services.[2]

To see how " maximizing revenues to the bar" works in practice, consider what happened for many years when shareholders brought lawsuits in Delaware trying to halt takeovers and mergers involving companies incorporated in the state.

Most shareholder challenges to business leaders' day-to-day decisions get dismissed by the Delaware courts.[3] But takeovers and mergers are different. Delaware courts scrutinize these claims more carefully and have to determine whether shareholders have been provided with adequate information about the proposed takeover or merger.

As a result, from 2009 to 2015 shareholders challenged around 90 percent of proposed takeovers and mergers valued at more than $100 million, up from less than 40 percent a decade earlier. Most of those suits settled, not with any money paid to the shareholders, but with corporate leaders providing more information about the proposed deal. In such a settlement, no one actually gets paid except the lawyers on both sides. As Sean J. Griffith, a law professor at Fordham University, observed,

> Merger litigation has devolved into a nonadversarial process in which attorneys on both sides of the "v" extract rents from corporations and their shareholders. The promise of serious judicial scrutiny over merger transactions has all but disappeared, replaced instead by a system that ensures a source of revenue for the corporate bar. . . . Only the lawyers get paid. The shareholders who pay them are doubly harmed by settlements that waive potentially valuable claims in exchange for meaningless disclosure relief.
>
> The incentive to protect shareholder rights is lacking on both sides. Plaintiffs' lawyers seeking disclosure settlements happily trade litigation rights into which they have invested little, if any,

real investigative effort. Meanwhile, defense counsel, who of course also collect fees ultimately funded by shareholders, broker the trades that result in the abandonment of shareholder rights.[4]

These "disclosure settlements" have since been curbed.[5] But they still stand as a powerful example of a system that works well for lawyers but offers no significant benefit to shareholders, and even less benefit to society as a whole. The Delaware system gives rise to "rent-seeking" by lawyers—they look to extract money by exploiting the rules rather than by adding value to the economy, the way most businesses do.

That is a world away from the official description of the Corporation Law Council, which, as Lawrence Hamermesh observes, is supposed "to maintain a balance among the interests of investors, managers, and society."[6] That description leaves out the most important constituency: the lawyers themselves.

You can't really blame the lawyers. They are bound to protect their own self-interest. Any other professional group given the same opportunities would probably behave in the same way. This is precisely the reason that our democratic system has regulation and checks and balances.

The culprit is the process itself, which allows lawyers to write the rules that govern their own industry, operating effectively without any oversight. The process enables Delaware lawyers to "enjoy a lucrative Wall Street practice in a comparatively pastoral setting," as William Cary observed.[7]

To reiterate: the corporate laws that Delaware writes effectively become the laws of the land. The US system of government is far from perfect. It could be argued, for example, that it allows lobbyists too much influence over the political process. But it is an even further step to hand over the ability to write the rules to an industry that stands to benefit from them. We would not allow US technology policy to be written exclusively in California. We do not let Michigan entirely dictate US industrial policy. We do not do these things for good reason: each of these states would just write the rules to benefit themselves, not with the broader interests of the entire United States in mind. Where we do exactly that—as the United States arguably does with farm subsidies, which are shaped in the agricultural Midwest, or with its policy toward Cuba, which is effectively created by exiles in Miami—the outcomes are less than optimal. Rational debate gives way to more base political calculations.[8]

There is one interesting parallel to the Delaware bar's control of the corporate code: the way that US intelligence and national security agencies craft defense policy largely in private, informing only a handful of members of Congress and telling them only what they want to tell them. As Norman Mineta, a former US member of Congress, once observed about these agencies, "We are like mushrooms. They keep us in the dark and feed us a lot of manure."[9] It would be hard to argue that we should replicate that model in other areas of policymaking.

Apart from lawyers, there is one other critical beneficiary of the process: the State of Delaware itself. The system as currently constituted works to Delaware's economic benefit. As William Cary observed in 1974 in his famous *Yale Law Journal* article, "Stimulating incorporation in Delaware has some of the flavor of a community chest drive. For revenue reasons, 'creating a favorable climate' is declared to be the public policy of the state. Perhaps there is no public policy left in Delaware corporate law except the objective of raising revenue."[10]

To question or try to reform the system would be to introduce political uncertainty, thereby frightening off investors and ultimately causing irreparable damage to the economy of the state.

Melanie George Smith and I had an enlightening conversation about this before she stepped down as a Delaware lawmaker in 2019. "A third of our budget comes from revenues spun off from corporations and alternative entities, and so it's kind of the golden goose, if you will," she told me.

> So we can't upset that apple cart and start running legislation where folks around the world are going to look and be like, "What just happened to the LLC world in Delaware?" We hunker down in the bunkers whenever Kowalko starts flashing around draft

legislation and stuff like that, part of the reason being that when he even introduces legislation, it becomes public. So the minute a legislator introduces legislation, whether it gets worked or not, it becomes public. As soon as the media picks up on that, and other lawyers pick up on it, now you've got companies in London or Tokyo or whatever calling Delaware law firms saying, "What the hell is going on?"[11]

This, then, is the economic aspect of the Delaware Way. Not only are lawmakers not entitled to independently propose amendments to the corporate code, they are not even entitled to discuss such amendments, for fear of raising eyebrows worldwide at companies that incorporate in Delaware, thereby potentially upsetting Delaware's entire business model.

As Charles Elson, a professor of corporate governance at the University of Delaware, puts it, "The development of its corporate statute and judicial appointments must be above the local political fray. Should Delaware fall, we all will lose."[12]

But let's be clear who Elson means when he says "we." It isn't society at large, whose democratic norms are undermined by "the process." It isn't even shareholders, whose interests can at times be pushed aside, as the "disclosure settlements" issue demonstrates. The "we" is the State of Delaware, whose government depends on incorporation fees, and the Wilmington lawyers who control the law and collect their fees. To question the system is to harm Delaware, even if no regulations actually change. Even *talking* about questioning the system is a no-no.

It's not just that Delaware is worried about someone killing the goose that lays the golden eggs. Delaware is so worried about losing the eggs that it wants to forbid any conversation about the goose in the first place.

And, until recently, everyone in Delaware—except for a few troublemakers such as John Kowalko—has been on the same page. That's obvious when you think about it—why would they want their state government's revenues to dry up? That might mean higher taxes or fewer services. Since Delaware is run like a corporation, it makes sense that it doesn't encourage its residents to engage in a frank conversation about its business model. As Delaware's own marketing materials put it, by the time the Corporation Law Council's proposals are up for a vote in the Delaware legislature, "Partisan divides are unheard of, because both political parties understand that trillions of dollars are invested in these corporations and respect the importance of ensuring that managers and investors can rely on a statute with real integrity, efficiency and reliability."[13] Debate, in other words, is not only unnecessary, but potentially damaging to this critical source of state revenue.

The economic Delaware Way essentially says that the Franchise shouldn't really be discussed in public, because if the process is questioned, everyone in Delaware will suffer the consequences. Delaware's elites want to be like stagehands, operating unobserved as they tweak America's corporate scenery. Their greatest fear is that someone will do something to focus the spotlight on them.

A long-standing Delaware tradition underlines this point. By custom, every departing Delaware secretary of state leaves a letter to their successor. No matter the author, the letter always ends, "Don't screw it up."[14]

——

The Corporation Law Council is only half the equation when it comes to Delaware corporate law. The other half is the Delaware Court of Chancery. The Chancery Court is unique, a hangover from the colonial era, when the original thirteen colonies imported the English concept of common law, with a separate Court of Chancery that handled issues of equity. All the other US states eventually abolished their Chancery Courts, merging their business with the regular courts, and even the United Kingdom did so in the 1870s. But Delaware clung on.

Today, the court, which hears almost exclusively business disputes, is critical to the state's business-friendly image. The court is probably Delaware's most important selling point for corporations. In theory, any other state could reproduce everything Delaware offers. But the

Chancery Court's long record of case law is unique to the First State. Judges at both the Chancery Court and the Delaware Supreme Court write opinions supporting their decisions. This case law is a useful guide for corporations about the likely outcomes of cases. The business and legal communities largely consider the two courts' judges to be experts in corporate law, well versed in its intricacies.

The overriding principle of Delaware corporate law is the "business judgment rule." This term came into use in Delaware in the 1970s, but there is nothing particularly Delawarean about it. The idea, which dates back at least to a case in Louisiana in the 1820s, is essentially that the law trusts the judgment of corporate leaders.[15] So, as long as most members of the board of a company do not have conflicts of interest, give due care to their decisions, and act in good faith, the Delaware courts will not hold them responsible for what happens, even if the results are bad for shareholders. In the words of William T. Allen, former chancellor of the Chancery Court, "In the absence of facts showing self-dealing or improper motive, a corporate officer or director is not legally responsible to the corporation for losses that may be suffered as a result of a decision that an officer made or that directors authorized in good faith."[16] The business judgment rule is a big reason that many critics characterize Delaware as pro-management (although, as we saw in the Introduction, this is a long-standing debate in academic circles). Delaware, observed prominent Wilmington lawyer Charles S. Crompton Jr., is the state "where any sensible businessman would want to be sued."[17]

Although the business judgment rule might suggest that the Chancery Court would always side with management over shareholders, the rulings don't always go that way. From the perspective of the Delaware courts it's important that those courts remain the chief venue for shareholder litigation. If the shareholders invariably got screwed, they would eventually stop bringing lawsuits, which would diminish the number of cases being brought in Delaware. A drop in cases would threaten lawyers' fees and, ultimately, diminish corporate America's notion of the centrality of the Delaware court system—and the Franchise itself. So the Chancery Court has a vested interest in not making its rulings too predictable.

Perhaps for this reason, many legal scholars find that while the Chancery Court judges are undoubtedly experts, their rulings are not always clear. "Commentators are in wide agreement that Delaware corporate law lacks clarity," observe Marcel Kahan of NYU and Ehud Kamar of Tel Aviv University.[18] A lot of this has to do with the business judgment rule itself. Take, for example, the notion that corporate leaders must act "in good faith." Legal experts think Delaware's courts have never given us a clear picture of precisely what "in good faith" means. "Delaware's inability to offer a clear, consistent conception of good faith is significant," says Clark W. Furlow, an emeritus law professor at Stetson University.[19] UCLA's Stephen M. Bainbridge and colleagues have observed that "new and unnecessary doctrinal uncertainties have been created" by the good faith rule.[20] Mae Kuyk-endall, a law professor at Michigan State, says she is "uncertain" if the phrase "in good faith" has any real substance at all.[21]

To be fair, the vagueness may be desirable. Some laws set clear rules, such as speeding limits. Other laws set general standards, such as a requirement to perform due diligence. There are good reasons for the Chancery Court to aim for the latter, because very clear rules can simply give clever lawyers an incentive to find a way around the letter of the law while breaking the spirit of the law. Setting standards rather than rules can help reduce the hunt for these loopholes.

Another advantage of this lack of clarity is that it keeps cases coming back to the courts. If the outcome of one case is not necessarily applicable to another case, the two sides cannot easily extrapolate from one to the other, so the only way to know the law would be to go to court. As Boston College's Kent Greenfield notes, "The judges decide cases in a way that will not show their expertise, but instead make it more necessary for them to rule. They're not that good at articulating really clear, precise judgments. They're better at reaching outcomes and then explaining those outcomes in ways that will leave the court itself the ability to decide differently in the next case."[22]

Rather than get lost in the details of individual decisions, it's instructive to look at how the Chancery Court operates. There are some parallels between the crafting of the corporate code by the

Corporation Law Council and the rulings on corporate law by the Chancery Court. In both, democracy and transparency are often sidelined in the name of efficiency, business-friendliness, and the Delaware Way.

First, it's clear that the lawyers who sit on the Corporation Law Council have an outsized impact on the life of corporate America. Similarly, because of Delaware's stature as the home of business formation in the United States, the Chancery Court's one chancellor and six vice chancellors are probably the most powerful judges in the United States when it comes to corporate law. One source of the uncertainty in judgments is that the Chancery Court judges clearly bring their own perspectives to cases. They are not completely homogeneous in their views, any more than the justices on the US Supreme Court. Yet, unlike that body, the chancellor and vice chancellors issue solitary rulings, which means it is critical for corporate lawyers to know their particular personalities and preferences.

The recent chancellor perhaps most renowned for his colorful character inside the courtroom was Leo Strine, who often meandered and digressed from the case at hand, attempting to enliven the proceedings with unpredictable, seemingly random repartee. In 2012, during Strine's two-and-a-half-year stint as chancellor, he received an unprecedented dressing-down from the Delaware Supreme Court (which he would shortly go on to lead). The Supreme Court slammed Strine for inserting a lengthy digression—an eleven-page rumination on limited liability companies—into his written opinion on a case that was actually about a golf course on Long Island in New York State. "The court's excursus on this issue strayed beyond the proper purview and function of a judicial opinion," the Supreme Court wrote. "We remind Delaware judges that the obligation to write judicial opinions on the issues presented is not a license to use those opinions as a platform from which to propagate their individual world views on issues not presented."[23]

Strine's distractable style was on full display in another 2012 case, a dispute between Tory Burch, the high-end fashion designer, and the ex-husband she had divorced five years earlier, Christopher. As the two sides discussed scheduling, Strine chimed in, "I didn't see any reason to burden anyone's Chanukah, New Year's, Christmas, Kwanzaa, Festivus with this preppy clothing dispute." The judge then wondered out loud why he appeared to be assigned all the cases involving preppy clothes, since he had recently presided over a case about J. Crew, the clothing retailer. That prompted a Strine digression on rain-appropriate footwear. "What's a duck shoe?" he asked. "You see all these freaks wearing this really ugly—I like LL Bean, but those duck shoes are ugly. I mean, there's no way around it." His meditation soon meandered into the general subject of shoes, as Strine recalled his confusion over his son's recent purchase of a pair of Top-Siders. "I'm like, what is this?" he recounted. "I mean, you know, how do you actually want to wear these things?" The hearing got back on track, but Strine's mind once again began to wander. He quizzed one of the lawyers in the case on Ralph Lauren's original surname, Lifschitz. The judge's thoughts then turned to culture in general. He told the hearing he was deep in "an autumnal Cheever phase," referring to the short-story writer John Cheever, the so-called Chekhov of the Suburbs. He urged the lawyers to read Cheever, to go and see the Broadway revival of Edward Albee's *Who's Afraid of Virginia Woolf?*, and to watch *Mad Men*, the TV series about New York advertising in the 1960s, the days of three-martini lunches. "We'll be all geared up and in the mood for this sort of drunken WASP fest," Strine said, which prompted him to start wondering about the litigants' religions. "Are the Burches WASPs?" he asked. Robert Isen, Tory Burch's chief legal officer, responded that his client was Jewish but her ex-husband was not. No matter, Strine's mind was already moving on. "But not Jewish doesn't make you a WASP, because it could make you an equally excluded faith like Catholic, right?" he continued. "I mean, that's not a WASP. You know, a WASP is a WASP."[24]

While such tangential musings were uniquely Strinean, they paint a picture of a system that is chummy and clubby, in which corporate experts debate technocratic details and individual judges decide on their own the judgments in cases on which billions of dollars depend and which set precedents for the responsibilities of corporate leaders across the United States and beyond. The perspectives of these individuals are untroubled by other judges, or by juries. For litigants, it's critical to get the "right" judge for the case. Corporations love the Chancery Court system's lack of a jury, comforted by the fact that ordinary men and women will have no say in the legal process.

The lack of a jury is just one way in which the Chancery Court avoids transparency. Unlike judges in some states, members of the Chancery Court are not elected. (Of course, systems in which judges are elected are replete with their own problems and do not tend to lead to more optimal judicial decisions.) Instead, Delaware's governor nominates the chancellor and vice chancellors, whom the state Senate confirms for twelve-year terms. The judges select which cases they wish to hear, and aren't required to disclose any conflicts of interest, or any income they receive outside their judicial salaries.

The other similarity between the way the Chancery Court operates and the way Delaware's corporate code gets written is that the rules are designed with the particular benefits, interests, and requirements of Delaware in mind. For one thing, each judge on the Chancery Court must be a Delaware citizen. The court has to be balanced in a highly political way. Delaware's constitution requires that the court should have an equal number of judges from the two main political parties. It obliges the governor to replace a retiring judge with another from the same political party. David Finger, a Delaware lawyer who challenged the rule in 2019, observed that this was a recipe for "political horsetrading" in the allocation of judicial seats, rather than finding and appointing the absolute best person available.[25] Finger's client, the retired attorney James Adams, sued Delaware's governor, John Carney, arguing that he was barred from joining the First State's judiciary, even if he were a "perfect candidate" supported by the governor and the legislature. "You cannot discriminate in public employment based on political affiliation," Finger noted. "But there's an exception for those who help the executive, be that the president, or governor, or mayor, implement policy."[26] In 2019, a federal court ruled against Carney, saying the political-balance rule violated the First Amendment of the US Constitution. The following year, the US Supreme Court ruled against Adams, but in a narrow way—determining that he had not shown that he was "able and ready" to apply for a Delaware judgeship, and so did not have a legal right to sue—without commenting on the merits of his actual case.[27]

Delaware's Chancery Court judges have gone far beyond their purely legal role, at times joining Delaware's powerful marketing efforts, promoting the First State and its incorporation system to companies in the United States and around the world. As Stuart Grant, one of Delaware's most prominent lawyers, told the *Financial Times* in 2018, "One of the things about Delaware—and I have some qualms about it—is that our judiciary considers themselves ambassadors for Delaware, unlike any other judiciary.... They'd have these junkets to talk about why Delaware law is so great, why the Delaware judiciary is great. And as part of that they'd spend a lot of time also at conferences, the overwhelming majority of which were sponsored by Corporate America and its lawyers."[28]

William Cary had observed the same thing back in 1974, drawing a contrast between the federal system and the murkier domains that governed in Delaware:

> The question arises why the federal courts should approach corporate standards in one way and the Delaware courts in an almost diametrically different way. It could be a difference in the interpretation of public policy or it could be that the federal courts have a tradition of independence and impartiality—freedom from a constrictive state policy. The fact is that these judges are chosen to serve for life and are not serving any constituency. Typically they do not resign to return to private practice and they would not entertain any feelings of disloyalty even if they were aware that their state or region would suffer by their judgments.[29]

But Stuart Grant, who has been observing Delaware's corporate law scene firsthand since moving to the state in the late 1980s, thinks things got worse following the 2007 to 2010 financial crisis, whose impact on Delaware's banking sector prompted the state's establishment to place its trust in a steadier flow of fees from business formation.

One incident provided a perfect example of how Delaware's judges are so heavily invested in providing revenues to the state while also playing to the corporate desire for secrecy. This was the Chancery Court's brief attempt to get into private arbitration in corporate disputes after the Delaware legislature enacted a 2009 bill to allow the Chancery Court to do so confidentially.

There were two main advantages to confidential private arbitration of business disputes. First, it provided companies with a way to settle corporate disputes away from the eyes of their shareholders, consumers, and clients, reducing the risk of class-action lawsuits that big court cases can draw. Secrecy was attractive since a "lot of people do business together and may not want to air their dirty linen in public, so to speak," observed Francis Pileggi, the prominent Delaware lawyer and blogger we met in the last chapter.[30] Arbitration also promised to generate healthy revenues for the State of Delaware. Those choosing to go to arbitration first had to pay a $12,000 filing fee and then a daily arbitration cost of $6,000. Although that was a lot of money for Delaware, it was often a very reasonable price tag for the companies involved, compared to the cost of corporate litigation. A broader aim, as the legislation itself noted, was "to preserve Delaware's pre-eminence in offering cost-effective options for resolving disputes, particularly those involving commercial, corporate, and technology matters."[31] Arbitration, then, would make Delaware even more attractive as the home of corporate disputes by offering a cheap and secretive legal service, provided by the very Chancery Court judges whose courts litigants were avoiding.

The system might have worked beautifully if not for the Delaware Coalition for Open Government, a local nonprofit that promotes government transparency and accountability. The group sued, claiming the arbitrations violated the First Amendment, which requires the public to have qualified access to civil and criminal trials. The federal courts upheld the challenge, killing Delaware's attempt to sell secrecy for a low price. "It's one thing for a dispute by two companies over a joint venture in a foreign country to arbitrate the dispute. And it makes sense for Delaware judges to be picked for this task," observed Steven Davidoff Solomon, a University of California, Berkeley law professor. "But when it is a dispute that directly implicates third parties like shareholders, the arbitration provision may go a bit too far."[32]

Delaware may have been stymied, but it had unwittingly revealed its instincts for self-enrichment and aversion to transparency—the very instincts at the heart of the Delaware Way.

10

Uncle Dupie

Joe Biden prides himself on being a centrist—the kind of guy who could take the Delaware Way to Capitol Hill and do deals across the aisle in the US Senate. But at times in his long Senate career, Biden also acted as something of a lobbyist for lenders against the interests of vulnerable borrowers, reflecting the interests of the financial sector and the predatory lenders who had been drawn to Delaware. "I spent most of my career representing the corporate state of Delaware," the president noted in 2021—or the "corporate whore state," as one former Biden staffer described it to *Harper's Magazine* two years earlier.[1]

Thanks to the 1981 Financial Center Development Act that we discussed in chapter 4, eleven big banks opened subsidiaries in Delaware by 1984, and eighteen money center and regional banks had set up Delaware holding companies by 1987.[2] By the 1990s, four of the five biggest US credit card issuers had relocated to Wilmington. Biden proved adept at using congressional procedures to protect them. In 1991, he voted in favor of an amendment to impose a cap on credit card interest rates, but as he explained on the Senate floor, he only did so because "I hoped it would kill this bill." The strategy worked: the bill died.

When he first entered the Senate, Biden was junior partner to Delaware's long-serving Republican senator William Roth, a fiscal

conservative who championed Reagan-era tax cuts and whose enduring legacy is the Roth IRA, a tax-advantaged individual retirement
account. Senators Biden and Roth worked together to defeat proposals to reduce how much time credit card companies would have
to collect debts from consumers.[3] The Delawarean duo thus ensured
that lenders could continue to hound borrowers for repayment.

In 1999, Roth and Biden again joined together to support the
Financial Services Modernization Act, which repealed Glass-
Steagall, the 1933 law that separated commercial and investment
banking. The change prompted massive bank consolidation and the
creation of "too big to fail" financial institutions. During the 2008
presidential election campaign, Barack Obama, with Biden as his
running mate, traced the origins of the 2008 financial crisis to the
1999 law. Biden would come to consider it his only Senate vote that
he regretted in a thirty-six-year Senate career, attributing his decision to his support for the financial sector. "I did it out of loyalty, and
I wasn't aware that it was gonna be as bad as it was," he said in 2014.[4]

By the time Biden became president in 2021, student loan debt
had become a national crisis. But many felt that Biden's voting record had helped to create that crisis, in part by removing bankruptcy
protection from those struggling under the burden of student loans,
a measure spurred by several high-profile cases of wealthy people
abusing the system. In 1978, Biden helped write a bill blocking
students from seeking bankruptcy protections on their loans after
graduating. In 1984, he worked to remove those protections for borrowers with loans for vocational colleges.

All this—and the 1990 Crime Control Act, which Biden sponsored, and which further restricted debtors' access to bankruptcy
protections—was merely a prelude to the Delaware senator's main
act for the credit card issuers: fundamental bankruptcy reform, a
cause that Biden took up in the late 1990s.

In 1999, the senator cosponsored the Bankruptcy Reform Act,
a bill that met fierce opposition from consumer groups, which
argued that the bill added so much paperwork to the process that
people who qualified for bankruptcy protection would need to hire
lawyers to steer them through the process. Congress passed the bill

the following year, but President Bill Clinton refused to sign it. He had apparently been influenced by Hillary Clinton, the First Lady and future US senator, who had been briefed on its shortcomings by another future US senator, Elizabeth Warren, then a Harvard Law professor.[5] Undeterred by President Clinton's veto, Biden continued to push the legislation, and Warren continued to call him out for it. "His energetic work on behalf of the credit card companies has earned him the affection of the banking industry and protected him from any well-funded challengers for his Senate seat," Warren wrote of Biden in 2002. "This important part of Senator Biden's legislative work also appears to be missing from his Web site and publicity releases."[6] When the two were running against each other for the 2020 Democratic presidential nomination, Warren often brought up the issue to attack Biden.

The legislation finally passed in 2005 and President George W. Bush signed it into law. Biden and his junior Senate partner from Delaware, Tom Carper (who had defeated Roth in the 2000 election), had been critical to its success. Orrin Hatch, the Utah Republican who had helped drive the bill, praised the pair, saying they had "worked tirelessly for years on this legislation, and they have taken some tough votes to get it done."[7] Elizabeth Warren agreed on that point, at least. "Senator Biden was twisting arms to get the bankruptcy bill through Congress," she noted at the time.[8]

The 2005 bill was able to pass because the Republicans had control of the Senate. Biden was not the only Democrat to support it—seventeen of his colleagues also did so, including his future boss, Barack Obama. But Biden and Obama found themselves on opposite sides when the senator from Delaware helped to defeat amendments that aimed to protect people who had been forced into bankruptcy because of large medical debts, as well as those serving in the military.

Biden did help to include some protections in the final version, which prioritized alimony and child-support payments above credit card bills in bankruptcy proceedings. The bill set out new disclosure requirements for credit card solicitations. There was an exemption for bankruptcy filers who took home less than their state's median income. The bill capped how much real estate rich debtors could hide from creditors.

But taken as a whole, the bill made it harder for consumers and students to qualify for traditional "clean slate" Chapter 7 bankruptcy, which would have forgiven their debts, and pushed them instead toward Chapter 13 bankruptcy, which puts debtors on payment plans under which their future income goes to paying back their creditors. Clearly, creditors prefer Chapter 13 to Chapter 7 (and consumers prefer Chapter 7 to Chapter 13).

Officially, a key justification Biden put forward was that the bankruptcy system was subject to widespread abuse. "An awful lot of people are discharging debt who shouldn't," he told a 2001 hearing.[9] But aside from media anecdotes, there was little solid evidence that the system was being widely misused by consumers.

One key backer for Biden's position was MBNA, a bank holding company headquartered in Wilmington, whose employees as a group made up Biden's biggest source of political contributions at the time. MBNA was one of the many success stories to spring from Delaware's 1981 Financial Center Development Act. The company had started as a unit of the Maryland National Bank, a financial institution that started in Baltimore in the early twentieth century. In the early 1980s, it unsuccessfully lobbied the Maryland legislature to allow higher interest rates on credit cards. Spurning its heritage, the bank spun off its credit card business and moved it to Delaware.

Over the next twenty years, MBNA transformed itself from a credit unit lopped off a financial grandee to a financial giant that dwarfed its ancestor. It began in 1982 with a five-person team operating out of a derelict former A&P supermarket in Ogletown, Delaware, on the outskirts of Newark, and grew rapidly to become the world's largest independent credit card issuer, based in palatial offices in more happening Wilmington that seated thirteen thousand employees. In 1991, MBNA became the first stand-alone credit card issuer to float on the New York Stock Exchange.

The man who drove this transformation was Charles Cawley, an old-school business tycoon whose vision was to turn MBNA into "the LL Bean of financial services companies."[10] A key part of

Cawley's strategy was to issue "affinity cards," branded credit cards for different groups. Fans of sports teams could have a credit card with their beloved team's logo. University alumni could use cards featuring their alma mater's branding. Charities and professional associations had their own affinity cards. There was even a special credit card for Frank Sinatra fans.

Cawley treated MBNA like an extension of his own colorful personality. He had the MBNA's offices decked out in a color scheme of Kelly green and tan. A lover of antique automobiles, he had the company buy a series of expensive vintage cars, including a Duesenberg, which took pride of place in its lobby. Under Cawley's guidance, MBNA also purchased a fleet of Gulfstream jets, helicopters, and yachts. Another of Cawley's big passions was art. He was particularly fond of Andrew Wyeth, the American realist painter, and once used $3.5 million of MBNA's money to buy an original painting directly from the artist.[11]

Keen to keep Washington on his side, Cawley also cultivated Joe Biden, who had been the state's senator since 1973. The Bidens flew on an MBNA-owned jet in 1997 to Maine, where Biden was speaking at an MBNA management conference, an annual jamboree with a price tag of more than $1 million, which always culminated in an address by a high-profile keynote speaker.[12] And when Biden became vice president, Cawley lent him an Andrew Wyeth painting from his personal collection to hang in Biden's official residence.[13] The ties between Biden and the credit card issuer were so strong that journalists teased the senator that he was "(D-MBNA)"—representing the financial institution first and foremost.[14] It struck a nerve. "I'm not the senator from MBNA," Biden retorted to the *Washington Post* in 1999.[15] But Joseph Pika, a former University of Delaware professor and longtime Biden watcher, pointed to how the state and the lender's motivations had become intertwined. "He was representing the interests of his state, which is one of the responsibilities of anybody elected to Congress," Pika observed.[16]

There was nothing particularly new in Delaware's particularly close connection between business and government. In 1973—the year Joe Biden entered the US Senate—Ralph Nader, the consumer activist, described in *The Company State* how DuPont dominated Delaware's politics, economics, and society to a larger extent than other businesses did in other states. At the time, DuPont employed one-quarter of the representatives in the state's part-time legislature and 10 percent of the state's workforce.[17] The chemicals giant was so influential that it was referred to locally as simply "the Company" or, more tenderly, "Uncle Dupie."[18]

As Nader described the buildings flanking Wilmington's Rodney Square, of course, he began with the most imposing edifice: the historic Hotel du Pont, which as well as being a hotel, also housed the DuPont theater and DuPont's corporate headquarters. Next door to that was a bank the du Pont family controlled. The du Ponts owned the state's two largest newspapers. The governor was a former DuPont executive. Delaware's member of Congress was Pierre Samuel du Pont IV. "General Motors could buy Delaware," Nader wrote, "if DuPont were willing to sell it."[19]

Pete du Pont's governorship showed that the name still wielded considerable influence nearly a decade after *The Company State* was published. By that point, the Company had begun a steady decline in presence and power in Delaware. Over the years, DuPont slashed its workforce, moved out of its historic headquarters, and ceded dominance to the financial industry. But what persisted was the same unique nexus between government and business that Nader had described. One of the main heirs was MBNA, which by 2002 had become the First State's biggest private employer.[20] The lender even bought up a string of old DuPont properties in Delaware, including office buildings and golf courses.

Apart from his own close ties to the credit card issuer and to Charles Cawley, Biden was also sensitive about the subject because in 1996, his son Hunter had been hired by MBNA straight out of Yale Law School and then landed an annual $100,000 consulting gig for the company. At the time, MBNA's biggest issue was promoting bankruptcy reform, although Joe Biden has stressed that Hunter was not a registered lobbyist and did not lobby on legislation for the company.

Bank of America bought MBNA in 2005, the same year the bank-ruptcy bill passed, but Biden was unable to shake the episode and the sense that a bank had bought his loyalty. In 2008, the aides to then presidential candidate Barack Obama who were charged with vetting potential running mates reportedly identified Biden's links to MBNA as his most sensitive issue.[21] In 2019, as Biden was mak-ing his own run for the White House, he was still forced to insist that his views had not been shaped by contributions. Even if they had turned against him, "MBNA could not beat me," he recalled.[22] He said he became involved in bankruptcy reform because it was going to pass anyway and he was trying to make it more consumer friendly.

But despite Biden's contention that he had softened the worst aspects of the law, its effect was decidedly one-sided. The legislation saved credit card companies billions of dollars, but their custom-ers' costs went up by 5 to 17 percent because of higher rates and late fees, according to one 2009 study.[23] A 2020 study found that the law actually did help reduce credit card interest rates by cutting the number of bankruptcy filings, but concluded that the legislation made it much harder for uninsured people with huge medical bills to declare bankruptcy.[24] In 2007, the year that observers first began to flag the danger of subprime mortgages—which would ultimately become the catalyst for the financial crisis of 2008 and the Great Recession—Credit Suisse reported that the 2005 law meant that sub-prime borrowers were now more likely to fail to stick to their bank-ruptcy payment plans, making the whole sector riskier.[25] The law caused an additional twenty-nine thousand foreclosures every three months—home losses that would not have happened had the bill not been enacted, according to a 2012 paper by Donald P. Morgan of the Federal Reserve Bank of New York, Benjamin Charles Iverson of Brigham Young University, and Matthew J. Botsch of Bowdoin Col-lege.[26] Prime defaults increased by 23 percent and subprime defaults by 14 percent after the bill became law, adding to the severity of the subsequent mortgage crisis.[27] The drop in bankruptcy filings that the bill prompted was mainly accounted for by poor people, who could no longer afford the increased cost of the bankruptcy process; wealthy people continued to file for bankruptcy at the same rate.[28]

Carper, who became the senior senator from Delaware when Biden became vice president, was an even more strident supporter of the financial industry than his former colleague had been. As a member of Congress with a seat on the House Banking Committee from 1983 to 1992, Carper had publicly pushed against credit card interest-rate caps, supported the repeal of Glass-Steagall, and urged the Federal Reserve to allow banks to enter the securities business, which sparked the growth in short-term shadow banking and helped lead to the 2007 financial crisis. When Carper, following a stint in Delaware's governor's mansion, was elected to the Senate in 2000, *American Banker* noted, "Financial services executives are finding comfort in the return to Washington of an old friend."[29]

Whereas Biden had tried to distance himself from MBNA, the credit card issuer praised Carper as "a steady supporter of the banking industry because the industry plays a big role in the state."[30] Carper cosponsored the 2005 bankruptcy bill and voted against several amendments that Biden had supported. These amendments had aimed to close loopholes for trusts that wealthy people used to hide their assets; to curb predatory lending; and to keep bankruptcy protection for caregivers, victims of identity fraud, and people with serious medical problems. Carper fought hard to represent the interests of the financial sector following the 2008 financial crisis. During negotiations on the 2010 Dodd-Frank Act, a package aimed at improving accountability and limiting the financial industry's excesses, he championed a clause that enabled the Office of the Comptroller of the Currency to preempt state consumer protection laws on nationally chartered banks—even overcoming resistance from the Obama White House on the issue. In 2014 and 2018, Carper joined Republicans to roll back key sections of Dodd-Frank, loosening restrictions, oversight, and disclosure requirements on the banks. Kamala Harris, the California senator who became Biden's vice president, was among those who voted against.

Delaware's 1981 legislation, which brought the big banks to Delaware, had been a fascinating case study in the Delaware Way and its effects. The support of Delaware's representatives in Congress projected the implications onto the national stage. When it comes to business, what happens in Delaware rarely stays there. The First State's corporate code is the United States' corporate code. Delaware's desire to attract financial services jobs helped companies bypass interest-rate caps elsewhere. The First State harms other states' finances by enabling tax dodging by corporations and wealthy individuals, and through its muscular pursuit of unclaimed property. Biden's and Carper's support for financial lenders had an outsized influence on financial policymaking and harmed consumers— especially the poor and vulnerable.

The Delaware Way made preservation of the Franchise and the role of Delaware as a financial center a top priority of policymaking in the First State. And in pursuit of that end, Delaware welcomed not only the wealthy and the powerful to operate in its jurisdiction, but also much more sinister individuals and organizations, who would cause untold damage around the world.

———

We know that Michael Cohen, Donald Trump's former lawyer, established a Delaware corporation to try to pay adult movie star Stormy Daniels to keep quiet about her alleged affair with the future president years after the fact. We know it because Cohen put his name on the paperwork to set up the shell company, Essential Consultants LLC. But had he checked the rules, Cohen might not have put his name on the documents. Delaware rules do not require the owners of companies to be identified. A more diligent lawyer than Cohen might well have left the LLC anonymous.

It's anonymity that traditionally made Delaware shell companies (and shell companies in most other US states) potentially so dangerous. Big corporations that list their shares on stock exchanges have always had to disclose a huge amount of information to regulators such as the Securities and Exchange Commission, to the exchanges that list their shares, and to shareholders. But these "C corps" have long been vastly outnumbered in Delaware by LLCs, which traditionally enjoyed the ultimate in corporate privacy: they did not identify their true owners, nor include any names of people involved in the new company on the forms of incorporation, which could be filed on behalf of the new company by a registered Delaware agent, who could put their own name and address on the forms.

It was not until 2021 that the US Congress acted decisively to address corporate anonymity, thirty-two years after Washington first pledged to collect information on who controls shell companies as part of the original FATF statement. On New Year's Day 2021, a few weeks before Joe Biden was sworn in as president, the United States passed the Corporate Transparency Act, which promised finally to bring the United States closer to other jurisdictions such as the European Union and the United Kingdom in creating a register of names of the people who actually control businesses registered in US states. The law will require businesses to supply the names of their owners to the US Treasury by 2023. (At the time of writing, the final rules are still being written.)

To be fair to Delaware, while Congress sat on its hands, the First State took several tentative steps toward transparency, but they were weak. In 2014, Delaware required registering agents (but not the Division of Corporations) to have a contact for someone—not necessarily one of the corporation's owners—who could act as a "contact person" for the owners. This effectively ordered agents to get the name of a guy who knew a guy who knew something about the corporation. The first person in this chain not only did not need to be formally connected to the corporation, they also did not need to reside in the United States, or even be a US citizen. In practice, it added another potential wall of secrecy between the beneficial owners and law enforcement.

In 2019, Delaware also started requiring agents to check the names of their clients against a US Treasury list of individuals and groups prohibited from conducting business in the United States. (As we saw in chapter 5, this was a rule first proposed by John Kowalko— only to be dismissed because it failed to follow "the process.") Doing a quick check that your clients are not internationally wanted criminals might seem like a pretty elementary step, but Jeffrey Bullock, the Delaware secretary of state, boasted that this measure would "deny access to those who attempt to use Delaware entities for nefarious purposes."[31] That seemed like a stretch: the agents were not actually required to verify their clients' identification, only to check it against the Treasury list. What's more, Delaware agents were not required to ask the names of anyone else associated with a corporation—its officers, directors, or members.[32] The State of Delaware gave agents no guidance as to how agents should check the Treasury lists, other than saying they could do so manually or using software. It specified no fines for failing to conduct such checks. Given that at least some agents in Delaware are small, mom-and-pop shops, that many businesses registered in the state are based overseas, and that shell companies have often been used to conduct international dirty business, the measure seemed a less-than-robust way to safeguard US national security.

In 2020, Delaware struck a long-overdue agreement with the US Treasury Department's Office of Foreign Assets Control to encourage information sharing and coordination on investigations, particularly in relation to attempts to evade US sanctions.[33]

Delaware officials always claimed that anonymity didn't help it get business. But at the same time, by adamantly stating that if it changed the system unilaterally, business might move to one of the other many states that provide corporate anonymity, the First State suggested that secrecy was at least one of the attractions.

Secrecy was certainly touted by the state's leading incorporating agents. "The privacy afforded to owners of Delaware corporations and LLCs is . . . incomparable," stated Harvard Business Services, one of the biggest agents. "The state of Delaware allows you to file your company without listing the names of the owners, which protects the owners' identities, personal information and privacy in general."[34] (As we'll discuss, even with the new registry in place, individual states will still not require businesses to identify their owners, although the US federal government will.)

The notion that Delaware did not sell secrecy is plainly disingenuous. A prime example is in real estate: many wealthy individuals have formed LLCs in Delaware to purchase real estate, precisely to avoid publicity. Many of these business dealings are legitimate. But the lack of transparency has undoubtedly attracted odious actors.

We touched on one such case in the introduction: a multibillion-dollar theft of Malaysian public funds that used eight Delaware companies to help launder the money. The scheme was cooked up by senior government employees working for 1MDB, a state-owned investment fund that Malaysian prime minister Najib Razak launched in 2009 with the aim of promoting economic development in a country where the median monthly paycheck is about $530.[35] Over six years, they and their associates stole more than $3.5 billion from the fund.[36]

The money was funneled through a complex web of shell companies in locations including Singapore and Switzerland, but about $1 billion of it was laundered through the United States, according to the US federal government. The perpetrators used the money to buy a $35 million jet, paintings by Vincent van Gogh and Claude Monet, and a stake in the publishing rights of EMI Music.

They funneled at least $64 million through a Delaware LLC to fund the production of the 2013 film *The Wolf of Wall Street*. The movie, directed by Martin Scorsese and starring Leonardo DiCaprio, covers the story of Jordan Belfort, a fraudster stockbroker who was indicted for securities fraud and money laundering in 1999 and served twenty-two months in jail. The irony was not lost on federal investigators, who launched a bid in 2016 to recover more than $1 billion of the stolen 1MDB money. "This is a case where life imitated art," said Assistant Attorney General Leslie Caldwell.[37] While the Hollywood angle caught the headlines, some of the 1MDB money was also used to purchase high-end real estate and hotels in Beverly Hills, New York, and London.[38]

The very thing that makes Delaware so attractive to wealthy individuals who want to keep their private affairs private has also traditionally made it attractive to the unethical individuals who want the same thing. That has been the cost of corporate anonymity.

11

In Good Standing

Delaware is to business formation what Facebook is to social media.

Facebook (or Meta, as the company renamed itself in 2021) allows people to set up profiles and to post and interact with content. In much the same way, Delaware allows companies to register themselves as legal entities and do business. Both have argued that what is good for them—facilitating online interactions, or providing dependable business services—is good for the world. Both portray themselves as enabling organizations, which help others to do what they want to do easily and efficiently. Both have been reluctant to police the behavior of those who use their services, until scandal has forced them to embrace the idea of enhanced oversight.

Before about 2014, Facebook was chiefly thought of as a way for individuals to connect with friends, find like-minded groups of people, brag about losing weight, display their cookie-making prowess, or share cute animal videos. But the company was widely criticized that year when it turned out to have conducted a psychology experiment on seven hundred thousand of its users without their awareness or informed consent.[1] "Our goal was never to upset anyone," one of the researchers said. "In hindsight, the research benefits of the paper may not have justified all of this anxiety."[2]

In the wake of the 2016 US presidential election and the United Kingdom's Brexit referendum earlier that year, Facebook's public reputation took a darker turn. It emerged that Cambridge Analytica, a political data-gathering firm (whose US operation was registered in Delaware), had gained access to private information on more than fifty million Facebook users, of whom only about 270,000 had consented. The firm had been using personal data to target political advertising on Facebook. One of Cambridge Analytica's clients was Donald Trump's election campaign (which was briefly run, as it happens, by Paul Manafort, not a stranger to the world of Delaware business incorporations). Another was the campaign team of Trump's rival for the Republican presidential nomination, Ted Cruz, a US senator from Texas. In the United Kingdom, a client was the Leave.EU group, led by Trump's British chum Nigel Farage, former head of the UK Independence Party, a fringe nationalist grouping. Cambridge Analytica was also tied to Vote Leave, the mainstream campaign for Brexit. In addition to the interventions by Cambridge Analytica, Facebook admitted to finding significant attempts by Russia to meddle in the US elections, saying content promoted by the Internet Research Agency, a Russian group tied to the Kremlin, had reached some 126 million Americans during the 2016 election.

When the news about Facebook's connection to Cambridge Analytica broke, Facebook shares plummeted 20 percent in a day, slashing $120 billion off its market value. Mark Zuckerberg, Facebook's founder, chairman, and CEO, was lambasted at congressional hearings, in some cases by lawmakers who clearly had little grasp of what Facebook was. Trillium Asset Management, an investment firm with a $10 million stake in Facebook, proposed that Zuckerberg be fired as the company's chairman.

Facebook responded by deleting pages and hiring a public relations firm to produce warm and fuzzy promotional videos and undermine its critics. Sheryl Sandberg, Facebook's chief operating officer, also asked staff to dig into George Soros's financial interests, after the polarizing hedge fund billionaire described the social media company as a "menace" to society and called for it to be regulated.

In March 2018, Alex Stamos, Facebook's outgoing head of security, sent an internal memo urging the company to take more responsibility for what appeared on the platform. "We need to be willing to pick sides when there are clear moral or humanitarian issues," Stamos wrote.[3]

But Facebook resisted the notion that it should take a fundamental look at its business model or that it should actively regulate the content on its platform, like a traditional publisher would. To many, this suggested that Facebook was essentially in denial about how it was used. As the *Financial Times* (my former employer) argued in December 2018, "The platform does not intentionally cause harm to users. Too often, however, Facebook's business model allows harm to occur."[4] That assessment may have been too generous: in 2021, whistleblower Frances Haugen, a former Facebook data scientist, claimed that the company had kept secret research showing that its platforms (including Instagram) increased suicidal thoughts and eating disorders among teenage girls, undermined democracy, and fanned ethnic violence.

It was not really until 2020—during the height of the COVID-19 pandemic and a scorched-earth US presidential election, both of which amplified conspiracy theories, misinformation, and downright lies—that Facebook bowed to relentless pressure to change its policies and tighten the boundaries around free speech on its platform. By 2021, Facebook was publicly calling for Washington to pass comprehensive laws on internet regulation.

Delaware's story is remarkably similar. The state has never deliberately crafted its business-formation industry with the aim of attracting hitmen, child-sex traffickers, and international criminals. But their existence and associated problems have long been documented, and Delaware historically showed little appetite for root-and-branch reform to get rid of them. It changed the system over the years, but only incrementally, and usually in response to scandals. Delaware always argued that the scandals were caused by the proverbial few bad apples. Just as Facebook is not the only online platform where objectionable material appears, so Delaware can point to disreputable activity in other states. But, like Facebook, what's different is the scale. While Delaware is not unique, it's by far the biggest center for out-of-state business formations. That enables unscrupulous actors to hide amid a sea of registered businesses. If you want to set up an organization for some sketchy end, Delaware has traditionally been a good place to avoid unwanted attention.

As well as the ability to bury oneself in a mound of business entitics, Delaware has also traditionally offered nefarious actors a comforting lack of transparency. Until the law changed in 2021, an LLC registering in Delaware, as in many states, was not obliged to state the names of the actual owners of the company. That allowed many unlawful and undesirable activities to funnel money through Delaware undetected. Delaware officials always maintained that the scandalous cases that were uncovered proved that wrongdoing could not go unexposed for long. But that would have meant that the cases that made the headlines accounted for *all* the misconduct carried out through Delaware. Is it really plausible that every time someone has tried to launder money through Delaware, or set up a company there with illicit or odious ends, their actions came to light? Did *no one* get away with *anything*? That stretches credulity.

As the state with the biggest interest in the issue, Delaware fought tooth and nail against forcing more transparency on US-based companies, until scandal after scandal changed its mind. Even then, the law it agreed to back only partially improved transparency and left open loopholes of corporate anonymity.

———

Red flags about the United States' vulnerability to money laundering and terrorist financing were first raised in the late 1970s. Yet the first "beneficial ownership" registry—identifying the true owners of US-registered companies—will be created only in 2023. Why did it take more than forty years for the United States to address the problem seriously?

One reason may be simply that too many powerful business interests, wealthy individuals, and influential politicians were entangled in the system and stood to lose from greater transparency.

In April 2016, Republican presidential hopeful Donald Trump held a rally at the Delaware State Fairgrounds as part of his presidential campaign. "I've known Delaware for a long time," Trump boasted to the crowd. "It's a great place and we're going to get rid of all of the bad stuff." In an attempt to highlight his love of the state, Trump told the crowd that he had recently asked his staff to find out how many entities he had registered in Delaware. "I figured they'd maybe say two or three, right?" Trump said. "We have 378 entities registered in the state of Delaware, meaning I pay you a lot of money, folks. I don't feel at all guilty, OK?"[5]

Trump's Federal Election Commission filing revealed that the 378 Delaware-registered businesses were out of a total of 515 companies the future president owned. His Delaware-registered entities included 40 Wall Street Corporation, the Trump Carousel in Central Park, and Hudson Waterfront Associates, a Trump partnership to develop more than $1 billion worth of luxury condos on the west side of Manhattan.

Hillary Clinton, Trump's 2016 Democratic challenger, had her own ties to the First State. Eight days after stepping down as US secretary of state in February 2013, she registered a holding company in Delaware through which she earned more than $16 million in public speaking fees and book royalties in 2014 alone. A campaign spokesman stressed that "no federal, state, or local taxes were saved by the Clintons as a result of this structure."[6] The candidate was following a tradition begun by her husband, former president Bill Clinton, who had set up his own Delaware-registered corporation in 2008 to collect consulting fees. Meanwhile, the Clinton Foundation operated three Delaware shell companies. And, of course, Trump and the Clintons are only three examples among a wide range of politicians who choose to set up political or business vehicles in Delaware, despite having no connection to the state. Political campaign organizations that form out-of-state entities typically do so in Delaware.[7] Even US representative Alexandria Ocasio-Cortez, the New York liberal Democrat who has campaigned fiercely for more transparency in campaign financing, has got tangled up in Delaware. Her chief of staff set up two political action committees that paid a company he ran—a Delaware LLC—more than $1 million in 2016 and 2017. Grilled about that on the conservative Fox News channel, Ocasio-Cortez could only say that there had been "no violation" of existing campaign finance laws.[8]

But in spite of these high-profile connections, these are not really the people who protected Delaware from efforts in Washington to shut down its secrecy peddling. Delaware didn't just sit back and wait for Congress to act against it. Over the years, the state and its representatives on Capitol Hill fought hard against legislation aimed at providing law enforcement officials with access to beneficial ownership information. On the state side, one person critical to this effort was Jeff Bullock, Delaware's appointed secretary of state. From his base in Dover, the sleepy Delawarean state capital, Bullock has exercised an outsize influence on US national politics that belies his folksy persona. On Capitol Hill, the state's US senators were instrumental—and one of them, for thirty-six years, was Joe Biden. Delaware is one of those small-population states whose national political clout comes mainly in the Senate. The state sends only one member to the US House of Representatives, whose state delegations are roughly proportional to their populations; California, the most populous US state, sends fifty-two, followed by Texas with thirty-eight. But like every other state, Delaware has two senators. Tom Carper, the senior of the First State's US senators, who was Biden's junior partner in the delegation for eight years, was particularly important in this regard. Carper and Bullock coordinated their efforts closely in their efforts to block greater transparency. Before he won his Senate seat in 2000, Carper had been governor of Delaware, and Bullock had been his chief of staff.[9]

To understand how Bullock and Carper worked together, you have to go back to 2006, when FATF, the group set up by the G7 to combat money laundering and terrorist financing, deemed the United States "non-compliant" with its anti–money laundering rules. FATF demanded that the United States enable federal authorities to obtain timely information about a company's real owners. Later that year, the US Government Accountability Office issued its report saying it was too easy for individuals to form companies anonymously, and it named Delaware as a favored destination for such companies.

Carl Levin, the then US senator from Michigan, took up the issue and pushed for a hearing before the Homeland Security Committee, where he served with Carper. The hearing was the opening salvo in what would become a multiyear tussle between the two Democrats over the issue. Levin and his ally in the House of Representatives, Carolyn Maloney of New York, repeatedly introduced bills to require states to collect beneficial ownership information at the point of business formation. Carper said that he understood the impulse to improve transparency, but pushed the idea that Levin's solution would be unduly burdensome on states, and that a federal agency—perhaps the Internal Revenue Service—should bear the costs instead.

In the 2006 hearing, in no uncertain terms, Levin laid out the case against Delaware and other states chasing business-formation revenue. "Our states have been competing with each other to set up new companies not only faster than ever, at less cost than ever, but with greater anonymity for the company's owners," Levin thundered. "The problem with incorporating nearly two million new US companies each year without knowing anything about who is behind them is that it becomes an open invitation for criminal abuse." The Michigan senator went on to display a website from a foreign incorporation company that was promoting "Delaware, an offshore tax haven for non-US residents."

Carper had invited Rick Geisenberger to testify. Geisenberger, then Delaware's assistant secretary of state and later its secretary of finance, started with a full-fledged assault on the idea of any form of collecting beneficial ownership information. If public companies were included, he said, it "would be a logistical and costly nightmare for corporate America." On the other hand, he noted, a registration system that excluded public companies "would have immense verification costs." Either way, Geisenberger continued, requiring companies to identify their true owners "would impose costs on legitimate private businesses that seem vast in relation to the benefits that are, at best, uncertain." He added that money launderers would likely get around the system by simply falsifying their identities. His biggest concern, Geisenberger said, was that Delaware's role would transform from "providing an attractive investment environment for domestic and international capital, one that values privacy, efficiency, and the ease of capital formation," to being forced to regulate millions of companies. Delaware, it seemed, was happy to enjoy the benefits of the Franchise, but reluctant to take any responsibility.

Unsurprisingly, Levin took exception to this opening gambit, and he and Geisenberger launched into a testy exchange. The senator pointed out that Massachusetts required corporate entities to maintain lists of shareholders, limited partners, or members, which law enforcement could access. Why, he wondered, was it not overly burdensome for Massachusetts, but it would be for Delaware? Because, Geisenberger responded, Delaware has more than five times as many new businesses registering in any year, and the cost would be oppressive. Besides, Geisenberger added, the benefits needed to be balanced against the interests of privacy and efficiency. "Don't they have those interests in Massachusetts?" Levin snapped back. Geisenberger began to respond, but Levin cut him off. "Let me tell you, they do," the senator continued, answering his own question. "They care just as much about their privacy and efficiency as people in Delaware or all over the world that use Delaware or Nevada or anyone else. There is no difference in terms of human beings wanting anonymity or privacy, but they just do not allow it in Massachusetts."[10]

In 2008, Levin introduced legislation to force states to collect information about the true owners of companies. The bill's other sponsors were Norm Coleman, a Republican from Minnesota, along with then senator Barack Obama, who would resign his seat later that year after he won the US presidential election. Their proposal had momentum: in 2009, the US Department of Justice, US Immigration and Customs Enforcement, and the Manhattan District Attorney's Office each testified on Capitol Hill that corporate secrecy was a growing problem that was hampering law enforcement.

Bullock, newly appointed as Delaware's secretary of state, set out to sink the legislation. He hired Peck Madigan Jones, a Washington lobbying firm, to work Capitol Hill on Delaware's behalf, becoming the only secretary of state in the United States with a taxpayer-funded lobbying firm.[11] (Bullock pointed out to me that unlike many other states, Delaware does not employ permanent staff on Capitol Hill, and so it hired lobbyists to represent the state on a wide range of issues.) But Bullock didn't depend solely on Peck Madigan Jones. He also marshalled the powerful National Association of Secretaries of State to his cause, writing a letter on the organization's behalf to FATF, calling its recommendations "impractical" and warning it against interfering with "the core principle of Constitutional state sovereignty."[12]

Meanwhile, Levin's bill languished in the Senate's Homeland Security and Government Affairs Committee, held up by objections from Carper, who was still arguing that states shouldn't be burdened with more work. Efforts to introduce greater transparency should not damage Delaware's "nurturing" business environment, he said. The bill died a slow death.

Bullock celebrated, bragging about how he had prevented the attempt at greater transparency. "With a hands-on approach, Secretary Bullock has led a coordinated effort to prevent passage of federal legislation that would jeopardize Delaware's unique position in corporate governance," his website proclaimed, a statement that was subsequently removed.[13] These days, Bullock is more modest, saying that lots of other secretaries of state felt the same way.

Levin tried again in 2011 with another bill, which President Obama's US Treasury Department endorsed. The bill required states to secure beneficial ownership information for companies formed within their borders and to give it to law enforcement if requested. Acknowledging Delaware's concerns about publicly traded companies, Levin's bill exempted those corporations, which already submit a great deal of information and whose ownership changes regularly as their stock is traded. But Carper also helped derail that effort, persuading Senator Joe Lieberman, the committee chairman from Connecticut, to prevent the bill from ever coming for a markup. Lieberman asked the senators to compromise on some kind of legislation, but they failed to agree, and that proposal too faded away.

Two years later, Levin tried one final time, avoiding the Homeland Security Committee—where Carper had now ascended to the chairmanship—and instead pushing his bill to the Judiciary

Committee, whose chairman was Patrick Leahy of Vermont. Bull-ock raised the issue at a meeting with other US secretaries of state, following which James Condos, Vermont's secretary of state, imme-diately wrote to Leahy to attack Levin's bill. Condos wrote that that legislation "would leave companies, especially small businesses, with additional costly and confusing layers of bureaucratic red tape."[14] It worked. The bill never made it out of the committee. Levin retired from the Senate in 2014 at eighty years of age, having lost his decade-long battle to bring more transparency to company ownership in the United States.

But not all was clear for Carper and Bullock. In the summer of 2013, leaders of the Group of Eight industrialized countries met in Northern Ireland and issued a statement demanding that its mem-bers curb anonymous shell companies. President Obama—backed by Delaware's longest-serving champion in Washington, Vice Presi-dent Biden—quickly followed up by calling on the US Treasury and other federal agencies to support measures for greater transparency. Clearly, Bullock and Carper needed to stop blocking others' propos-als and start making proposals of their own. Among the secretaries of state, Bullock put forward a plan that relied on the information that the Internal Revenue Service collects from companies. This enabled Bullock to proclaim that he was the only secretary of state in the United States who was actively trying to do away with corporate anonymity, noting that he was doing so in a way that could draw bipartisan support—ignoring that at least some of Levin's proposals had been backed by Republicans such as Coleman. In fact, Bullock's plan appeared to be set up to fail. The IRS has historically restricted the information it provides to law enforcement and it doesn't collect beneficial ownership information—only the names of "responsible parties," who might not be the actual company owners.

In 2014, a group of international business leaders, including Vir-gin boss Richard Branson, HuffPost founder Arianna Huffington, and Unilever CEO Paul Polman, wrote an open letter to the Group of Twenty organization of the world's most powerful governments and central banks, demanding a crackdown on shell companies and corporate anonymity. Looking to burnish their reputations, more and more global companies joined the call for transparency, arguing that knowing who you are dealing with is just good business.

Feeling the heat, Delaware took the very timid step of requiring LLCs to provide the name and telephone number of a person who has access to a list of the names and last known addresses of each of its members and managers. But there was a big loophole: these could themselves be other companies with hidden ownerships or nominees. Watchdog groups such as Global Witness decried the measure as little more than "window dressing" that would do little to stop criminals and other nefarious actors from using Delaware companies for malign ends. Clark Gascoigne of the Financial Accountability and Corporate Transparency Coalition called the requirement "a roundabout way of still shielding who actually owned the company."[15]

By 2016, pressure to act had grown more intense as news about international money laundering, tax dodging, and other sketchy uses of shell companies came thick and fast. The TV show *60 Minutes* aired an investigation by Global Witness, which caught a string of top New York real estate lawyers on camera—including a recent president of the American Bar Association—providing advice on how to move suspect money into the United States. The Obama administration put out a statement calling on Congress to craft legislation to identify companies' beneficial owners.

FinCEN issued a rule requiring US title insurance companies to identify the beneficial owners behind shell companies in real estate transactions, although it only applied to "all-cash" purchases of high-end residential real estate, and was only in effect in New York City, Miami, Los Angeles, San Francisco, San Diego, and San Antonio. These geographic targeting orders (GTOs) were spurred by long-standing concerns about money laundering through cash real estate deals. At best, the measure was insufficient in itself to tackle the problem, given that nearly half of the most expensive residential properties in the United States are purchased anonymously through shell companies, according to FATF, and many of these transactions are a vehicle for money laundering. As Transparency International noted in a summary of FATF's 2016 report: "While the US has made some progress in collecting beneficial ownership information for high-end real estate in some markets, what is really needed is to put an affirmative obligation on the real estate sector to conduct customer due diligence."[16]

Using Bullock's IRS idea, Carper introduced a bill in the Senate in 2016 for the IRS to collect the information. The cosponsors were Chris Coons, a Democrat who had filled Biden's Senate seat when he vacated it to become vice president, and Dean Heller, a Republican from Nevada—another state popular with those seeking to form shell corporations.

In the absence of legislation, FinCEN began in 2018 to require US financial institutions to step up their due diligence by verifying the beneficial owners of new accounts opened with them. This Customer Due Diligence Rule was enough to secure a much more favorable report from FATF in 2020—although FATF also noted that the system was less than comprehensive.[17]

In fact, the due diligence rule had several loopholes. For one thing, a beneficial owner was defined as anyone whose stake in the company is more than 25 percent, which meant that four owners could avoid identifying themselves if they could bring on one more owner and split the ownership between them to give each a 20 percent stake. Then, instead of naming a beneficial owner, all they had to name was a manager, who need not be one of the owners. Second, such anti–money laundering rules do not apply to state-chartered banks, which are not regulated by a federal agency. And there are a range of "shadow banks"—financial services companies that operate outside the supervision or obligations that apply to traditional banks, such as payment processors, check consolidation companies, and cash vault service providers. The US government estimates that there are at least 669 such institutions in the United States.[18]

In any case, it was reasonable to be skeptical about the banks' commitment to addressing the issue. FinCEN has long required banks to file "suspicious activity reports" to flag possible financial crimes that may be linked to drug or people trafficking, money laundering, or terrorism. But once they have reported the suspected wrongdoing, the banks often continue doing business with the account holders whom they have reported. Even in the most extreme cases, it is rare for the accused to get anything more than a deferred prosecution agreement—essentially a fine and a slap on the wrist. Big global banks such as JPMorgan Chase, HSBC, Standard Chartered, Deutsche Bank, and Bank of New York Mellon continued to move money for suspected criminals even after they were prosecuted or fined for financial misconduct, according to a 2020 BuzzFeed investigation.[19]

By 2020, two years after the Customer Due Diligence Rule came into effect, the US Treasury itself expressed skepticism about its effectiveness in combating money laundering, concluding that "it is not a comprehensive solution to the problem and a crucial gap remains."[20]

One of the challenges of the rule was that it established a marked contradiction between the regimes for banks, which were required to identify their customers, and for incorporating states such as Delaware, which are not. This made the rules around corporate anonymity a bit like those for marijuana, which is often legal at the state level but illegal under federal law. In the case of corporate transparency, rather than trying to standardize and improve federal anti–money laundering laws by overriding the patchwork of state rules, federal authorities were trying to work around them, and imposing the costs of compliance on financial institutions.[21]

The banks were keen to rid themselves of the extra paperwork burden that had been forced on them in the absence of any federal law securing more corporate transparency. And given the political and economic clout of the financial sector in the United States, they were going to get their way. From the banks' perspective, they were being asked to do work that should really have been done either by the registering states or by the companies themselves. The obvious answer was that the paperwork should be shoved onto one or the other via legislation that would either require companies to disclose their beneficial owners to the US federal government, or require states to collect that information when a business was registered. The cost of greater transparency had to be shifted either to the states or to businesses.

As an important home to many of the big players in the financial sector, Delaware was feeling the pressure. And on top of that, scandals continued to come out, with fingers often pointing at Delaware and other states that fight for a share of the business-formation market, such as Nevada and Wyoming. The First State was getting so much bad publicity that the consequence of doing nothing might have been a fundamental overhaul of the Franchise, gouging an unfillable hole in Delaware's state finances.

Perhaps the final straw came in April 2018, when US federal law enforcement officials seized the website Backpage amid allegations of child sex trafficking.

Federal authorities charged Backpage founders Michael Lacey and James Larkin and five other executives with knowingly publishing ads that enabled child sex trafficking and prostitution. They had aggressively sought to hide that fact: Andrew Padilla, Backpage's operations manager, threatened to fire any employee who put down in writing that the escorts depicted in the ads on the company's website were actually prostitutes. When the website discovered ads that indicated underage girls were available, it edited them to remove the offending language, rather than removing the ads altogether, effectively aiding child sex trafficking, according to a US Senate investigation.[22] The company even hired a call center in the Philippines to solicit and create sex-related ads to win business.[23]

The scale of the Backpage case was astonishing: the company was involved in nearly three-quarters of the ten thousand child trafficking reports received annually by the National Center for Missing and Exploited Children, the organization said in 2017, and had been repeatedly sued by state prosecutors, victims of sex trafficking, and campaigning groups. The site earned $500 million from prostitution-related ads, according to federal investigators. When banks raised concerns about the revenues, the company's executives laundered the proceeds instead, wiring them to foreign banks and converting them into cryptocurrency such as Bitcoin. A few days after the indictment was announced, Carl Ferrer, Backpage's CEO, pleaded guilty to money laundering and conspiracy to facilitate prostitution, and agreed to testify against his cofounders.

A particular focus of media attention was that for at least six months after federal authorities finally acted against the website,

Backpage was still officially considered to be a Delaware registered limited liability company "in good standing." Backpage, a classified ads site, was actually owned by a limited liability company in the Netherlands; its principal place of business was in Dallas; and it maintained its bank accounts and servers in Arizona. But the website was registered in Delaware, and as long as its fees were paid up, the Delaware authorities classified it as being in good standing. It was not until November 2018, seven months after federal authorities finally acted against the website, that the First State's attorney general moved to dissolve the company.[24]

Delaware justifiably came in for a good deal of unwanted attention because of Backpage, and it was in this context that Bullock abandoned the IRS proposal and came to the next least-worst option. If beneficial ownership information had to be collected, then at the very least, it should be collected by a federal agency and not by the states themselves. As to how the information was to get to the federal government, better to force companies to report it (and punish them if they fail to do so) than oblige registering agents to ask and verify. In this way, Delaware saw an opportunity to resolve the corporate anonymity issue with minimal possible damage to the Franchise. If there was a burden to be borne, it should fall on the businesses that were incorporating and the federal government. Let Delaware keep the revenues, and make others absorb the costs. In June, two months after the Backpage raid, Bullock publicly backed a bill proposed by Carolyn Maloney, Levin's old ally from the House of Representatives, who to her credit had continued plugging away at the transparency issue. The bill required companies to register the names of their beneficial owners with the US Treasury. With Bullock's blessing, the bill passed the House in 2019, and the Senate in 2021.

It was a highly significant moment—the first piece of legislation mandating companies to supply information about their real owners. The Corporate Transparency Act enjoyed bipartisan support—and support from the Trump administration—but because Delaware had managed to shove the costs of compliance onto companies, it was opposed by small-business groups such as the National Federation of Independent Business, the National Restaurant Association, and the Real Estate Roundtable. These groups argued that the legislation would essentially shift the reporting burden from large banks to small businesses. They were right. Of course, whatever the system, businesses themselves would have to give the information. But the legislation obliged them to send that information directly to the federal government, rather than simply include it in their state filing application. The law set up a bifurcated system in which businesses had two lots of paperwork: first to register in a US state; and then to send ownership details to the federal government. Delaware, meanwhile, had dodged any responsibility for solving the problem.

Given the state's track record, one would be forgiven for thinking that the motivation behind Delaware's change of heart was a fear that if it did not help America to clean up its act over corporate anonymity, the federal reaction to the outrage over the growing number of scandals linked to the First State could kill off the Franchise. Did Delaware adopt its new position out of a concern that federal authorities might question the wisdom of leaving business formation in the hands of the states and reopen the issue of whether both incorporations and the collection of beneficial ownership should be done at the national level?

Another plausible motivation is that Delaware was simply representing the interests of the financial sector, as it had many times in the past. The banks were keen to offload the responsibility to collect ownership information that FinCEN had imposed on them in 2018, the same year that Jeff Bullock publicly changed his mind on a national beneficial ownership registry.

Whatever its motivations, Delaware is to be commended for belatedly coming round to the view that something needed to be done. The First State had certainly changed its tune since Geisenberger's concerns about burdensome costs and "uncertain" benefits. Such a Damascene conversion a decade or two earlier might well have been prevented a great deal of wrongdoing.

Much as the law meant the United States was taking a huge step toward combating money laundering and international criminal activity, it was still essentially catching up with the rest of the world. Many countries were far ahead in establishing mechanisms to collect beneficial ownership information for the companies created under their jurisdictions, including countries of the European Union, Afghanistan, Canada, Cyprus, Ghana, Kenya, Luxembourg, Nigeria, South Africa, the Ukraine, the United Kingdom, and others.

The law also leaves open a loophole. For one thing, it may not apply to all legal entities, meaning that sketchy actors could switch from LLCs to trusts or other structures not covered by the new rules. This would leave a significant gap in the law, especially after the Pandora Papers revealed how extensively the wealthy and powerful use trusts to hide their fortunes. It also raises the question of whether the United States' bifurcated system for creating companies—formed at the state level but regulated at the federal level—makes sense, or whether it creates a new gap for wrongdoing to continue.

More fundamentally, there is the question of who has access to the beneficial ownership information. The rules are aimed at combating money laundering, and consequently, they envisage that corporate privacy continues—the registries of beneficial ownership they establish would be visible only to federal authorities and not to the media or the general public. (The exception is for companies that receive contracts or grants from the federal government, for whom ownership information will be public.) By contrast, the European Union in 2018 passed a directive requiring each of its member states to set up public registries of beneficial owners.[25] The United Kingdom, Canada, the British Virgin Islands, the United Arab Emirates, and Ukraine are making their registries public.

The privacy of the US registry worries James Henry, a fellow at Yale University, former chief economist at McKinsey & Company, and investigative journalist. For Henry, a big problem with a private registry that depends on self-reporting is who will be responsible for updating and verifying the information, and making sure it is current. Several million new entities are formed in the United States every year, and the ownership of the tens of millions that already exist can change day to day. Henry doubts that the US federal government will commit significant enough resources to ensure the information stays up to date. "There's always an issue there with who's going to maintain the thing and make sure that it's accurate,"

Henry says. The Corporate Transparency Act did not specify additional funds to build up the team at FinCEN, the Treasury unit that will be responsible for the database, leaving the funding of the registry at the whims of the Congressional budget process. The answer, Henry thinks, is to make the registry public. "The best people to do that are journalists. They have access to the data, and they can make sure that there's somebody actually auditing the system."[26] The Pandora and Panama Papers have demonstrated the power of journalism to bring transparency to the global financial system. Making the registry public would enable US authorities to harness that power.

There is also a democratic cost to keeping a registry private: it still leaves the American public in the dark about who is behind, for example, the political donations that influence US elections. A public registry could help shed light on practices that are not necessarily illegal but may still be in need of reform.

Even with this landmark reform, then, the United States will not have introduced transparency in the democratic sense, only the law enforcement sense. Illegal activity may be crimped, but unethical behavior that abuses corporate privacy seems likely to continue unhampered.

———

Does it really matter if the registry of company owners is private or public? Isn't the important point that the registry exists?

The 2021 Corporate Transparency Act was a huge step forward in one important aspect: it should work as a deterrent to those who want to use US shell companies to conduct illegal activity. But keeping the registry out of the public eye enables a whole host of unseemly yet legal behavior to continue unmonitored. And the line between the two can be blurry. As the University of Chicago's Kimberly Kay Hoang notes: "There is no neat dichotomy between legal and illegal, licit and illicit. The illegal and the illicit facilitate legal and licit market-making."[27] Two examples of this type of behavior—political "dark money" and tax dodging—show how it shapes US society. These examples demonstrate that beyond the money laundering, corruption, and kleptocracy, Delaware has historically protected all sorts of harmful activity—activity that will remain private even under the new law.

Consider tax dodging first. Because of its focus on criminal activity, the Corporate Transparency Act will do little to address the sorts of tax-dodging schemes revealed in the Pandora and Panama Papers. By keeping the registry of corporate owners private, it will continue to protect those who use complex legal structures to shield themselves from the scrutiny of the public gaze. A private registry may turn out to be inadequate to address and police the increasing complex maze of "spiderweb capitalism." Indeed, the small-business coalition campaigning against the 2021 law argued that "this legislation would impose a 'look-through' reporting requirement, necessitating small business owners to look through every layer of corporate and LLC affiliates to identify if any individuals associated with such entities are qualifying beneficial owners. Ownership of an entity by one or more other corporations or LLCs is common." [28] In other words, so many small businesses have complex structures that even for them to identify their own owners is an unduly burdensome task. If that really is the case, we cannot be optimistic about investigators' ability to untangle this web.

As for money in politics, one of the most interesting tales about the secret flows of political donations comes from Stephen Colbert, the TV show host. Although the story dates back to the time before the Corporate Transparency Act, the law will do little to help the public understand who is buying influence in their national politics, since it addresses anonymity (companies have to report their owners) but retains privacy (the information will not be made public). In this way, the difference between the anonymity that was on offer previously and the privacy that remains is somewhat academic.

In an age of polarized cable news channels and opinion journalism, comedians such as Colbert, John Oliver, and Jon Stewart have arguably produced some of the most probing exposés of the darker sides of US politics. During the 2012 US election cycle, Colbert—at the time, host of *The Colbert Report*, before he took over at *The Late Show* in 2015—offered a powerful illustration of how anonymous shell corporations combined with unlimited political donations to create an explosive cocktail.

The year 2012 saw the first presidential election since the US Supreme Court's 2010 *Citizens United* decision, which established the right of corporations to spend unlimited money with the aim of swaying US elections, in the name of free speech. By 2011, as Colbert later explained, "We'd done jokes on *Citizens United* for about a year, and then I realized, 'Oh, well, this is what the whole year is about. It's really about this whole new flush of cash into our political system that is in large part untraceable or traceable only after the fact when it's too late, after the primaries, after the election is over.'"[29]

Colbert's response was to set up his own super PAC—a political action committee with the catchy moniker "Americans for a Better Tomorrow, Tomorrow." But Colbert lamented that he didn't receive the flood of large donations and corporate cash that he had anticipated. Thankfully, US corporate anonymity rules came to the rescue.

Trevor Potter, a former chair of the Federal Election Commission and the general counsel to John McCain's 2000 and 2008 presidential campaigns, explained to the TV host that companies might be reluctant to donate to his super PAC because direct donations to super PACs have to be disclosed, and corporations might fear the transparency could expose them to a negative reaction from their shareholders or customers.[30] So Potter recommended that if Colbert wanted big companies and überwealthy individuals to donate to the fund, he should set up a Delaware shell corporation, enabling big donors to give anonymously. "I don't have to *go* to Delaware, do I?" Colbert fretted, wiping his brow in relief when Potter assured him he did not, and all the paperwork had been taken care of. Potter had set up a Delaware shell company named "Anonymous Shell Corporation," which not only did not have to reveal the names of its owners, but, thanks to *Citizens United*, could also receive unlimited donations and never had to report anything about its donors. Anonymous Shell Corporation was set up as a 501(c)(4) organization, a tax-exempt entity that is required to disclose the source of its donations only when it spends money given for a specific purpose. Unlike with super PACs, direct donations to 501(c)(4)s do not have to be reported. (Americans for a Better Tomorrow, Tomorrow, Colbert's super PAC, reported donations of $1.23 million to the Federal Election Commission in 2011 to 2012.)[31] The US government stipulates that a 501(c)(4) is a tax-exempt entity that must be organized not to make a profit and "operated exclusively to promote social welfare."[32] Strictly speaking, these nonprofit groups are prohibited from making politics their primary purpose, but that rule is largely ignored by the tax authorities.[33] Most super PACs receive anonymous donations from 501(c)(4) and other 501(c) organizations. ("What's the difference between that and money laundering?" Colbert quizzed Potter. "It's hard to say," the former FEC chair admitted.)[34]

To formalize Colbert's anonymous shell corporation, the only piece of remaining business was to transfer the ownership to Colbert (who would be anonymous, of course). In order to do so, Anonymous Shell Corporation had to call a board meeting. Potter explained that he had helpfully configured the corporation's board to be solely made up of Colbert. As the lone director, Colbert duly called a board meeting live on air, appointed himself president, treasurer, and secretary, and authorized the corporation to file its paperwork with the Internal Revenue Service in May 2013, six months *after* the election it was trying to sway—and even then, it would not be required to identify its donors. Brandishing the papers, Colbert summed up the situation, "Without this, I am transparent; with this, I am opaque."[35] The difference was the Delaware corporation.

Colbert's stunt (which won him a Peabody Award in 2013) proved prescient: in the subsequent presidential election, political influence became an issue of global geopolitics and international relations. Colbert had helped raise the public's awareness of the lack of transparency over corporate political donations, but in 2016 the US elections were subject to manipulation by Russia, in a "sweeping and systematic" manner, according to Robert Mueller, the former FBI director, who led a two-year special counsel investigation into the matter.[36]

But Colbert had actually only scratched the surface of the influence of anonymous money in US politics. Even when super PACs (or, less commonly, 501(c)(4)s) report donations, the donors they identify are often LLCs without any named owner. Transparency campaigners complain that the lack of beneficial ownership information helps hide how money influences US politics, echoing some of the frustrations expressed by John Cassara. The 2021 Corporate Transparency Act will set up a registry of beneficial owners, but by making it private, the donations from LLCs publicly disclosed by super PACs will be no more enlightening than they have historically been.

Historically, corporate anonymity rules in many US states meant it was impossible to know the true extent to which Delaware shell corporations were used as part of any campaign to influence US politics with "dark money" from abroad.

While the Corporate Transparency Act should deter foreign money from influencing US elections, super PACs will still be allowed to accept donations from US subsidiaries of foreign corporations, so long as foreign nationals are not formally involved in the decision-making process. Colbert was shocked by the ease with which US companies can exert immeasurable and untraceable influence on the political process. We should be even more concerned about the ability of non-American corporations to do so.

Joe Biden observed in 2018 that anonymity was undermining the integrity of the US democratic process. "The lack of transparency in our campaign finance system combined with extensive foreign money laundering creates a significant vulnerability for our democracy," Biden noted. "We don't know how much illicit money enters the United States from abroad or how much dark money enters American political campaigns. . . . As we take on the threats posed by cyber attacks and disinformation from foreign actors, we can't ignore the threat posed by foreign dark money."[37]

And Biden admitted that foreign dark money has frequently flowed through Delaware. To take just one example, Lev Parnas and Igor Fruman, two Soviet-born Americans, were indicted in 2019 by federal authorities for allegedly using a Delaware LLC to funnel millions of dollars of political donations from Russia to US political campaigns. Parnas and Furman had been intercepted together at Dulles International Airport outside Washington in October 2019, moments away from successfully fleeing the country. Each had been closely associated with Rudy Giuliani, President Trump's personal lawyer, and with the Trump administration's attempts to gather damaging information in Ukraine about the president's future opponent, Joe Biden—attempts that would lead directly to Trump's impeachment in December 2019. At Dulles, Parnas and Furman were in the process of boarding a Lufthansa flight to Frankfurt amid a gaggle of first-class passengers before plainclothes officers stopped the two and led them back to the terminal, where they were arrested. Both of the men had one-way tickets, en route to Vienna and perhaps various points east. A judge set bail at $1 million for each of them. Prosecutors alleged that the pair had "conspired to circumvent the federal laws against foreign influence by engaging in a scheme to funnel foreign money to candidates for federal and state office so that the defendants could buy potential influence with candidates, campaigns, and the candidates' governments."[38]

To cover their tracks, Parnas and Fruman set up Global Energy Producers, an LLC formed in Delaware in April 2018 by an individual named John Gelety. (In a twist that recalled Colbert's Anonymous Shell Corporation, Parnas controlled several other Delaware entities, including two named, helpfully, Fraud Guarantee LLC and Fraud Guarantee Holdings LLC.) The notion that Global Energy Producers was in any way connected with energy was false. Rather, the federal investigators said, Parnas and Fruman "intentionally caused certain large contributions to be reported in the name of GEP instead of their own names." As part of that plan, in May 2018, $325,000 was officially donated by the LLC to America First Action SuperPac, a political action committee supporting Donald Trump's reelection campaign.

As his underground activity was exposed, Lev Parnas made a revealing comment. "This is what happens when you become visible," an associate noted to him, as they hit the news headlines. "The buzzards descend." Parnas responded, "That's why we need to stay under the radar."[39] Foreign money wanted to buy influence undetected. For decades, Delaware-style corporate anonymity helped achieve just that.

The Corporate Transparency Act should in theory end the flow of foreign money into US politics, but since the registry of corporate owners will be visible only to government agencies, the political donations of US-based corporations and wealthy individuals that aren't out-and-out illegal will remain in the dark.

The issue isn't just the secrecy surrounding the money that flows into political campaigns. Increasingly, political candidates have also used LLCs to conceal how they spend the donations they receive. This was a particular concern during the Trump era, when the suspicion among transparency campaigners was that political donations to the Trump campaign were being routed through a web of companies and potentially ending up being paid to businesses owned by the Trump Organization. If true, this would be a clear case of corruption concealed by corporate anonymity. A more quotidian example is how the Trump campaign used LLCs to hide who was it was paying and how much. Although this was a more significant issue with the Trump campaign, given that his children and their significant others were on the payroll, the ability to hide information about how campaigns spend their donations is a more general phenomenon. "That use of opacity on the outgoing side is one of the new fronts on our battle against this that we'll have to address in the coming years," says Adav Noti of the Campaign Legal Center, a nonpartisan group that campaigns for more transparency in US politics, founded by Trevor Potter (Colbert's foil in the superPAC segment).[40]

The Corporate Transparency Act should limit the flow of illegal dark money into US politics. But until the beneficial ownership registry is made public, other types of dark money will continue to flow unmonitored—the unlimited donations that businesses use to buy candidates and shape the political agenda. Without media and watchdog access to that information, the American public will still be in the dark about how the US political system really operates.

12

Conclusion

NO MORE HIDING IN PLAIN SIGHT

This is not a book full of revelations. To experts, it is old news. Everything in it was already hiding in plain sight. Delaware's great achievement has been to blend into the background enough that we think of the Franchise as an integral part of American capitalism, too humdrum and technical to be analyzed or debated.

If the Franchise is a problem, it's a chronic problem, not an acute one. The issues are complex. The interests are entrenched. The challenge for most of us is to follow the tangle of threads and to pay attention.

There has been some progress. Publicly, the world's most powerful leaders have acknowledged the need to change the financial architecture that enables money laundering and tax evasion. Countries, now including the United States, have started to set up registries of beneficial owners of companies registered in their jurisdictions. Transparency campaigners see that as an important first step toward a more concerted effort to tackle the misuse of US business entities.

In Delaware, there are signs that the mood is slowly changing. While support for the Franchise remains strong, there is growing concern—about the way it has been abused and the effect that has had on Delaware's reputation, and about the state's financial dependence on Franchise fees and related revenue such as unclaimed property. The 2020 election ushered into the state's legislature a new group of radical lawmakers who may well challenge the Delaware Way. Senator Carper, an archetype of the Delaware Way, has faced challenges in the past two elections from candidates who have campaigned against traditional dealmaking and entrenched interests, although Carper easily brushed off both. In 2021, a public outroar forced Delaware officials to withdraw a proposal that would have given the state more reasons to deny requests for public records under Delaware's Freedom of Information Act and would have required people seeking public records to pay new fees.[1]

The United States took a big step forward with the 2021 Corporate Transparency Act, which will establish a registry of corporate owners. But if that is the only step it takes, it will only have half-solved the problem it was trying to address. Given that it took decades to pass legislation enabling law enforcement to know the most basic information about shell companies, there may be little appetite to tackle the remaining issues. Yet even when the registry is set up in the United States in 2023, access to it will be limited to officials. That is a good distance from Louis Brandeis's dictum that "sunlight is said to be the best of disinfectants." In effect, the American people will remain in the dark about how corporate structures registered in the United States are being used.

The Corporate Transparency Act leaves open loopholes. Structures such as trusts will not be subject to the new rules and can remain anonymous. Like the decision to keep the registry private—visible only to law enforcement—leaving those loopholes was driven by understandable concerns about privacy, and because identifying the owners was not deemed necessary for US national security or anti–money laundering efforts. But there is a need for a national conversation—perhaps via congressional hearings—about whether that privacy outweighs the costs, such as the possibility of continued wrongdoing using business entities and the free flow of large anonymous donations through political campaigns. If the act is successful in limiting illicit behavior using corporate structures, it should beg the question of whether it could help curb the unethical use of other entities such as trusts.

More generally, the Corporate Transparency Act sets the responsibility for probity on the federal government and on companies themselves. Accompanying rules also place responsibilities on banks to know their customers. But the Pandora and Panama Papers revealed a broad community of secrecy enablers such as lawyers, accountants, art dealers, and investment advisers, along with corporate service providers such as registering agents. The law could be strengthened by explicitly obliging these actors to provide information that could be used to verify information on registries of beneficial owners and similar databases.

A lack of transparency is also a hallmark of the Delaware Way. Under the process, the Corporation Law Council operates in private and features almost exclusively lawyers who represent either companies or shareholders. The setup is clubby and exclusive, with a chronic lack of democratic oversight and accountability. The changes the council recommends to the Delaware legislature are typically rubber-stamped by a poorly informed, part-time legislature that is incapable of effectively scrutinizing their suggestions.

We do not need to assume venality to want the system to open up. It may be that the members who serve want above all else to produce the most technically superior corporate legislation. If so, they should have little to fear from making their deliberations more public, enabling legal experts to parse them and explain the implications for shareholders, stakeholders, and companies. In the absence of adequate supervision by the legislature, this could provide a kind of crowdsourced technical oversight.

The Corporation Law Council uses an outdated model for an era in which the wider implications of corporate action are increasingly under scrutiny. Part of opening up could include widening the council to include legal experts representing stakeholders beyond shareholders, such as consumer groups, environmental organizations, and employee associations. A strong argument against "stakeholder capitalism" has been that it is unclear what metrics should be used to gauge the performance of corporate leaders, and how to measure them. Even if the law were to mandate that CEOs must balance the interests of shareholders and stakeholders, that could still amount to little more than "a license for directors to do whatever they want," observes the University of Chicago's Luigi Zingales.[2] Many smart people are working on addressing the issue of how to measure performance beyond financial statements.[3] But in the meantime, opening the process up to stakeholders could enable a wider sense of what the United States expects from its corporate leaders. Even corporate leaders who have pledged themselves to "stakeholder capitalism" have mostly done little to change their behavior, research suggests.[4] Greater scrutiny could help hold them accountable to their stated goals.

Four specific steps could start to address these concerns.

First, the US federal government should make public its registry of corporate owners, as many other jurisdictions, including the European Union, the United Kingdom, and Canada, have done or have signaled that they will do. The database should be published online, and there should be no cost to search it, as in countries including Bulgaria, Croatia, Denmark, France, Latvia, Poland, Portugal, Slovenia, and the United Kingdom.[5]

Second, the US Congress could enhance the Corporate Transparency Act by closing loopholes that exempt certain kinds of legal entities, such as trusts, from registering their owners. If it can be established that no public interest would be served by making those names publicly available, they could be treated differently from corporate entities and excluded from the public registry. But in the wake of the Pandora Papers, that may be a tough case to make. Congress should also require secrecy enablers such as accountants, art dealers, asset-protection companies, real-estate agents, and registering agents to conduct due diligence on their clients and their sources of funding.

Third, Delaware's Corporation Law Council should make its proceedings public and allow time for expert opinion to inform debate in the Delaware legislature. Members of the council should also be required to explain to the legislature in straightforward terms why any changes in the law are needed.

Fourth, the council could be expanded to include legal experts specifically representing stakeholders other than shareholders, who could begin a process of formalizing a wider and more objective set of management performance benchmarks that would update the "business judgment" rule with clear criteria relating to the wider impact of corporate decisions.

These are not radical proposals. Many countries have already made their corporate registries public. Closing privacy loopholes and obliging secrecy enablers to conduct due diligence are nothing more than extensions of existing law. The Delaware Corporation Law Council should have little to fear from deliberating in public. And expanding the purview of corporate directors to their societal impact is proposed by none other than Leo Strine, the former head of both Delaware's Chancery Court and its Supreme Court.

These proposals, then, should be seen as a minimum. But they also raise the need for a broader national conversation about how and where US companies should be created. Again, congressional hearings may be the best way to restart this conversation. If companies have to identify their beneficial owners to the federal government, the natural question is why the Franchise remains in the hands of individual states, where oversight is more likely to be partial and weak. Incorporation at the state level can seem something of a relic, ill-suited to the global economy. Periodically, the question arises as to whether business registration should instead be made a standardized, federal process. No doubt, such a system would have its own weaknesses, but the gap that the Corporate Transparency Act has created between forming businesses locally and identifying their owners nationally may force the issue to the surface once again. Often, that conversation has been prompted by scandals. Why wait for that? Having a rational discussion about the optimal way to structure business formation and corporate oversight might help prevent scandals in the first place.

After all, the Delaware Way might not be the best way.

ACKNOWLEDGMENTS

The original idea for this book was not mine. Joe Jackson, my editor, first came up with the notion of digging into Delaware's outsized role in the US corporate landscape, and we discussed it over many lunches at Salonica in Hyde Park, Chicago. We strategized about who might be interested in writing such a book. Joe approached several possible authors, all of whom turned him down. The main reason seemed to be that Delaware appeared too small a topic, and when the writers dug into it, they became more attracted by the bigger global themes such as money laundering or tax dodging. But to me, the smallness of Delaware was what made the project attractive. It grounded these big themes in a place that may have seemed to others overwhelmingly humdrum.

Taking on the project myself turned out to be a great decision, and one of the main joys of writing this book was getting to work with Joe. Throughout, he was unflappable, patient, and encouraging. Joe guided me through the entire process with grace and kindness.

I am grateful to the many people who supported me early on in this project and set me on the right track. Brendan Pedersen helped with critical initial research and data collection. Conversations with Luigi Zingales, Gabriel Zucman, Guy Rolnik, Amy Merrick, Michael Polsky, Chipo Nyambuya, Ryan Coyne, Matthew Weitzman, Adam Roberts, Jonathan Russ, Becky Yerak, and Doug Denison were immensely helpful in giving me food for thought and questions to research.

A large number of people agreed to be interviewed, too many to mention individually. While most of them are quoted in this book, many are not. I appreciate the time and insights all of them gave me.

I drew a great deal from the hard work done by transparency campaigners and journalists, and in particular, by reporters at the *News Journal* in Delaware. Reading their work, years after leaving daily journalism myself, reminded me of the importance of on-the-ground local reporting in holding public figures and businesses accountable.

I am thankful to the many people who read parts or all of the manuscript and offered helpful feedback: David Weitzman, Emily Lambert, Jeff Cockrell, Chuck Burke, Josh Stunkel, Simone Cavallaro, Chelsea Vail, Lynne Marek, Nick Wasileski, Ram Shivakumar, John Paul Rollert, Lior Strahilevitz, Eduardo Frajman, Jeff Pruzan, Francine McKenna, Brian Schwartz, Nat Grotte, Jim Binder, and Kimberly Kay Hoang. Special thanks to Mitch Tobin and Susan Jacobson, who were kind enough to read the manuscript several times and engage in discussions about it. Of course, any errors or misjudgments in the text are mine alone.

In the latter phases, I received tremendous support from Josh Drake at Princeton University Press, Erin Davis at Westchester Publishing, and Emily Treptow at the University of Chicago Library. Thank you for your punctiliousness, diligence, and responsiveness.

I am grateful for encouragement from my parents, Avis and David Weitzman, and my parents in-law, Kate and Ian Campbell.

My children, Orlie, Tess, Ray, and Josephine, boosted me along with their love, enthusiasm, and energy. I am sorry to them for not going with their proposed title, "Delaware Doubts"—maybe we can revisit that for the sequel (or the movie version)?

My wife, Lorna, is a wonderful human being, my copilot, "good companion," partner in crime, cheerleader, and the only other person I know who appreciates obscure 1980s British cultural references as much as I do. Tato: Slàinte Mhath and L'Chayim—this book is dedicated to you.

NOTES

Preface

1. David Shukman, "Diary: The Amazon Rainforest," BBC News, July 19, 2006, http://news.bbc.co.uk/2/hi/science/nature/5184332.stm.

2. Leonard David, "Water Found in Sunlight and Shadow on the Moon," *Scientific American*, October 26, 2020.

3. Ian Johnston, "Antarctic Iceberg Quarter the Size of Wales Splits from Ice Shelf," *Independent*, July 12, 2017.

4. See Marwa Eltagouri and Chris Mooney, "These Close-Up Images from NASA Show One of the Largest Icebergs to Ever Split Off from Antarctica," *Washington Post*, November 15, 2017; Jugal K. Patel and Justin Gillis, "An Iceberg the Size of Delaware Just Broke Off a Major Antarctic Ice Shelf," *New York Times*, July 12, 2017.

5. Jonathan Gilbert, "Argentina Scrambles to Fight Biggest Plague of Locusts in 60 Years," *New York Times*, January 26, 2016.

6. Doyle Rice, "2 Months Later, Massive Canadian Wildfire Finally 'under Control,'" *USA Today*, July 5, 2016.

7. "Gulf Waters Eating Away at Louisiana Coast," CBS News, August 14, 2015, https://www.cbsnews.com/news/gulf-waters-eating-away-at-louisiana-coasts/.

8. "Wales' Sheep Numbers Rise Above the 10 Million Mark," BBC News, December 15, 2017, https://www.bbc.com/news/uk-wales-42371973.

Chapter 1

1. John A. Cassara, phone interview with the author, February 23, 2017.

2. John A. Cassara, "Delaware, Den of Thieves?," *New York Times*, November 1, 2013.

3. You may say "tchotchke," I say "tchatchke."

4. Adam Duvernay and Margie Fishman, "Arrested Klansman is 'Belligerent' Leader of KKK Splinter Group," *News Journal*, August 31, 2017.

5. Quoted in Bill Schneider, "An Honest Man in Washington?," CNN, June 24, 2005, http://www.cnn.com/2005/POLITICS/06/24/grosh/.

6. I use the term "corporate" in this book as an adjective to mean both registered corporations and LLCs, even though LLCs, strictly speaking, are companies and not corporations.

7. Quoted in Jerry W. Markham, *A Financial History of Modern U.S. Corporate Scandals: From Enron to Reform* (London: Routledge, 2015), page 250.

8. Joseph F. Mahoney, "Backsliding Convert: Woodrow Wilson and the 'Seven Sisters,'" *American Quarterly* 18, no. 1 (Spring 1966): page 72.

9. Mahoney, page 72.

10. Quoted in "Law for Sale: A Study of the Delaware Corporation Law of 1967," *University of Pennsylvania Law Review* 117 (1969): page 861.

11. Quoted in Sung Hui Kim, "The Failure of Federal Incorporation Law," in *Can Delaware Be Dethroned? Evaluating Delaware's Dominance of Corporate Law*, edited by Stephen M. Bainbridge, Iman Anabtawi, Sung Hui Kim, and James Park (New York: Cambridge University Press, 2018), page 83.

12. Quoted in Kim, page 85.

13. Quoted in Kim, page 87.

14. Quoted in Mahoney, "Backsliding Convert," page 72.

15. Quoted in Henry Jones Ford, *Woodrow Wilson: The Man and His Work* (New York: D. Appleton, 1916), pages 152–53.

16. Quoted in Mahoney, "Backsliding Convert," page 75.

17. Quoted in Mahoney, page 76.

18. Mahoney, page 71.

19. Sarath Sanga, "The Origins of the Market for Corporate Law," Northwestern University, January 2021, http://dx.doi.org/10.2139/ssrn.3503628.

20. Robert M. Daines, "The Incorporation Choices of IPO Firms (Initial Public Offerings)," *New York University Law Review* 77 (2002): page 1572.

21. "2018 Annual Report," Delaware Division of Corporations, accessed October 6, 2021, https://corp.delaware.gov/stats/2018-annual-report/.

22. "2020 Annual Report Statistics," Delaware Division of Corporations, accessed October 18, 2021, https://corpfiles.delaware.gov/Annual-Reports/Division-of-Corporations-2020-Annual-Report.pdf.

23. "2020 Annual Report Statistics."

24. Lynn M. LoPucki, *Courting Failure: How Competition for Big Cases Is Corrupting the Bankruptcy Courts* (Ann Arbor: University of Michigan Press, 2006), page 53.

25. Cassara, interview with the author, February 23, 2017.

Chapter 2

1. Of the forty-seven US states that have secretaries of state, thirty-five are elected and twelve are unelected.

2. "Why Businesses Choose Delaware," Delaware.gov, accessed September 26, 2021, https://corplaw.delaware.gov/why-businesses-choose-delaware/.

3. John Williams, "Delaware Is the Best State for Incorporating," *Delaware Business Times*, April 17, 2017.

4. LoPucki, *Courting Failure*, pages 51–52

5. Delaware Economic and Financial Advisory Council (DEFAC) General Fund Revenue Forecast, Delaware.gov, October 2020, accessed October 18, 2021, https://financefiles.delaware.gov/DEFAC/06-21/Revenues.pdf.

6. US Census Bureau, Annual Survey of State Government Tax Collections 2020, https://www.census.gov/programs-surveys/stc.html.

7. The thirty-minute service, which was introduced in 2009, is not advertised on the Delaware Division of Corporations website, and is only available through online registered agents.

8. DEFAC General Fund Revenue Forecast.

9. Bill Freeborn, "Opinion: Delaware Is in Real Trouble If It Loses Corporation-Revenue Dominance," *Delaware News Journal*, December 10, 2018.

10. US Census Bureau, State Government Tax Collections 2020.

11. James Butkiewicz, professor of economics, University of Delaware, interview with the author, May 8, 2018.

12. Juan Carlos Suárez Serrato and Owen Zidar, "The Structure of State Corporate Taxation and Its Impact on State Tax Revenues and Economic Activity" (NBER working paper 23653, July 2018), https://www.nber.org/papers/w23653. See Table A13.

13. U.S. Bureau of Labor Statistics, "Economy at a Glance: Delaware," https://www.bls.gov/eag/eag.de.htm.

14. Scott Goss, "Ashland Moving Corporate Headquarters to Delaware by 2020," *Delaware News Journal*, August 2, 2018.

15. See Sarah Gamard and Jared Whalen, "These 7 Charts Show Exactly What Happened to Delaware's Economy," *Delaware News Journal*, April 1, 2021.

16. "Study: Delaware 2nd among States Seeing the Worst Economic Recovery," First State Update, October 16, 2020, http://firststateupdate.com/2020/10/study-delaware-2nd-among-states-seeing-the-worst-economic-recovery/.

17. See "Total State Expenditures per Capita" (data for financial year 2019), KFF.com, accessed October 26, 2021, https://www.kff.org/other/state-indicator/per-capita-state-spending; "Total State Goverment Expenditures," Ballotpedia, accessed September 26, 2012, https://ballotpedia.org/Total_state_government_expenditures.

18. Adam McCann, "Tax Burden by State," WalletHub, March 31, 2021, https://wallethub.com/edu/states-with-highest-lowest-tax-burden/20494.

19. Although the state has no sales tax, it does charge a "gross receipts tax" on sellers for certain businesses, rather than consumers. The rate varies between 0.1 and 0.7 percent. Delaware also levies excise taxes on products such as gas, alcohol, and cigarettes.

20. Freeborn, "Delaware Is in Real Trouble."

21. William L. Cary, "Federalism and Corporate Law: Reflections upon Delaware," *Yale Law Journal* 83, no. 4 (March 1974): page 663.

22. Quoted in David Margolick, "William Carey, Former S.E.C. Chairman, Dies at 72," *New York Times*, February 9, 1983.

23. Quoted in Markham, *Financial History*, page 253.

24. Cary, "Federalism and Corporate Law," pages 665, 666, and 700.

25. Frank H. Easterbrook, "The Race for the Bottom in Corporate Governance," *Virginia Law Review* 95 (2009): page 686.

26. See, for example, Lucian Bebchuk, Alma Cohen, and Allen Ferrell, "Does the Evidence Favor State Competition in Corporate Law?," *California Law Review*

90, no. 6 (2002): pages 1775–1821; Guhan Subramanian, "The Disappearing Delaware Effect," *Journal of Law, Economics, & Organization* 20, no. 1 (April 2004): pages 32–59.

27. See, for example, Ralph K. Winter Jr., "State Law, Shareholder Protection, and the Theory of the Corporation," *Journal of Legal Studies* 6, no. 2 (June 1977): pages 251–92.

28. Daines, "Incorporation Choices of IPO Firms," page 1573.

29. Myron T. Steele, "Sarbanes-Oxley: The Delaware Perspective," *New York Law School Law Review* 52 (2007/8): page 507.

30. Mark J. Roe, "Delaware's Competition," *Harvard Law Review* 117 (2003): page 590.

Chapter 3

1. Home Depot, Inc. v. Arizona Department of Revenue, 314 P.3d 576 (Ariz. Ct. App. 2013).

2. See Title 30, Delaware Code online, accessed September 26, 2021, http://delcode.delaware.gov/title30/c019/index.shtml.

3. Sheldon Pollack, "Is Delaware a Tax Haven? Maybe," *News Journal*, July 12, 2014.

4. Vivian Lei, "Geoffrey v. Commissioner: The Fall of 'Toys R Us' and the Rise of 'Tax R Us,'" *Houston Business and Tax Law Journal* 10, no. 3 (2010): page 341.

5. Scott D. Dyreng, Bradley P. Lindsey, and Jacob R. Thornock, "Exploring the Role Delaware Plays as a Domestic Tax Haven," *Journal of Financial Economics* 108, no. 3 (June 2013): page 769.

6. Dyreng, Lindsey, and Thornock, page 751.

7. Dyreng, Lindsey, and Thornock, page 753.

8. Glenn R. Simpson, "Diminishing Returns: A Tax Maneuver in Delaware Puts Squeeze on States," *Wall Street Journal*, August 9, 2002; Dyreng, Lindsey, and Thornock, "Exploring the Role Delaware Plays," pages 763–65.

9. Quoted in Howard Fischer, "Court Rules Home Depot Can't Minimize AZ Tax Liability," Capitol Media Services, December 23, 2013, https://tucson.com/business/local/court-rules-home-depot-can-t-minimize-az-tax-liability/article_3ebd923b-90b2-510d-838e-8f0c840d1fa3.html.

10. Home Depot Inc v. Arizona Department of Revenue.

11. Geoffrey, Inc. v. Commissioner of Revenue, 453 Mass. 17 (2009).

12. Carrick Mollenkamp and Glenn R. Simpson, "WorldCom Tax Strategy May Have Saved Millions," *Wall Street Journal*, August 14, 2003; Dyreng, Lindsey, and Thornock, "Exploring the Role Delaware Plays," pages 766–68.

13. Dyreng, Lindsey, and Thornock, "Exploring the Role," page 752.

14. Dyreng and his coauthors find that companies using the Delaware Loophole saw their tax savings fall by 25–41 percent from the first half to the second half of their sample period (1995–2009), which they attribute to legislative action by other states.

15. David Brunori, interview with the author, April 26, 2018.

16. Michael Mazerov, interview with the author, December 12, 2018.

17. Susan Steblein, "Global Intangible Low Tax Income (GILTI) and Foreign-Derived Tangible Income Taxes (FDII)," *Summing It Up* (blog), Freed Maxick, January 23, 2018, https://blog.freedmaxick.com/summing-it-up/global-intangible-low-tax-income-gilti-and-foreign-derived-tangible-income-taxes-fdii.

18. LeAnn Luna, interview with the author, May 7, 2018.

19. Professor Luna was kind enough to share her advice for the State of Tennessee with me, in email correspondence on May 7, 2018.

20. Richard Waters, "Google to End Use of 'Double Irish' as Tax Loophole Set to Close," *Financial Times*, January 1, 2020.

21. Edward Helmore, "Google Says It Will No Longer Use 'Double Irish, Dutch Sandwich' Tax Loophole," *Guardian*, January 1, 2020.

22. Bret Bogenschneider and Ruth Heilmeier, "Google's 'Alphabet Soup' in Delaware," *Houston Business and Tax Law Journal* 1 (2016): page 4.

23. Taylor Rock, "Reddit Thread Slams Applebee's with Scathing Reviews," *The Daily Meal* (blog), January 17, 2018, https://www.thedailymeal.com/eat/reddit-thread-negative-applebees-review/011718.

24. Mark Davis, "Applebee's to Move Headquarters to California, Lay Off Some Area Employees," *Kansas City Star*, September 4, 2015.

25. For the lower figure, see Timothy J. Bartik, "A New Panel Database on Business Incentives for Economic Development Offered by State and Local Governments in the United States," Pew Charitable Trusts, February 2017, https://research.upjohn.org/reports/225/; Kenneth P. Thomas, *Investment Incentives and the Global Competition for Capital* (Basingstoke, UK: Palgrave Macmillan, 2011), page 96. The higher figure is cited in "Episode 699: Why Did the Job Cross the Road?," *Planet Money* (podcast), NPR, May 4, 2016, https://www.npr.org/sections/money/2016/05/04/476799218/episode-699-why-did-the-job-cross-the-road.

26. Morgan Scarboro, "State Corporate Income Tax Rates and Brackets for 2018," Tax Foundation, February 7, 2018, https://taxfoundation.org/state-corporate-income-tax-rates-brackets-2018/.

27. Jeff Mordock, "Delaware OKs $7.9M for Chemours, but It Might Not Matter," *News Journal*, May 23, 2016.

28. Jack Markell, "Let's Stop Government Giveaways to Corporations," *New York Times*, September 21, 2017.

29. Jack Markell, interview with the author, May 16, 2019.

30. Serrato and Zidar, "Structure of State Corporate Taxation," page 16.

31. US Census Bureau, State Government Tax Collections 2020.

32. Elissa Braunstein, "Declining Corporate Income Taxes in the 1990s: A State-by-State Analysis of Effective Tax Rates" (PERI working paper no. 91, 2004), https://scholarworks.umass.edu/cgi/viewcontent.cgi?referer=https://www.google.com/&httpsredir=1&article=1075&context=peri_workingpapers.

33. California, Connecticut, Florida, Illinois, Massachusetts, New Jersey, New York, and Pennsylvania collected more in state corporate income tax in 2020. US Census Bureau, State Tax Collections 2020.

34. As Nicholas Shaxson notes, "At the last count the Big Four earned nearly $30 billion a year from tax advice alone, helping private clients both to comply with tax laws and to escape tax, usually both at the same time. To get a sense of how those apparently opposite functions work together, ponder the word 'loophole'" (Nicholas Shaxson, *The Finance Curse* [London: The Bodley Head, 2018], page 237).

35. Cited in Brian Bowling, "Cut in Corporate Tax Rate, Loophole Fix Could Generate $330M," AP News, March 22, 2018, https://apnews.com/article/64d4 6ea3a70b40c5bd3605fd4eba44da.

36. Jack Markell, interview with the author, May 2, 2018.

37. "Facts and Myths," Delaware.gov, accessed September 26, 2021, https:// corplaw.delaware.gov/facts-and-myths/.

38. Richard A. Gordon, *Tax Havens and Their Use by United States Taxpayers—an Overview: Report to the Commissioner of Internal Revenue, the Assistant Attorney General (Tax Division) and the Assistant Secretary of the Treasury (Tax Policy)* (Washington, DC: Internal Revenue Service, 1981), page 89.

39. Dyreng, Lindsey, and Thornock, "Exploring the Role Delaware Plays," page 752.

40. Gabriel Zucman, interview with the author, May 10, 2018, Chicago.

41. Scott Dyreng, interview with the author, May 3, 2018.

42. At the time of writing, as measured by market capitalization.

43. Stephen Long, "US Oil Giant Chevron Faces $300 Million Tax Bill after ATO Court Victory," ABC, April 20, 2017, https://www.abc.net.au/news/2017-04-21 /chevron-faces-massive-tax-bill-after-ato-court-victory/8460874; "Chevron Drops Appeal over Landmark Australian Tax Ruling," Reuters, August 17, 2017, https:// www.reuters.com/article/australia-chevron-taxavoidance-idUSL4N1L41TK.

44. LeAnn Luna, interview with the author, May 7, 2018.

45. David Brunori, interview with the author, April 26, 2018.

Chapter 4

1. Art Basel and UBS Global Art Market Report 2019, March 2019, https:// artbasel.com/news/art-market-report.

2. Gráinne Gilmore, "New Order," *The Wealth Report 2018*, Knight Frank, 2018, https://content.knightfrank.com/resources/knightfrank.com/wealthreport2018 /the-wealth-report-2018.pdf; P. Espinoza Revollo, "The Inequality Virus" (Oxfam Briefing Paper, January 2021), https://oxfamilibrary.openrepository.com /bitstream/handle/10546/621149/bp-the-inequality-virus-summ-250121-en.pdf.

3. Cited in Margie Fishman and Scott Goss, "Delaware Provides Tax Shelter for Multimillion-Dollar Masterpieces," *News Journal*, September 30, 2017.

4. Clare McAndrew, "The Art Market 2018," Art Basel and UBS Report, page 17, https://d2u3kfwd92fzu7.cloudfront.net/Art%20Basel%20and%20UBS_The%20 Art%20Market_2018.pdf.

5. Melanie Gerlis, "The Art Market in 2018: The Year of Banksy and Blockchain Auctions," *Financial Times*, December 28, 2018.

6. "The Art Industry and US Policies that Undermine Sanctions," staff report, Permanent Subcommittee on Investigations, United States Senate, July 29, 2020.

7. "Portman, Carper: Bipartisan Report Reveals How Russian Oligarchs Use Secretive Art Industry to Evade US Sanctions" (media release), Permanent Subcommittee on Investigations, July 29, 2020.

8. Sophie Kalkreuth, "Meet the Man Who Found the da Vinci That Sold for a Record US$450 Million," *South China Morning Post*, May 12, 2018.

9. Josh Spero, "Hunt for New Master of Record-Breaking Da Vinci," *Financial Times*, November 16, 2017.

10. Gerlis, "Art Market in 2018." There is vast speculation over why the painting has not been exhibited. See, for example, Jonathan Jones, "The Da Vinci Mystery: Why Is His $450m Masterpiece Really Being Kept under Wraps?," *Guardian*, October 15, 2018.

11. This is made up of a city sales tax rate of 4.5 percent, the New York State sales and use tax of 4 percent, and the Metropolitan Commuter Transportation District surcharge of 0.375 percent. See "New York States Sales and Use Tax," NYC Department of Finance, accessed September 27, 2021, https://www1.nyc.gov/site/finance/taxes/business-nys-sales-tax.page.

12. Fishman and Goss, "Delaware Provides Tax Shelter."

13. Fritz Dietl, interview with the author, May 14, 2018.

14. See Darla Mercado, "The Holiday Is Over: Amazon Will Collect Sales Taxes Nationwide on April 1," CNBC, March 24, 2017, https://www.cnbc.com/2017/03/24/the-holiday-is-over-amazon-will-collect-sales-taxes-nationwide-on-april-1.html.

15. Margie Fishman and Scott Goss, "Some of Delaware's Most Famous Art Will Never Be Seen," *News Journal*, September 27, 2017.

16. Fishman and Goss, "Delaware's Most Famous Art."

17. Michael Cooper, John McClelland, James Pearce, Richard Prisinzano, Joseph Sullivan, Danny Yagan, Owen Zidar, and Eric Zwick, "Business in the United States: Who Owns It and How Much Tax Do They Pay?," *Tax Policy and the Economy* 30, no. 1 (2016): pages 91–128.

18. Paulina Likos, "How to Invest in the Private Market," US News & World Report, January 26, 2021, https://money.usnews.com/investing/investing-101/articles/how-to-invest-in-the-private-market.

19. Allison Herren Lee, "Going Dark: The Growth of Private Markets and the Impact on Investors and the Economy; Remarks at The SEC Speaks in 2021," October 12, 2021, https://www.sec.gov/news/speech/lee-sec-speaks-2021-10-12?utm_medium=email&utm_source=govdelivery#_ftnref2.

20. Thomas Piketty and Emmanuel Saez, "Income Inequality in the United States, 1913–1998," *Quarterly Journal of Economics* 118, no. 1 (February 2003): page 9; N. Gregory Mankiw, "Defending the One Percent," *Journal of Economic Perspectives* 27, no. 3 (Summer 2013): page 22.

21. Juliana Menasce Horowitz, Ruth Iglielnik, and Rakesh Kochhar, "Trends in Income and Wealth Inequality," Pew Research Center, January 9, 2020, https://www.pewresearch.org/social-trends/2020/01/09/trends-in-income-and-wealth-inequality/.

22. Russ Buettner, Mike McIntire, Susanne Craig, and Keith Collins, "Trump Paid $750 in Federal Income Taxes in 2017. Here's the Math," *New York Times*, September 29, 2020.

23. Jesse Eisinger, Jeff Ernsthausen, and Paul Kiel, "The Secret IRS Files: Trove of Never-Before-Seen Records Reveal How the Wealthiest Avoid Income Tax," ProPublica, June 8, 2021, https://www.propublica.org/article/the-secret -irs-files-trove-of-never-before-seen-records-reveal-how-the-wealthiest-avoid -income-tax.

24. Matt Viser and Anu Narayanswamy, "Joe Biden Earned $15.6 Million in the Two Years after Leaving the Vice Presidency," *Washington Post*, July 10, 2019.

25. Darla Mercado, "Joe Biden Used This Strategy to Trim His Tax Bill. You Can, Too," CNBC, August 6, 2019, https://www.cnbc.com/2019/08/06/joe-biden -used-this-strategy-to-trim-his-tax-bill-you-can-too.html.

26. Nicholas Shaxson, *The Finance Curse: How Global Finance Is Making Us All Poorer* (London: The Bodley Head, 2018), page 178.

27. E.g., Chris Isidore, "Buffett Says He's Still Paying Lower Tax Rate Than His Secretary," CNN Business, March 4, 2013, https://money.cnn.com/2013/03 /04/news/economy/buffett-secretary-taxes/index.html. Buffett paid a "true tax rate" (taxes paid on wage income and dividends as a proportion of increase in wealth) of 0.1 percent from 2014 to 2018, according to ProPublica. See Eisinger et al., "Secret IRS Files."

28. Jeffrey A. Winters, "Oligarchy and Democracy," *American Interest* 7, no. 2 (2011).

29. Paul Kuhns, interview with the author, May 30, 2018.

30. "Delaware Property Taxes,"Tax-Rates.org, accessed October 6, 2021, http://www.tax-rates.org/delaware/property-tax.

31. Joe Heim and Carol D. Leonnig, "We Can Say the President Lives Here," *Washington Post*, November 29, 2020.

32. Ashley Parker, "'Corporations Are People,' Romney Tells Iowa Hecklers Angry over His Tax Policy," *New York Times*, August 11, 2011.

33. Colorado, New Mexico, and Connecticut also allow nonresident voting. See Margie Fishman, Gray Hughes, and Taylor Goebel, "Rehoboth Proposal to Let LLC Owners Vote Creates Stir," *News Journal*, December 2, 2017.

34. Karl Baker, "Newark, Delaware, Where Some People Can Vote More Than Once," *News Journal*, June 29, 2018.

35. Jan Konesey, interview with the author, May 23, 2018.

36. Karl Baker and Jeanne Kuang, "How Much Small-Business Relief Money Really Flowed to Delaware?," *Delaware News Journal*, July 18, 2020.

37. W. Gardner Selby, "Ken Paxton Draws on Debunked Figures, Says 'Illegals' Committed 600,000 Crimes in Texas since 2011," PolitiFact, September 7, 2018, https://www.politifact.com/factchecks/2018/sep/07/ken-paxton/ken-paxton -draws-debunked-figures-says-illegals-co/.

38. Emma Platoff, "As Ken Paxton Faces Criminal Allegations, an Agency at War with Itself Must Carry on the State's Business," *Texas Tribune*, October 5, 2020.

39. Doina Chiacu, Jon Herskovitz, and Tom Hals, "Twenty-One U.S. States Sue Delaware over Unclaimed Checks," Reuters, June 9, 2016.

40. See Robert Teitelman and Lawrence C. Strauss, "Unused Gift Cards: Lost but Not Forgotten," *Barron's*, January 2, 2016; Jeff Mordock, "Spend Your Gift Card before Delaware Takes It," *News Journal*, January 13, 2017.

41. DEFAC General Fund Revenue Forecast.

42. "Justices Hint at Property-Seizure Overhaul," Courthouse News Service, February 29, 2016, https://www.courthousenews.com/justices-hint-at-property-seizure-overhaul/.

43. Karl Baker, "Taking Unclaimed Property Keeps Delaware Taxes Low—but Other States Cry Foul," *News Journal*, March 22, 2019.

44. Jessica Masulli Reyes, "Federal Judge Blasts Delaware's Abandoned Property Practice," *News Journal*, June 29, 2016.

45. "Temple-Inland Decision and Settlement Open the Door to Changes in Delaware," *Unclaimed Property Focus* (blog), Unclaimed Property Professionals Organization, August 18, 2016, https://www.uppo.org/blogpost/925381/254979/Temple-Inland-decision-and-settlement-open-the-door-to-changes-in-Delaware.

46. Matthew Albright, "State Overhauling Unclaimed Property Law," *News Journal*, January 19, 2017.

47. "Delaware Jury Finds Retailer Liable for Gift Card Breakage in *qui tam* Escheat Litigation," Eversheds Sutherland, September 28, 2018, https://us.eversheds-sutherland.com/NewsCommentary/Legal-Alerts/214608/Legal-Alert-Delaware-jury-finds-retailer-liable-for-gift-card-breakage-in-qui-tam-escheat-litigation.

48. Tom McParland, "Jury Hits Overstock.com with $3M Verdict in Del. Unclaimed Property Case," *Delaware Law Weekly*, September 24, 2018.

49. Quoted in Jonathan Starkey, "Abandoned Property: Millions for Markell-Linked Firms," *News Journal*, May 17, 2014.

50. Jack Markell, interview with the author, May 16, 2019.

51. Quoted in Starkey, "Abandoned Property."

52. Claire Tsosie, "Why So Many Credit Cards Are from Delaware," *Forbes*, April 14, 2017.

53. Robert D. McFadden, "Pete du Pont, Ex-Delaware Governor Who Ran for President, Dies at 86," *New York Times*, May 9, 2021.

54. Bill Kauffman, "Tentatively Bold," *Reason*, December 1987.

55. Jeff Gerth, "New York Banks Urged Delaware to Lure Bankers," *New York Times*, March 17, 1981.

56. Du Pont quoted in William W. Boyer, *Governing Delaware: Policy Problems in the First State* (Newark: University of Delaware Press, 2000), page 62. James R. Dickenson, "The '88 Aspirants: Resumes and Reputations," *Washington Post*, August 11, 1986.

57. Quoted in Scott Goss, "Frank Biondi, Delaware Banking Law Architect, Honored," *News Journal*, January 11, 2016.

58. Gerth, "New York Banks."

59. Quoted in Boyer, *Governing Delaware*, page 64.

60. McBride and McDowell quoted in Gerth, "New York Banks."

61. In the interests of transparency, I should disclose that I once worked briefly for PIRG, in the summer of 1993.

62. Du Pont quoted in Jeff Gerth, "Law Freeing Banks Near in Delaware," *New York Times*, February 4, 1981.

63. Boyer, *Governing Delaware*, page 65.

64. See David Dayen, "Tom Carper's 40-Year Record of Defending Banks Is Being Challenged by Kerri Harris in a Democratic Primary," *The Intercept*, August 22, 2018.

65. Quoted in Goss, "Frank Biondi."

66. Pew Charitable Trusts, Payday Lending in America (series), March 27, 2015, https://www.pewtrusts.org/en/research-and-analysis/articles/2014/12/payday-lending-in-america.

67. Jeremy Pelofsky, "AIG Units Settle Mortgage Discrimination Case," Reuters, March 4, 2011, https://www.reuters.com/news/picture/aig-units-settle-mortgage-discrimination-idUSTRE6233K020100304.

68. Claire M. DeMatteis, "Women and the Delaware Bar and Bench: It Takes Generations," *Delaware Law Review* 14, no. 2 (2014): page 132.

69. Jeff Mordock, "Sid Balick, a Giant in Politics and Law, Will Be Remembered Thursday," *News Journal*, June 21, 2017.

70. LoPucki, *Courting Failure*, page 57.

71. "Helen Balick's Bailiwick Is a Backwater No More," *BusinessWeek*, November 30, 1992.

72. Lynn M. LoPucki and Joseph W. Doherty, "Delaware Bankruptcy: Failure in Ascendancy," *University of Chicago Law Review* 73 (2006): pages 1387–88.

73. Robert K. Rasmussen and Randall S. Thomas, "Whither the Race? A Comment on the Effects of the Delawarization of Corporate Reorganizations," *Vanderbilt Law Review* 54, no. 2 (March 2001): page 283.

74. Maureen Milford, "Companies Turn to Delaware to Survive Bankruptcy," *News Journal*, September 19, 2014; Kenneth M. Ayotte and David A. Skeel Jr., "Why Do Distressed Companies Choose Delaware? An Empirical Analysis of Venue Choice in Bankruptcy," Legal Scholarship Repository at Penn Law, May 21, 2003, https://scholarship.law.upenn.edu/faculty_scholarship/20/.

75. Quoted in Milford, "Companies Turn to Delaware."

76. See LoPucki, *Courting Failure*, pages 97–122.

77. LoPucki and Doherty, "Delaware Bankruptcy," pages 1418–19.

78. "Trends in Large Corporate Bankruptcy and Financial Distress (Midyear 2021 Update): Venues and Market Indicators," *National Law Review*, August 25, 2021.

79. "Trends in Large Corporate Bankruptcy."

80. William L. Cary, "Federalism and Corporate Law: Reflections upon Delaware," *Yale Law Journal* 83, no. 4 (March 1974): page 698.

Chapter 5

1. "Drugs, Law Enforcement and Foreign Policy," report prepared by the Sub-committee on Terrorism, Narcotics and International Operations of the Committee on Foreign Relations, United States Senate, December 1988.

2. James Henry, interview with the author, November 27, 2020.

3. "The Library Card Project: The Ease of Forming Anonymous Companies in the United States" (Global Financial Integrity, March 2019), https://gfintegrity.org/report/the-library-card-project/.

4. See "National Strategy for Combating Terrorist and Other Illicit Financing" (US Department of the Treasury, 2020), https://home.treasury.gov/system/files/136/National-Strategy-to-Counter-Illicit-Financev2.pdf.

5. "Library Card Project."

6. "Why Businesses Choose Delaware," Delaware.gov, accessed on October 20, 2021, https://corplaw.delaware.gov/why-businesses-choose-delaware/.

7. Jack Markell, interview with the author, May 16, 2019.

8. Michael Findley, Daniel Nielson, and Jason Sharman, "Global Shell Games: Testing Money Launderers' and Terrorist Financiers' Access to Shell Companies" (Centre for Governance and Public Policy, Griffith University, October 2012), page 2.

9. "Episode 390: We Set Up an Offshore Company in a Tax Haven," *Planet Money* (podcast), NPR, July 27, 2012, https://www.npr.org/sections/money/2016/03/16/470722656/episode-390-we-set-up-an-offshore-company-in-a-tax-haven.

10. FUSION, "How to Start an Anonymous Shell Company for Your Cat: Dirty Little Secrets," March 30, 2016, YouTube video, 2:09, https://www.youtube.com/watch?v=R0nHETD1wxg.

11. "Brother of Drug Lord Šarić Charged with Money Laundering," Organized Crime and Corruption Reporting Project, February 21, 2012, https://www.occrp.org/en/daily/28-ccwatch/cc-watch-indepth/1350-brother-of-drug-lord-ari-charged-with-money-laundering.

12. Milica Stojanovic, "Serbia Sentences Convicted Drugs Baron Saric for Money Laundering," Balkan Insight, July 31, 2020, https://balkaninsight.com/2020/07/31/serbia-sentences-convicted-drugs-baron-saric-for-money-laundering/; Filip Rudic, "Serbian Court Convicts Saric of Drug Smuggling," Balkan Insight, December 10, 2018, https://balkaninsight.com/2018/12/10/serbian-court-convicts-alleged-balkans-drug-lord-12-10-2018/.

13. Melanie Hicken and Blake Ellis, "These US Companies Hide Drug Dealers, Mobsters and Terrorists," CNN Money Investigates, December 9, 2015, https://money.cnn.com/2015/12/09/news/shell-companies-crime/index.html.

14. John A. Cassara, interview with the author, February 23, 2017.

15. John A. Cassara, interview with the author, February 23, 2017.

16. "State Minimum Wages," National Conference of State Legislatures, April 20, 2021, https://www.ncsl.org/research/labor-and-employment/state-minimum-wage-chart.aspx.

17. Clark Gascoigne, interview with the author, March 8, 2017.

18. Mark Hays, interview with the author, March 9, 2017.

19. Quoted in Christopher Maag, "President-Elect Joe Biden's Hometown of Wilmington, Delaware Is a Hub for Secrets," NorthJersey.com, November 13, 2020, https://www.northjersey.com/story/news/columnists/christopher-maag/2020/11 /13/joe-biden-wilmington-delaware-hub-secrets/6225673002/.

20. Ed Luce, "How Money Laundering Is Poisoning American Democracy," *Financial Times*, November 28, 2019.

21. Quoted in "The Al-Qa'idah Group Had nothing to Do with the 11 September Attacks," khilafah.com (taken from BBC Monitoring Service), September 28, 2001, https://web.archive.org/web/20020111073623/http:/www.khilafah.com /1421/category.php?DocumentID=2392.

22. John A. Cassara, interview with the author, February 23, 2017.

23. "Anti–Money Laundering and Counter-Terrorist Financing Measures: United States, Mutual Evaluation Report," Financial Action Task Force and Asia/Pacific Group on Money Laundering, December 2016, page 4, https:// www.fatf-gafi.org/media/fatf/documents/reports/mer4/MER-United-States -2016.pdf.

24. "Company Formations: Minimal Ownership Information Is Collected and Available," Report to the Permanent Subcommittee on Investigations, Committee on Homeland Security and Governmental Affairs, U.S. Senate, April 2006, page 1, https://www.gao.gov/assets/gao-07-196t.pdf.

25. Max Heywood, "The FATF Report on the USA: More Roof Than Holes on Average," Transparency International blog, December 5, 2016, https://blog .transparency.org/2016/12/05/the-fatf-report-on-the-usa-more-roof-than-holes -on-average/index.html.

26. John A. Cassara, interview with the author, February 23, 2017.

27. Mark Hays, interview with the author, March 9, 2017.

28. Emile van der Does de Willebois, Emily M. Halter, Robert A. Harrison, Ji Won Park, and J. C. Sharman, "The Puppet Masters: How the Corrupt Use Legal Structures to Hide Stolen Assets and What to Do About It," Stolen Asset Recovery Initiative, 2011, page 26, https://openknowledge.worldbank.org/bitstream/handle /10986/2363/9780821388945.pdf?sequence=6&isAllowed=y.

29. Julie Satow, "Seizing Iran's Slice of Fifth Avenue," *New York Times*, September 24, 2013.

30. Angelique Chrisafis, "Son of Equatorial Guinea's President Is Convicted of Corruption in France," *Guardian*, 27 October 2017; "Teodorin Obiang: French Court Fines Equatorial Guinea VP," BBC News, February 10, 2020, https://www .bbc.com/news/world-europe-51449951.

31. "Federal Real Property: GSA Should Inform Tenant Agencies When Leasing High-Security Space from Foreign Owners" (US Government Accountability Office, January 3, 2017), https://www.gao.gov/products/gao-17-195.

32. John A. Cassara, interview with the author, February 23, 2017.

33. See Daniel Hemel, "South Dakota's Tax Avoidance Schemes Represent Federalism at Its Worst," *Washington Post*, October 7, 2021.

34. Quoted in Steven J. Horowitz and Robert H. Sitkoff, "Unconstitutional Perpetual Trusts," *Vanderbilt Law Review* 67, no. 6 (November 2014): page 1784.

35. Michael Rainey, "America's $500 Billion Tax Haven on the Prairie," Yahoo!, October 14, 2021, https://www.yahoo.com/now/america-500-billion-tax-haven -224102003.html.

36. See Howard Gleckman, "South Dakota Turned Itself into a Tax Haven. But Why?" *Forbes*, October 14, 2021, https://www.forbes.com/sites/howardgleckman /2021/10/14/south-dakota-turned-itself-into-a-tax-haven-but-why/?sh =55f0efe72f25.

37. Ben Butler, "Panama Papers Law Firm Mossack Fonseca Sues Netflix over The Laundromat," *The Guardian,* October 16, 2019.

38. "Financial Secrecy Index 2020: Narrative Report on United States of America," Tax Justice Network, released February 18, 2020, https://fsi.taxjustice.net /PDF/UnitedStates.pdf.

39. Mike Findley, Daniel Nielson, and Jason Sharman, *Global Shell Games* (New York: Cambridge University Press, 2014), page 32.

40. "Death and Taxes: The True Toll of Tax Dodging," Christian Aid report, May 2008, https://www.christianaid.org.uk/sites/default/files/2017-08/death-and -taxes-true-toll-tax-dodging-may-2008.pdf.

41. US Department of the Treasury, "National Strategy," page 14.

42. Quoted in Eric Lipton and Julie Creswell, "Panama Papers Show How Rich United States Clients Hid Millions Abroad," *New York Times*, June 5, 2016.

43. Kimberly Kay Hoang, *Spiderweb Capitalism: How Global Elites Exploit Frontier Markets* (Princeton: Princeton University Press, forthcoming 2022.) As political scientists Ronen Palan and Anastasia Nesvetailova put it, "Underlying the evolution of offshore financial havens and the shadow banking universe has been the factor of 'elsewhere': the principle of not being recognized, registered, accounted for, taxed, regulated, detected or understood well, has been the engine being the growth of the offshore political economy" ("Elsewhere, Ideally Nowhere: Shadow Banking and Offshore Finance," *Tidsskriftet Politik* 16, no. 4 [December 2013]).

44. "Concealment of Beneficial Ownership" (Financial Action Task Force– Egmont Group Report, July 2018), https://www.fatf-gafi.org/media/fatf /documents/reports/FATF-Egmont-Concealment-beneficial-ownership.pdf.

45. Joseph Biden and Michael Carpenter, "Foreign Dark Money Is Threatening American Democracy," Politico, November 27, 2018, https://www.politico.com /magazine/story/2018/11/27/foreign-dark-money-joe-biden-222690/.

46. Nicholas Confessore, "How to Hide $400 Million," *New York Times Magazine*, November 30, 2016.

47. Alexandra Scaggs, "Delaware Loophole Could Leave Creditors Holding the Bag," *Barron's*, August 27, 2018.

48. "How Trucking Companies Use Shell Companies to Avoid Liability," Amaro Law Firm blog, October 19, 2016.

Chapter 6

1. The 2020 celebration was canceled due to the COVID-19 pandemic.

2. Maddy Lauria and Scott Goss, "Return Day, 200-Year Delaware Tradition, Briefly Makes Friends of Political Enemies," *News Journal*, November 8, 2018.

3. See, e.g., Elizabeth Williamson, "In Biden's Home State, G.O.P. Centrism Is Overtaken by Fringe," *New York Times*, October 5, 2020; David Alff, "Joe Biden's Love of Amtrak Tells Us How He Would Govern," *Washington Post*, October 20, 2020; Gerald Joseph McAdams Kauffman Jr., "The Delaware Way Could Be the National Key to Tackling Climate Change," USA TODAY network, April 21 2021, https://www.delawareonline.com/story/opinion/2021/04/21/delaware-way -could-national-key-tackling-climate-change/7303157002/.

4. Melanie Mason, "Joe Biden Personifies the 'Delaware Way.' In Wilmington, That Clubby Style of Politics Is Being Questioned," *Los Angeles Times*, February 23, 2020.

5. "Character Sketches of Delegates to the Federal Convention," Teaching American History, accessed November 7, 2021, https://teachingamericanhistory .org/document/character-sketches-of-delegates-to-the-federal-convention/.

6. "John Dickinson Plantation," Delaware.gov, accessed September 29, 2021, https://history.delaware.gov/john-dickinson-plantation/.

7. Quoted in Lesley Kennedy, "Caesar Who? The Founding Father You've Probably Never Heard Of," History.com, September 18, 2020, https://www.history.com /news/founding-father-you-never-heard-of-caesar-rodney.

8. James Pennewill and Rodney Macdonough, *Addresses Delivered at the Unveiling of a Memorial Tablet to Commodore Thomas Macdonough* (Wilmington: Historical Society of Delaware, 1908), page 16.

9. Edmund Cody Burnett, ed., *Letters of Members of the Continental Congress*, vol. 6, *August 29, 1774, To July 4, 1776* (Whitefish, MT: Kessinger Publishing, 2010), page 528.

10. Worthington Chauncey Ford, ed., *Journals of the Continental Congress, 1774–1789: Jan. 1–May 21, 1777* (Washington, DC: US Government Printing Office, 1907), page 83.

11. Richard F. Miller, ed., *States At War: A Reference Guide for Delaware, Maryland, and New Jersey in the Civil War* (Hanover, NH: University Press of New England, 2015), page 67; Peter T. Dalleo, "The Growth of Delaware's Antebellum Free African American Community," in *A History of African Americans of Delaware and Maryland's Eastern Shore*, ed. Carole C. Marks (Wilmington: Delaware Heritage Press, 1998), page 123.

12. James E. Newton, "Black Americans in Delaware: An Overview," University of Delaware, 1997, https://www1.udel.edu/BlackHistory/overview.html.

13. W. Emerson Wilson, ed., *Delaware in the Civil War* (Dover, DE: Civil War Centennial Commission, 1964), page 82.

14. A few days later, Saulsbury publicly apologized to avoid being expelled from the Senate. See "The Battle of Three Brothers," US Senate, accessed September 30, 2021, https://www.senate.gov/artandhistory/history/minute/The_battle _of_three_brothers.htm.

15. The Delaware Grays, August 21, 2021, https://www.descv.org/Delaware Confederates.html.

16. *Miscellaneous Documents of the House of Representatives for the First Session of the Fifty-First Congress, 1889–'90* [United States Congressional Serial Set, Volume 2773] (Washington, DC: US Government Printing Office, 1891), page 655.

17. Quoted in James A. McGowan, *Station Master on the Underground Railroad: The Life and Letters of Thomas Garrett* (Jefferson, NC: McFarland, 2009), page 65.

18. Quoted in Andrew Cockburn, "No Joe!," *Harper's Magazine*, March 2019.

19. Quoted in Yohuru R. Williams, "Permission to Hate: Delaware, Lynching, and the Culture of Violence in America," *Journal of Black Studies* 32, no. 1 (September 2001), page 8.

Chapter 7

1. For a contemporary account of the White lynching, see Associated Press, "Negro Flames for Mob in Delaware," *North Carolinian*, June 25, 1903.

2. The Ferris School for Boys is still in operation. See "Ferris School," Delaware.gov, accessed September 29, 2021, https://kids.delaware.gov/yrs/ferris.shtml.

3. Quoted in Williams, "Permission to Hate," page 12.

4. Quoted in Harry Themal, "New Castle County's Gruesome 1903 Lynching by Fire," *News Journal*, January 9, 2017.

5. Roosevelt quote cited in Jessica Bies, "Historical Marker in Memory of the Only Documented Lynching in Delaware Is Unveiled," *News Journal*, June 23, 2019; *New York Times* and Czar Nicholas cartoon quoted in Themal, "New Castle County's Gruesome 1903 Lynching."

6. The AP article was run by many newspapers, including, for example, the *San Francisco Call*, in its issue of June 23, 1903, and the *Plymouth Tribune* (Indiana) on June 25, 1903.

7. Quoted in Williams, "Permission to Hate," page 17.

8. Quoted in Dennis B. Downe, "The Lord's Messenger: Racial Lynching and the Church Trial of Robert Elwood," *Journal of Presbyterian History* 79, no. 2 (Summer 2001): page 137.

9. Quoted in Williams, "Permission to Hate," page 4.

10. See Williams, "Permission to Hate."

11. Quoted in Williams, page 13.

12. Cited in Williams, page 19.

13. Quoted in Downe, "Lord's Messenger," page 140.

14. Quoted in Downe, page 142.

15. Quoted in Williams, "Permission to Hate," page 26.

16. Quoted in Williams, page 24.

17. Quoted in Williams, page 22.

18. James E. Newton, "Black Americans in Delaware: An Overview," in *A History of African Americans of Delaware and Maryland's Eastern Shore*, ed. Carole C. Marks (Wilmington: Delaware Heritage Press, 1998), page 24; Charles Fred Hearns, "The Birth of a Nation: The Case for a Tri-Level Analysis of Forms of Racial Vindication," M.A. Thesis, University of South Florida, November 7, 2014, page 61, https://scholarcommons.usf.edu/etd/5366.

19. Newton, "Black Americans in Delaware," page 22.

20. Judgment of Vice Chancellor Seitz, Parker v. University of Delaware, Court of Chancery of Delaware, New Castle, August 9, 1950, https://law.justia.com/cases /delaware/court-of-chancery/1950/75-a-2d-225-4.html.

21. Quoted in Caleb Owens, "The University Says that Hugh M. Morris Fought for Campus Desegregation—History Says Otherwise," *Review: The Independent Student Newspaper of the University of Delaware*, November 13, 2018.

22. Quoted in Owens, "University Says."

23. Quoted in Harry Themal, "Jack Greenberg Also Brought Desegregation to UD," *News Journal*, October 21, 2016.

24. Parker v. University of Delaware, 75 A.2d. 225 (250).

25. Owens, "University Says."

26. Quoted in Brett Gadsden, "'He Said He Wouldn't Help Me Get a Jim Crow Bus': The Shifting Terms of the Challenge to Segregated Public Education, 1950–1954," *Journal of Black History* 90, no. 1/2 (Winter 2005): page 9.

27. Quoted in Gadsden, page 10.

28. Richard Kluger, *Simple Justice: The History of* Brown v. Board of Education *and Black America's Struggle for Equality* (New York: Vintage Books, 2004), page 433.

29. Quoted in Kluger, page 450.

30. Quoted in Kluger, pages 450–51.

31. Quoted in Jeff Brown, "Segregation Issues in Dover Helped Spur Changes in Delaware Law," *Dover Post*, February 5, 2014.

32. Quoted in Andrew Glass, "Ghana Finance Minister Denied Service, Oct. 10, 1957," Politico, October 10, 2013, https://www.politico.com/story/2013/10/this -day-in-politics-098073.

33. Quoted in Brown, "Segregation Issues."

34. Quoted in Brown.

35. Quoted in Brown.

36. Don Flood, "History of Milford Eleven Helped Form Delaware's Present," *Cape Gazette*, February 25, 2014.

37. Quoted in Alton Hornsby Jr., ed., *Black America: A State-by-State Historical Encyclopedia* (Santa Barbara, CA: Greenwood, 2011), page 139.

38. Quoted in Boyer, *Governing Delaware*, page 58.

39. Quoted in Boyer, page 57.

40. Quoted in Boyer, page 58.

41. Steve Inskeep, "Biden Vows to Ease Racial Divisions. Here's His Record," NPR, October 14, 2020, https://www.npr.org/2020/10/14/920385802/biden -vows-to-ease-racial-divisions-heres-his-record.

42. Jane Harriman, "Joe Biden: Hope for Democratic Party in '72?," *Evening Journal*, November 11, 1970.

43. Joe Farley, "An Interview: Senator Joseph R. Biden, Jr.," *People Paper*, September 13, 1975 (reprinted in the *Congressional Record*—Senate, October 2, 1975).

44. In a Senate speech in December 1974, for example, Biden said, "I have become more and more disenchanted with busing as a remedy. . . . It is increasingly apparent that busing is a dire step. I have always believed that busing should

be undertaken only under extreme circumstances—and even then I would have serious doubts about its effectiveness—about the impact upon students who are assembled in classrooms not to be bused but to be educated" (*Congressional Record*—Senate, December 14, 1974). Biden spent much more time criticizing busing in general than in distinguishing which types of busing he supported and opposed. "I don't know whether he's just reconstructed this history in his own mind, but he's factually untruthful, that's for sure," Gary Orfield, a Distinguished Research Professor at UCLA, told the *New York Times* in 2019 (Astead W. Herndon and Sheryl Gay Stolberg, "How Joe Biden Became the Democrats' Anti-Busing Crusader," *New York Times*, July 15, 2019). Busing, Orfield said, was "a real test of conscience and courage. I think he failed." Brett Gadsden, a Northwestern University historian who is an expert on the fight for desegregation in Delaware, thinks Biden was being disingenuous when he said he supported school integration but opposed busing. "To oppose busing remedies specifically designed to remedy segregation is to oppose desegregation," Gadsden notes. Instead, Gadsden sees Biden's mid-1970s stance on busing as a reflection of white prejudice in the Wilmington suburbs. "When white people opposed busing, that's when Biden raised his voice," he noted (Jeanne Kuang, "Joe Biden's Complicated Opposition to Busing for School Desegregation," *Delaware News Journal*, April 20, 2019).

45. "Busing Clash Wins Biden Few Friends," *Morning News*, July 10, 1974.

46. Quoted in Cockburn, "No Joe!"

47. Quoted in Inskeep, "Biden Vows."

48. Joe Biden, *Promises to Keep* (New York: Random House, 2007), page 125.

49. *The 14th Amendment and School Busing Hearings before the Subcommittee on the Constitution of the Committee on the Judiciary, US Senate, First Session, on the 14th Amendment and School Busing, May 14 and June 3, 1981* (Washington, DC: US Government Printing Office, 1982).

50. Arielle Niemeyer, with Jennifer Ayscue, John Kuscera, Gary Orfield, Genevieve Siegel-Hawley, "Courts, the Legislature and Delaware's Resegregation: A Report on School Segregation in Delaware, 1989–2010" (Civil Rights Project / Proyecto Derechos Civiles, December 19, 2014), https://files.eric.ed.gov/fulltext/ED558742.pdf.

51. See Jeanne Kuang and Natalia Alamdari, "Settlement of Delaware Education Suit Promises Historic Changes," *Delaware News Journal*, October 12, 2020; Jeanne Kuang and Natalia Alamdari, "What a Delaware Lawsuit Settlement Means for Education—If It Gets the Votes," *Delaware News Journal*, October 14, 2020.

52. Jeanne Kuang, Marina Affo, Patricia Talorico, and Ira Porter, "Wilmington Removes Caesar Rodney, Christopher Columbus Statues Friday amid Calls for Change," *Delaware News Journal*, June 12, 2020.

53. Xerxes Wilson, "As Nation Grapples with Symbols and Racism, Delaware to Remove Public Whipping Post," *Delaware News Journal*, June 30, 2020; "Georgetown Removes Whipping Post" (video), *Delaware News Journal*, July 1, 2020.

54. Jeff Neiburg, "New Castle County Rejected Its Black Students. Now the County Will Help Tell the Story," *Delaware News Journal*, July 29, 2020.

55. Busing was not the only chapter of Biden's past that irked liberals. Another was his support for the 1994 crime bill, which included the notorious "three strikes and you're out" provision, expanded the number of crimes that were eligible for the death penalty, and offered states money to build more prisons. The bill capped more than a decade in which Biden worked to establish his "tough on crime" credentials. "Whenever people hear the words 'drugs' and 'crime,' I want them to think 'Joe Biden,'" he reportedly told his staff at the time (quoted in Cockburn, "No Joe!"), Some would consider the law responsible for the subsequent steep increase in the number of Black people behind bars, although at the time, many Black leaders supported the legislation. See, for example, Yolanda Young, "Analysis: Black Leaders Supported Clinton's Crime Bill," NBC News, April 8, 2016, https://www.nbcnews .com/news/nbcblk/analysis-black-leaders-supported-clinton-s-crime-bill-n552961.

56. See P. R. Lockhart, "Joe Biden's Record on School Desegregation Busing, Explained," Vox, July 16, 2019, https://www.vox.com/policy-and-politics/2019/6 /28/18965923/joe-biden-school-desegregation-busing-democratic-primary; Amy Sherman, "Joe Biden Oversimplifies His School Busing Record in Miami Debate," Politifact, June 28, 2019, https://www.politifact.com/factchecks/2019/jun/28/joe -biden/joe-biden-oversimplifies-his-record-school-busing-/.

Chapter 8

1. "Delaware's Alternatives to Corporations," Delaware.gov, accessed September 28, 2021, https://corplaw.delaware.gov/delawares-alternatives-corporations/.

2. At the time of writing, Morris, Nichols Arsht & Tunnell LLP has three members and one former partner on the committee, while Potter Anderson & Corroon LLP and Richards, Layton & Finger, PA both have three. Morris James LLP, Skadden, Arps, Slate, Meagher & Flom LLP, Smith, Katzenstein & Furlow LLP, and Young Conaway Stargatt & Taylor, LLP each have two members, while the following firms have one representative each: Prickett, Jones & Elliott, PA, Grant & Eisenhofer PA, Connolly Gallagher LLP, The Delaware Counsel Group, LLP, Ashby & Geddes, PA, Heyman Enerio Gattuso & Hirzel LLP, and Ross Aronstam & Moritz LLP. See "About the Section," Delaware State Bar Association, accessed October 2, 2021, https://www.dsba.org/sections-committees/sections-of-the-bar /corporation-law/.

3. Lawrence Hamermesh, interview with the author, November 19, 2018. See also S. Samuel Arsht, "A History of Delaware Corporation Law," *Delaware Journal of Corporate Law* 1, no. 1 (1976): pages 1–22.

4. Stephen Labaton, "A Debate over the Impact of Delaware Takeover Law," *New York Times*, February 1, 1988.

5. Jeffrey M. Jones, "U.S. Stock Ownership Down among All but Older, Higher-Income," Gallup, May 24, 2017, https://news.gallup.com/poll/211052/stock -ownership-down-among-older-higher-income.aspx.

6. "Union Thug James Maravelias' Boorish Leadership Had Few, If Any, Followers at the Labor Day Parade Today," *Delaware Way* (blog), September 1, 2014, http:// delawareway.blogspot.com/2014/09/union-thug-james-maravelias-boorish.html.

7. Melanie George Smith, interview with the author, May 31, 2018.

8. Stephen Labaton, "A Debate over the Impact of Delaware Takeover Law," *New York Times*, February 1, 1988.

9. See, for example, Guhan Subramanian, Steven Herscovici, and Brian Barbetta, "Is Delaware's Antitakeover Statute Unconstitutional? Evidence from 1988–2008," *Business Lawyer* 65, no. 3 (May 2010): pages 685–752.

10. Ryan S. Starstrom, "Delaware's Ban on Fee-Shifting: A Failed Attempt to Protect Shareholders at the Expense of Officers and Directors of Public Corporations," *Brooklyn Law Review* 82, no. 3 (2017): pages 1355–56.

11. Lawrence A. Hamermesh, "The Policy Foundations of Delaware Corporate Law," *Columbia Law Review* 106, no. 7 (November 2006): pages 1778–89.

12. "About Delaware's General Corporation Law," Delaware.gov, accessed Oct 22, 2021, https://corplaw.delaware.gov/delawares-general-corporation-law/.

13. Chad Selweski, "Michigan Gets F Grade in 2015 State Integrity Investigation," Center for Public Integrity, November 12, 2015, https://publicintegrity.org/politics/state-politics/state-integrity-investigation/michigan-gets-f-grade-in-2015-state-integrity-investigation/.

14. Jonathan Starkey, "Delaware Gets F Grade in 2015 State Integrity Investigation," Center for Public Integrity, November 12, 2015, https://publicintegrity.org/politics/state-politics/state-integrity-investigation/delaware-gets-f-grade-in-2015-state-integrity-investigation/.

15. Brian Quinn, interview with the author, June 20, 2018.

16. Francis G. X. Pileggi, "Delaware Proposes New Fee-Shifting and Forum Selection Legislation," *Delaware and Corporate Litigation Blog*, March 6, 2015, https://www.delawarelitigation.com/2015/03/articles/commentary/delaware-proposes-new-fee-shifting-and-forum-selection-legislation/.

17. Jeff Bullock, interview with the author, May 29, 2018.

18. Raghuram Rajan, *The Third Pillar: How Markets and the State Leave the Community Behind* (New York: Penguin, 2019), page 110.

19. Jen Fifield, "State Legislatures Have Fewer Farmers, Lawyers; But Higher Education Level," Pew Charitable Trusts, December 10, 2015, http://www.pewtrusts.org/en/research-and-analysis/blogs/stateline/2015/12/10/state-legislatures-have-fewer-farmers-lawyers-but-higher-education-level; Adam McCann, "Most & Least Educated States in America," WalletHub, February 16, 2021, https://wallethub.com/edu/e/most-educated-states/31075#cinda-klickna.

20. Transparency campaigners in Delaware have lobbied for an independent counsel to investigate the changes proposed by the Corporation Law Council, without success.

21. Larry E. Ribstein, "Delaware, Lawyers, and Contractual Choice of Law," *Delaware Journal of Corporate Law* 19 (1994): pages 1009–10, http://www.djcl.org/wp-content/uploads/2014/08/Delaware-LAWYERS-AND-CONTRACTUAL-CHOICE-OF-LAW.pdf.

22. Milton Friedman, "The Social Responsibility of Business Is to Increase Its Profits," *New York Times Magazine*, September 13, 1970.

23. Kent Greenfield, "End Delaware's Corporate Dominance," *Democracy* 39 (Winter 2016), https://democracyjournal.org/magazine/39/end-delawares-corporate-dominance/.

24. Rajan, *Third Pillar*.

25. "A Sense of Purpose," Larry Fink's 2018 letter to CEOs, accessed October 22, 2021, https://www.blackrock.com/corporate/investor-relations/2018-larry -fink-ceo-letter.

26. Oliver Hart and Luigi Zingales, "Companies Should Maximize Shareholder Welfare Not Market Value" (New Working Paper Series No. 12, Stigler Center for the Study of the Economy and the State, University of Chicago Booth School of Business, July 2017), https://research.chicagobooth.edu/~/media/A51FEA9DB BF7409E84C381919F4925F6.pdf.

27. Leo E. Strine Jr., interview with the author, May 30, 2018.

28. Tom Hals, "Retiring Judge Strine Calls on Funds to Protect US Workers," Reuters, July 9, 2019, https://www.reuters.com/article/us-usa-courts-strine -workers-idUSKCN1U32N0.

29. Leo E. Strine Jr., "Human Freedom and Two Friedmen: Musings on the Implications of Globalization for the Effective Regulation of Corporate Behavior," *University of Toronto Law Journal* 58, no. 241 (2008): pages 24–41, https:// scholarship.law.upenn.edu/cgi/viewcontent.cgi?article=1179&context=faculty _scholarship.

30. Colin Mayer, Leo E. Strine Jr., and Jaap Winter, "The Purpose of Business Is to Solve Problems of Society, Not to Cause Them," ProMarket, Stigler Center for the Study of the Economy and the State, Chicago Booth, October 9, 2020, https://promarket.org/2020/10/09/purpose-business-solve-problems-society -not-cause-them-friedman/.

31. Alina Dizik, "When It Makes Sense to Pollute—and How to Change the Equation," *Chicago Booth Review*, August 28, 2018, https://review.chicago booth.edu/economics/2018/article/when-it-makes-sense-pollute-and-how -change-equation#:~:text=To%20change%20the%20equation%2C%20 make,%E2%80%9Cit%20can%20happen%20anywhere.%E2%80%9D. The paper the article is based on is Roy Shapira and Luigi Zingales, "Is Pollution Value-Maximizing? The DuPont Case" (NBER Working Paper No. 23866, September 2017), https://www.nber.org/system/files/working_papers/w23866/w23866.pdf.

32. George Stigler, "American Capitalism at High Noon," *Chicago Booth Review*, April 2, 1981, https://review.chicagobooth.edu/economics/archive/american -capitalism-high-noon.

Chapter 9

1. Joseph W. Bishop Jr., "Sitting Ducks and Decoy Ducks: New Trends in the Indemnification of Corporate Directors and Officers" (Yale Faculty Scholarship Series paper 2830, 1968), page 1084, https://digitalcommons.law.yale.edu/fss _papers/2830/.

2. Jonathan R. Macey and Geoffrey P. Miller, "Toward an Interest-Group Theory of Delaware Corporate Law," *Texas Law Review* 65, no. 3 (February 1987): pages 472–73, https://digitalcommons.law.yale.edu/cgi/viewcontent.cgi?referer =https://www.google.com/&httpsredir=1&article=2789&context=fss_papers.

3. Because of the business judgment rule. Sean J. Griffith, "Product Differentiation in the Market for Corporate Law: A Regulatory Alternative to Delaware Corporate Law," in Bainbridge et al., *Can Delaware Be Dethroned?*, 18; Stephen M. Bainbridge, "The Business Judgment Rule as Abstention Doctrine," *Vanderbilt Law Review* 57, no. 1 (2004): page 101.

4. Griffith, page 20.

5. Following the Court of Chancery's 2016 decision in the *Trulia* case.

6. "Faculty Directory: Lawrence Hamermesh," Delaware Law School, Widener University, accessed October 3, 2021, https://delawarelaw.widener.edu/current-students/faculty-directory/faculty/112/.

7. Cary, "Federalism and Corporate Law," page 687.

8. This is also, of course, frequently the case at the federal level, where lobbyists and special interest groups have buried self-serving provisions in lengthy laws such as the tax code or appropriations bills.

9. Quoted in Rahul Sagar, *Secrets and Leaks: The Dilemma of State Secrecy* (Princeton: Princeton University Press, 2013), page 47.

10. Cary, "Federalism and Corporate Law," page 684.

11. Melanie George Smith, interview with the author, May 31, 2018.

12. Charles M. Elson, "Delaware Must Retain Its Corporate Dominance," in Bainbridge et al., *Can Delaware Be Dethroned?*, page 237.

13. "About Delaware's General Corporation Law," Delaware.gov, accessed October 23, 2021, https://corplaw.delaware.gov/delawares-general-corporation-law/.

14. Freeborn, "Delaware Is in Real Trouble."

15. S. Samuel Arsht, "The Business Judgment Rule Revisited," *Hofstra Law Review* 8, no. 1 (1979): pages 93–134.

16. Quoted in Lawrence A. Hamermesh and Leo E. Strine, "Fiduciary Principles and Delaware Corporation Law: Searching for the Optimal Balance by Understanding that the World is Not" (University of Pennsylvania, Institute for Law & Economics Research Paper No. 17-40, October 2017), https://papers.ssrn.com/sol3/papers.cfm?abstract_id=3044477.

17. "Dogsbodies of the DGCL: Revisiting Roles in the Landmark Achievement," *Delaware Lawyer*, Spring 2008, page 13.

18. Marcel Kahan and Ehud Kamar, "Price Discrimination in the Market for Corporate Law," *Cornell Law Review*, 2001, page 1233, footnote 120.

19. Clark W. Furlow, "Good Faith, Fiduciary Duties, and the Business Judgment Rule in Delaware," *Utah Law Review*, 2009, page 1062.

20. Stephen M. Bainbridge, Star Lopez, and Benjamin Oklan, "The Convergence of Good Faith and Oversight," *UCLA Law Review* 55, no. 599 (February 2008): page 559.

21. Quoted in Kent Greenfield, "Law, Politics, and the Erosion of Legitimacy in the Delaware Courts," *New York Law School Law Review* 55, 2011, page 494.

22. Kent Greenfield, interview with the author, April 24, 2018.

23. Gatz Properties, LLC v. Auriga Capital Corporation, Delaware Supreme Court ruling, November 7, 2012.

24. Peter Lattman, "In Unusual Move, Delaware Supreme Court Rebukes a Judge," DealBook, *New York Times*, November 9, 2012, https://dealbook.nytimes .com/2012/11/09/in-unusual-move-the-delaware-supreme-court-rebukes-a-judge/.

25. Karl Baker, "Federal Appeals Court Takes on Delaware Question of Partisan Judges," *Delaware News Journal*, August 20, 2018.

26. Sophia Schmidt, "Federal Appeals Court Rules against Delaware Judicial Balance Requirements," Delaware Public Media, February 5, 2019, https://www .delawarepublic.org/post/federal-appeals-court-rules-against dclaware-judicial -balance-requirements.

27. Amy Howe, "Opinion Analysis: Court Throws Out Challenge to Delaware Rules on Bipartisanship in Judiciary," SCOTUSblog, December 10, 2020, https:// www.scotusblog.com/2020/12/opinion-analysis-court-throws-out-challenge-to -delaware-rules-on-bipartisanship-in-judiciary/.

28. Sujeet Indap, "Delaware's Feared Litigator Rounds on State's Judges," *Financial Times*, June 18, 2018.

29. Cary, "Federalism and Corporate Law," page 695.

30. Quoted in Steven David Solomon, "The Life and Death of Delaware's Arbitration Experiment," DealBook, *New York Times*, August 31, 2012, https://dealbook .nytimes.com/2012/08/31/the-life-and-death-of-delawares-arbitration-experiment/.

31. Quoted in Gellaine T. Newton, "Like Oil and Vinegar, Sitting Judges and Arbitrators Do Not Mix: Delaware's Unique Attempt at Judicial Arbitration," *Arbitration Law Review* 5, no. 449 (2013): page 450.

32. Solomon, "Life and Death."

Chapter 10

1. "Remarks by President Biden at Signing of an Executive Order Promoting Competition in the American Economy," July 9, 2021, https://www.whitehouse .gov/briefing-room/speeches-remarks/2021/07/09/remarks-by-president-biden -at-signing-of-an-executive-order-promoting-competition-in-the-american -economy/; Cockburn, "No Joe!"

2. David S. Swayze & David B. Ripsom, "The Delaware Banking Revolution: Are Expanded Powers Next?" *Delaware Journal of Corporate Law* 13, no. 1 (1988), page 44.

3. Tim Murphy, "House of Cards," *Mother Jones*, November 2019.

4. Evan Osnos, "Will Joe Biden's History Lift Him Up or Weigh Him Down?," *New Yorker*, April 26, 2019.

5. Cockburn, "No Joe!"

6. Elizabeth Warren, "What Is a Women's Issue: Bankruptcy, Commercial Law, and Other Gender-Neutral Topics," *Harvard Women's Law Journal* 25 (Spring 2002): page 20.

7. Quoted in Theodoric Meyer, "Inside Biden and Warren's Yearslong Feud," Politico, March 12, 2019, https://www.politico.com/magazine/story/2019/03/12 /biden-vs-warren-2020-democratic-primaries-bankruptcy-bill-225728/.

8. Jack Bohrer, "'It Is a Pleasure to Blog with You': Elizabeth Warren's Early Years Online," NBC News, January 6, 2019, https://www.nbcnews.com/politics /politics-news/it-pleasure-blog-you-elizabeth-warren-s-early-years-online -n954961.

9. Quoted in Meyer, "Biden and Warren's Yearslong Feud."

10. Kevin L. McQuaid, "Charging Forward," *Baltimore Sun*, February 2, 1997.

11. Lowell Bergman and Patrick McGeehan, "Co-founder of MBNA Meets an Anxious Board, and Loses," *New York Times*, March 7, 2004,

12. Bergman and McGeehan, "Co-founder of MBNA"; Julie Bykowicz and Ted Mann, "On Wall Street Regulation, Biden Keeps Everyone Guessing— Progressives, Moderates Vie for Candidate's Ear as He Edges Left," *Wall Street Journal*, October 14, 2020.

13. Bykowicz and Mann, "Wall Street Regulation."

14. This title has been periodically recycled. See, e.g., Will Bunch, "Sen. Joe Biden (D-MBNA)—Why He's No Friend of the Working Class and Why the GOP Can't Use It against Him," *Philadelphia Inquirer*, August 25, 2008.

15. Dan Morgan, "Creditors' Money Talks Louder in Bankruptcy Debate," *Washington Post*, June 1, 1999.

16. Heidi Przybyla, "Joe Biden's Record Could Pose Difficulties for 2016 White House Bid," *USA TODAY*, September 30, 2015.

17. Joseph N. DiStefano, "Latest Move Hastens DuPont's Exit from Wilmington," *Philadelphia Inquirer*, December 23, 2014.

18. Patricia Talorico, "Hospital Dropping DuPont Name: Is This Erasing Delaware History?," *Delaware News Journal*, May 26, 2021.

19. Reprinted in Ralph Nader, "The Case for Federal Chartering," in *Federal Charters for Energy Corporations—Selected Materials* (Washington, DC: US Government Printing Office, 1974), page 20.

20. LoPucki, *Courting Failure*, pages 54–55.

21. Christopher Drew and Mike McIntire, "Obama Aides Defend Bank's Pay to Biden Son," *New York Times*, August 24, 2008.

22. Michael Steinberger, "Joe Biden Wants to Take America Back to a Time before Trump," *New York Times Magazine*, July 23, 2019.

23. Michael Simkovic, "The Effect of BAPCPA on Credit Card Industry Profits and Prices," *American Bankruptcy Law Journal* 83, no. 1 (2009): pages 1–26.

24. Tal Gross, Raymond Kluender, Feng Liu, Matthew J. Notowidigdo, and Jialan Wangk, "The Economic Consequences of Bankruptcy Reform" (University of Chicago Becker Friedman Institute for Economics Working Paper no. 26234, July 2020), https://www.nber.org/papers/w26254.

25. "Subprime HEAT Update" (Credit Suisse, March 8, 2007), https:// bankruptcylitigationblog.lexblogplatform.com/wp-content/uploads/sites/427 /Credit_Suisse_HEAT_bk_report.pdf.

26. Donald P. Morgan, Benjamin Charles Iverson, and Matthew J. Botsch, "Subprime Foreclosures and the 2005 Bankruptcy Reform," *Economic Policy Review* 18, no. 1 (March 2012): pages 47–57.

27. Wenli Li, Michelle J. White, and Ning Zhu, "Did Bankruptcy Reform Cause Mortgage Defaults to Rise?," *American Economic Journal: Economic Policy* 3 (November 2011): page 1.

28. Stefania Albanesi and Jaromir Nosal, "Insolvency after the 2005 Bankruptcy Reform" (NBER Working Paper no. 24934, August 2018), https://www.nber.org /papers/w24934.

29. "Delaware Senator-Elect Sounds Like Bank Ally," *American Banker*, November 29, 2000, https://www.americanbanker.com/news/delaware-senator -elect-sounds-like-bank-ally.

30. Quoted in Dayen, "Tom Carper's 40-Year Record."

31. "2018 Annual Report: A Message from the Secretary of State," Delaware Division of Corporations, accessed October 6, 2021, https://corp.delaware.gov /stats/2018-annual-report.

32. From the Delaware Division of Corporations website: "**Does this new regulation require registered agents to collect additional information?** No. By statute, they are only required to obtain the communications contact information for the entity. If a registered agent collects *or* is provided additional information, such as names of officers, directors, members, etc., then the registered agent **MUST** check this information against the OFAC lists." OFAC is the Office of Foreign Assets Control, a division of the US Treasury. "Registered Agent Customer Entity Verification Requirements," Delaware Division of Corporations, accessed October 7, 2021, https://corp.delaware.gov/reg519/.

33. Jack Hagel, "Agreement Intended in Part to More Quickly Investigate Potential Violations by Companies Whose Beneficial Owners May Be Concealed," *Wall Street Journal*, September 7, 2020.

34. "Why Incorporate in Delaware?," Harvard Business Services, accessed October 3, 2021, https://www.delawareinc.com/.

35. Official 2017 income data. See Toh Kar Inn, "Median Salary for Employees in Malaysia Increased by 7.7% in 2017," *The Star*, May 8, 2018.

36. "United States Seeks to Recover More Than $1 Billion Obtained from Corruption Involving Malaysian Sovereign Wealth Fund," US Department of Justice, July 20, 2016, https://www.justice.gov/opa/pr/united-states-seeks-recover-more -1-billion-obtained-corruption-involving-malaysian-sovereign.

37. "United States Seeks to Recover More Than $1 Billion."

38. "Combating Terrorist and Other Illicit Financing," page 17.

Chapter 11

1. Adam D. I. Kramer, Jamie E. Guillory, and Jeffrey T. Hancock, "Experimental Evidence of Massive-Scale Emotional Contagion through Social Networks," *PNAS* 111, no. 24 (June 17, 2014): pages 8788–90.

2. Robinson Meyer, "Everything We Know about Facebook's Secret Mood Manipulation Experiment: It Was Probably Legal. But Was It Ethical?," *Atlantic*, June 28, 2014.

3. Ryan Mac and Charlie Warzel, "Departing Facebook Security Officer's Memo: 'We Need to Be Willing to Pick Sides,'" BuzzFeed News, July 24, 2018, https://www.buzzfeednews.com/article/ryanmac/facebook-alex-stamos-memo-cambridge-analytica-pick-sides.

4. "Facebook Must Recognise It Is More Than a Platform," *Financial Times*, December 2, 2018.

5. Harper Neidig, "Trump Has 378 Businesses Registered in Delaware," The Hill, April 22, 2016, https://thehill.com/blogs/ballot-box/presidential-races/277326-trump-has-378-businesses-registered-in-delaware.

6. Rupert Neate, "Trump and Clinton Share Delaware Tax 'Loophole' Address with 285,000 Firms," *Guardian*, April 25, 2016.

7. Adav Noti, Senior Director, Trial Litigation, and Chief of Staff, Campaign Legal Center, interview with the author, November 30, 2020.

8. See Michelle Ye Hee Lee, "Payments to Company Owned by Ocasio-Cortez Aide Come under Scrutiny," *Washington Post*, March 7, 2019; Meredith Newman, "Ocasio-Cortez's Campaign Funding Controversy Tied to—You Guessed It—Delaware LLC," *News Journal*, March 6, 2019.

9. Revolving political chairs is nothing new in Delawarean politics. For example, current governor John Carney was formerly Delaware's US House representative, lieutenant governor, and secretary of finance.

10. Hearing before the Permanent Subcommittee on Investigations of the Committee on Homeland Security and Governmental Affairs, United States Senate, November 14, 2006.

11. Karl Baker, "Delaware Seeks Compromise in Anti–Money Laundering Fight," *News Journal*, September 16, 2016.

12. Quoted in Suzanne Barlyn, "Special Report: How Delaware Kept America Safe for Corporate Secrecy," Reuters, August 24, 2016, https://www.reuters.com/article/us-usa-delaware-bullock-specialreport-idUSKCN10Z1OH.

13. At the time of writing, the statement is still visible in Jeff Bullock's bio from "Unclaimed Property Update," BDO Knowledge Webinar, May 24, 2017, https://www.bdo.com/BDO/media/Professional-Profile-Images/BDO-Webinar-Handout.pdf.

14. Quoted in Barlyn, "How Delaware Kept America Safe."

15. Clark Gascoigne, interview with the author, March 8, 2017.

16. Heywood, "The FATF Report on the USA."

17. "United States: Anti–Money Laundering and Counter-Terrorist Financing Measures, 3rd Enhanced Follow-up Report & Technical Compliance Re-rating" (Financial Action Task Force, March 2020), https://www.fatf-gafi.org/media/fatf/documents/reports/fur/Follow-Up-Report-United-States-March-2020.pdf.

18. See "Combating Terrorist and Other Illicit Financing," page 19.

19. Jason Leopold et al., "The FinCEN Files" BuzzFeed News, September 20, 2020, https://www.buzzfeednews.com/article/jasonleopold/fincen-files-financial-scandal-criminal-networks.

20. "Combating Terrorist and Other Illicit Financing," page 15.

21. See, e.g., Aaron D. Klein, "State Incorporation Laws: Good for Crooks, Bad for Banks," *American Banker*, April 9, 2017, https://www.americanbanker.com /opinion/state-incorporation-laws-good-for-crooks-bad-for-banks?feed=00000158 -080c-dbde-abfc-3e7d1bf30000.

22. "Backpage.com's Knowing Facilitation of Online Sex Trafficking," Staff Report of the Permanent Subcommittee on Investigations, Committee on Home-land Security and Governmental Affairs, United States Senate, January 10, 2017, page 2, https://www.hsgac.senate.gov/imo/media/doc/Backpage%20Report%20 2017.01.10%20FINAL.pdf.

23. Tom Jackman and Jonathan O'Connell, "Backpage Has Always Claimed It Doesn't Control Sex-Related Ads. New Documents Show Otherwise," *Washington Post*, July 11, 2017.

24. Cris Barrish and Zoe Read, "Delaware Attorney General Will Seek to Dissolve Backpage.com," WHYY, August 20, 2018, https://whyy.org/segments /delaware-attorney-general-will-seek-to-dissolve-backpage-com/.

25. Directive (EU) 2018/843 of the European Parliament and of the Council, May 30, 2018.

26. James Henry, interview with the author, November 27, 2020.

27. Kimberly Kay Hoang, *Spiderweb Capitalism: How Global Elites Exploit Fron-tier Markets* (Princeton: Princeton University Press, forthcoming 2022).

28. Letter from business groups urging members of the US House of Repre-sentatives to vote "no" on the Corporate Transparency Act of 2019, October 21, 2019, National Federation of Independent Business website, https://www.nfib.com /assets/Small-Business-Coalition-Opposition-to-Corporate-Transparency-Act -October-2019-2.pdf.

29. "Colbert: 'Re-Becoming' the Nation We Always Were," *Fresh Air*, NPR, October 4, 2012, https://www.npr.org/2012/10/04/162304439/colbert-re-becoming -the-nation-we-always-were.

30. "Colbert Super PAC—Trevor Potter & Stephen's Shell Corporation," *The Col-bert Report*, Comedy Central, September 29, 2011, https://www.cc.com/video/3yzu4u /the-colbert-report-colbert-super-pac-trevor-potter-stephen-s-shell-corporation.

31. Melissa Yeager, "It's Been 4 Years since Stephen Colbert Created a Super PAC—Where Did All That Money Go?," Sunlight Foundation, September 30, 2015, https://sunlightfoundation.com/2015/09/30/its-been-four-years-since-stephen -colbert-created-a-super-pac-where-did-all-that-money-go/.

32. "Social Welfare Organizations," Internal Revenue Service, accessed Octo-ber 4, 2021, https://www.irs.gov/charities-non-profits/other-non-profits/social -welfare-organizations.

33. John Dunbar, Center for Public Integrity, "What's a Super PAC? A Cam-paign Finance Glossary," NBCNews.com, April 7, 2016, https://www.nbcnews.com /news/investigations/what-s-super-pac-campaign-finance-glossary-n552036.

34. "Colbert Super PAC."

35. "Colbert Super PAC."

36. "Mueller: The 'Russian Government Interfered in Our Election in Sweeping and Systematic Fashion,'" CNN Politics, July 24, 2019, https://edition.cnn.com/politics/live-news/robert-mueller-congress-testimony/h_55da883cd3e8311bedf62aa60cac4f7b.

37. Joseph Biden and Michael Carpenter, "Foreign Dark Money Is Threatening American Democracy," Politico, November 27, 2018, https://www.politico.com/magazine/story/2018/11/27/foreign-dark-money-joe-biden-222690/.

38. "Lev Parnas and Igor Fruman Charged with Conspiring to Violate Straw and Foreign Donor Bans" (press release), US Attorney for the Southern District of New York, October 10, 2019, https://www.justice.gov/usao-sdny/pr/lev-parnas-and-igor-fruman-charged-conspiring-violate-straw-and-foreign-donor-bans.

39. "Lev Parnas and Igor Fruman Charged."

40. Adav Noti, interview with the author, November 30, 2020.

Chapter 12

1. Sarah Gamard, "Delaware Lawmaker Drops Plans for FOIA 'Abuse' Bill. Here's Why," *Delaware News Journal*, June 14, 2021.

2. Luigi Zingales, "Friedman's Legacy: From Doctrine to Theorem," ProMarket, Stigler Center for the Study of the Economy and the State, Chicago Booth, October 13, 2020, https://promarket.org/2020/10/13/milton-friedman-legacy-doctrine-theorem/.

3. See, e.g., Jingwei Maggie Li, Shirley Lu, and Salma Nassar, "Corporate Social Responsibility Metrics in S&P 500 Firms' 2017 Sustainability Reports" (Chicago Booth Rustandy Center research report, May 2021), https://www.chicagobooth.edu/-/media/research/sei/docs/csr-metrics-rustandy-center-report_final.pdf; Jon Lukomnik, "State of Integrated and Sustainability Reporting 2018," Harvard Law School Forum on Corporate Governance, December 3, 2018, https://corpgov.law.harvard.edu/2018/12/03/state-of-integrated-and-sustainability-reporting-2018/.

4. See Lucian A. Bebchuk and Roberto Tallarita, "Will Corporations Deliver Value to All Stakeholders?" (working paper, August 4, 2021), https://papers.ssrn.com/sol3/papers.cfm?abstract_id=3899421.

5. At the time of writing, not all EU countries have complied with the 2015 fourth EU Anti–Money Laundering Directive, which required member states to set up beneficial ownership registries. See "404 Beneficial Owner Not Found: Are EU Public Registers in Place and Really Public?," Transparency International, May 26, 2021, https://www.transparency.org/en/news/eu-beneficial-ownership-registers-public-access-data-availability-progress-2021.

INDEX

A NOTE ON THE TYPE

This book has been composed in Adobe Text and Gotham.
Adobe Text, designed by Robert Slimbach for Adobe,
bridges the gap between fifteenth- and sixteenth-century
calligraphic and eighteenth-century Modern styles.
Gotham, inspired by New York street signs, was designed
by Tobias Frere-Jones for Hoefler & Co.